IRRECONCILABLE
DIFFERENCES?

IRRECONCILABLE DIFFERENCES?

INTELLECTUAL STALEMATE IN THE GAY RIGHTS DEBATE

THOMAS C. CARAMAGNO

Westport, Connecticut
London

Library of Congress Cataloging-in-Publication Data

Caramagno, Thomas C.
    Irreconcilable differences? : intellectual stalemate in the gay rights debate /
    Thomas C. Caramagno.
        p.   cm.
    Includes bibliographical references and index.
    ISBN 0–275–97711–0 (alk. paper)—ISBN 0–275–97721–8 (pbk. : alk. paper)
    1. Gay rights.   2. Homosexuality—Religious aspects.   3. Homosexuality.
    I. Title.
    HQ76.5.C37   2002
    305.9'0664—dc21   2002022474

British Library Cataloguing in Publication Data is available.

Library of Congress Catalog Card Number: 2002022474
ISBN: 0–275–97711–0
        0–275–97721–8 (pbk.)

First published in 2002

Praeger Publishers, 88 Post Road West, Westport, CT 06881
An imprint of Greenwood Publishing Group, Inc.
www.praeger.com

Printed in the United States of America

The paper used in this book complies with the
Permanent Paper Standard issued by the National
Information Standards Organization (Z39.48–1984).

10 9 8 7 6 5 4 3 2 1

This book is dedicated to the memory of
Joseph Chadwick
and
Jean Selden

It is better to debate a question without settling it than to settle a question without debating it.

—*Joseph Joubert*

Contents

Preface   ix

1   The New Cold War   1

2   Group Affiliations and Post-Consensus Politics   11

Part One: Religious and Sexual Diversity   **21**

3   Religious Views: Past and Present   23

4   Biblical Scholarship: Texts, Errors, and Methods   35

5   Textual Ambiguities and the Scriptures   47

6   The Theological Meaning of Sex   75

Part Two: Science and Uncertainty   95

7   The Etiology of Homosexuality: Biology and/or Culture?   97

8   Diversity within Diversity: Postmodern Sexual Identities   119

9   Define "Illness": Rival Theories of Pathology
     and "Ex-Gay" Ministries   141

Part Three: Politics and Sexual Diversity   163

10   Demonizing the Enemy   165

11   Gay Bashing and Social Control   179

12   Pluralism versus Dogma: Public Spaces and Private Beliefs   191

Works Cited   207
Index   229

Preface

What has happened to the "debate" in "the gay rights debate"? Why does each side resort to moral condemnations and demonizing stereotypes instead of extended, useful dialog? The disputants have become "perfect enemies" (Gallagher and Bull 3), divided on every issue with such intensity that consensus—or even detente—seems impossible. The issue of sexual orientation is so interwoven with American notions of self, society, and God that many people can imagine no other resolution than abdication by one side or the other. The debate is important because it intersects with such a large field of related issues: the tensions between religious dogma and secular pluralism, the rival authorities of science and religion, the rights of minorities and majorities, and the diverse meanings and practices of sexual relationships. But it also risks becoming a futile spectacle that hardens opposition further because fundamental conflicts in how the disputants think about spirituality, human behavior, and freedom have so complicated conceptions of sexual diversity that resolving the latter may require comprehensive resolutions of the former.

For many Americans, listening to the debate is "like being deluged with competing theories of advanced physics without first having mastered basic math" (Gallagher and Bull 3). This textbook does not pursue a narrow or partisan thesis but is intended to give students an introductory view of the basic math of pro-gay and anti-gay rights perspectives. It does not pander to the "already converted" or demonize any group; nor is it reductionistic. No single profile for homosexuals exists that can encompass the diverse

individuals who comprise the lesbian, gay, bisexual, or transgendered/
transsexual (LGBT) population, just as there is no monolithic model for
heterosexuals who oppose legal protections for LGBTs. The gay rights
debate is stalemated because each side oversimplifies and pathologizes the
other's perspective. Assuming that both pro-gay and anti-gay positions
bring something valuable to the debate, I show how these ideologically
opposed groups marshal evidence to muster public support but without
addressing the conceptual changes needed to conduct a more profitable dialog. I am careful to separate fact from myth, summarizing a broad range of
religious, sociological, psychological, and historical material to give an
accurate picture of sexual diversity, but I also draw attention to those areas
where science or scholarship cannot supply a definitive answer—questions
about meaning and value, some of which inform the assumptions of the
very science being used. I invite students to participate in the exploration of
meaning. My aim is not closure but to encourage continued thinking.

The book is organized around three fields of study—religion, science, and
politics. Chapter 1, "The New Cold War," introduces sexual diversity as the
new ideological battleground in American politics, dividing people into
adamantly opposed groups that cast orthodox believers as homophobic fascists and LGBTs as sinners corrupting America's moral fiber. Both sides are
pathologized by their views, for sex has become a metonym for mind in this
debate: pro-gay advocates often assume that *liberated sex produces a liberated mind;* anti-gay rights groups reverse the polarity: *depraved sex produces a depraved mind.* Can a consensus be forged when each side discounts the other side's ability to think? The tenuous political position each
side occupies is exacerbated by conflicting sodomy laws from state to state,
reinforced by *Bowers v. Hardwick* (1986). School curricula and library
holdings are largely censored to avoid references either to sexual orientation or Christianity as if both were an "abductive ideology."

Chapter 2, "Group Affiliations and Post-Consensus Politics," shows how
oversimplifying each side's agenda and membership obscures important ideological distinctions within the "gay community" and anti-gay rights
groups. Conflicts among the Christian Right, mainline, and progressive
Christians roughly follow liberal, moderate, and conservative categories,
but within each branch numerous factions have emerged that are politically
and socially diverse. It is also impossible to typify LGBTs, for they range
from liberal Democrats to conservative Republicans and can be found in
virtually every religious sect. This is more than a simple political conflict
between monolithic camps oversimplified as "conservative" and "liberal"
or "gay" and "straight"; it cuts across social, cultural, sexual, and religious
lines in ways that are surprising. How it is being discussed reveals how
democracy works (or doesn't work) in a multicultural, post-consensus age.

Both pro- and anti-gay groups make appeals to the past to justify their
positions, but, as Chapter 3, "Religious Views: Past and Present," shows,

heated debates about sexual diversity existed in the ancient world, focusing on the same unresolved issues: whether it was natural or unnatural, biologically ordained or a moral failing, fated or a matter of choice. A number of ancient religions found social and spiritual value in sexual diversity, where orthodox Christianity found only degradation and sin, perhaps because the Judeo-Christian God was considered a singular perfection while many non-Christian religions saw good and evil as conjoined aspects. Christianity has in the past adjusted its teachings in response to changes in scientific knowledge and cultural values, but the issue of whether dogma should evolve over time is controversial. Revelation is the cornerstone of both Judaism and Christianity, but it is a matter of intense debate between Judeo-Christian sects about *how* God intrudes upon history and *what* constitutes obedience. Is revelation complete, or are more prophets to come? Is compromise even possible if the question of how to view LGBTs becomes a litmus test for religious commitment? Just as in Christ's day, deciding who is the pharisee and who is the heretic depends on deciding who speaks for God.

Chapter 4, "Biblical Scholarship: Texts, Errors, and Methods," discusses the historical and linguistic problems scholars face when translating ancient Hebrew and Greek into modern English. Interpretive approaches are split along ideological lines since editors work according to guiding principles that reflect their theologies. The history and the form of biblical texts made errors during copying inevitable, and the pedigree of the King James Version (KJV), its editors, and their justification for rewording passages as an inspired interpretation further complicate how modern readers interpret the Bible for themselves.

Chapter 5, "Textual Ambiguities and the Scriptures," discusses the recent work of revisionist theologians and historians who argue that mistranslations, produced either by error, accident, ignorance, or a translator's cultural biases, are responsible for Christianity's condemnation of sexual diversity. John Boswell, Daniel Helminiak, and Paul Halsall recast Levitican Purity Laws and St. Paul's view of the "unnatural" as culturally unique to the ancients, not universal moral laws. But while it is true that various Levitican taboos are no longer followed, there is no universally accepted policy on when to revise the Bible. Revision is acceptable when the evidence for it is "compelling," but what "compelling" means varies according to one's theology. When does selective literalism become prejudice? Whose self-validating interpretive strategy will be used? If different theologies shape the way different Christians read the Bible and non-biblical supporting evidence, then radically different interpretations are not only possible; they all find some validation. Christianity's position on homosexuality may not be reduced simply to a prejudice that can be legislated away. It is a complex amalgam of scholarship, philosophy, mystery, and human experience, and it will take much more research and discussion to make any progress.

Chapter 6, "The Theological Meaning of Sex," moves from Aquinas' view of "natural law" and Philo's concept of "one flesh" to John Finnis' recent model of a spiritual transaction analogized by anatomical structure: the joining of opposites, the experience of the human "other" (in marital, vaginal intercourse only) in order to invite the divine "Other." This view assumes that metaphorical analogies between body parts and mentality or spirituality are stable and universally applicable. Finnis' critics argue that the spiritual correctness of heterosexual intercourse cannot be refuted or verified through reason or evidence, and that when heterosexual theologians conceive of the metaphorical meaning of "homosexual sex," they see it only in gendered, heterosexual terms. This suggests three presently unanswerable questions: are heterosexuals prevented from knowing what homosexuals know of the spirituality of their desire? What is the purpose of a lesbian or gay life when it is the excess that gender metaphors cannot account for? Can we conceive of gendered persons without reducing them to simplistic binaries based strictly on anatomical difference?

Chapter 7, "The Etiology of Homosexuality: Biology and/or Culture?," considers the controversial findings of genetic, brain, and neuroendocrine research into the origins of sexual orientation. Methodological problems, objections to applying scientific knowledge to issues of value and meaning, and the question of how much science has been ideologically contaminated have diminished hopes that a "gay gene" will be found. Moreover, gay rights advocates are divided about the implications of biological evidence for their cause. Do genes limit freedom, reinforcing old stereotypes about LGBTs as inherently defective? Are Christians using dogma to define contradicting evidence as false? Are LGBTs embracing science to reduce sexuality to mere biology? Cultural anthropologists and sociologists argue that sexuality may be as much a product of history, culture, and ideology as it is of nature. Is it even possible to decide which aspects of sexuality are innate and which are learned when biological systems are so responsive to environmental conditions and when the hypotheses that hard science tests contain concepts that are themselves socially constructed? If sexuality is a cultural product, its expression may be part of a larger system of meaning that science cannot reduce to a manageable focus. And if the modern LGBT is a product of the times, on what basis can sexual minorities lobby for protected status? Neither biological essentialism nor social constructionism is necessarily gay-affirmative since anti-gay rights groups freely use both to justify discrimination.

Many pro-gay activists claim that 10% of the public is homosexual, while anti-gay groups insist on 1–2%; each side uses figures to calculate how much political influence LGBTs should enjoy. In Chapter 8, "Diversity within Diversity: Postmodern Sexual Identities," I show how methodological and theoretical issues affect the results of sex surveys and the meaning of these results. Deciding who is "really" gay or "really" lesbian or "really" bisexual depends on how well human beings fit into rigid categories, but for many people sexual orientations seem fluid rather than stable. Should identity be determined by sexual behavior, fantasy, desire, ideology, personal aims, or some combination? Do different individuals stress each component differently? At what percentile of same/opposite sex interactions do we decide *who* is *what* orientation? How is bisexuality misconceived in sex survey questions? Do sexual categories disserve LGBTs because defining who is considered a "real" gay or lesbian marginalizes and polices individuals who do not behave, feel, or identify the same way?

Chapter 9, "Define 'Illness': Rival Theories of Pathology and 'Ex-Gay' Ministries," shows how different schools of psychology conceive of sexual pathology in different terms that cannot be adequately correlated. "Anti-gay" therapists use psychoanalytic theory, which considers orientation as a problem in gender identity, while "pro-gay" psychologists and psychiatrists rely on behavioral studies, which focus on overt signs of pathology. The former argue that homosexuality is a pathological lifestyle, a neurotic or addictive condition resulting from poor parenting; the latter argue that homosexuals resemble heterosexuals in social functioning, emotional well-being, and personality characteristics. Some psychoanalysts claim that homosexuality can be cured but provide no consistent, replicable documentation that it is a developmental disorder or that patients have changed sexual orientation; behavioralists claim that homosexuality is an immutable condition which cannot be "cured" without harm to the individual's emotional makeup, self-image, and identity structure. Two fundamentally different approaches to understanding human behavior have created a long paper trail of published articles and books that flatly contradict each other. Sifting through these competing views requires not just separating evidence from hypothesis but understanding the relative merits of Freudian and behavioral approaches to human psychology.

Chapter 10, "Demonizing the Enemy," considers the contested connection between inflammatory rhetoric and public fear. Portraying LGBTs as "perverts" or fundamentalists as "fascists" rallies the troops but spreads propaganda that can be long-lived in spite of evidence against it. But will a kinder, gentler approach avoid demonizing stereotypes and advance the debate? Does a middle ground even exist on which either side can find an ideologically sound position? How does one even take the first step: deciding if an opponent's beliefs are a satanic conspiracy or bigotry, or if they are part of an exploration of—and passionate disagreement about—the meaning and value of life? The two sides can't even agree on whether inflammatory rhetoric is hate speech or protected speech.

Chapter 11, "Gay Bashing and Social Control," considers the parallels between antisemitism, racism, and anti-gay rhetoric, as well as Louis Farrakhan's racial theory of homosexuality and the question of identity for African American LGBTs. Most Christians who oppose expanding gay rights also condemn violence, but does anti-gay ideology incite violence against gays? What distinguishes a personal prejudice from misconceptions/prejudices that are already integrated into a conceptual system that makes sense of the way we experience and evaluate evidence? To complicate matters, anti-gay groups are extremely diverse, and not everyone agrees on what righteousness allows them to say or do about other people's "sins."

As illustrated in Chapter 12, "Pluralism versus Dogma: Public Spaces and Private Beliefs," pluralism, easy to understand in the abstract, can be difficult to define in practice, for it is interpreted in two very different ways in the gay rights debate. Liberals, libertarians, and Goldwater conservatives tend to view it as a "live and let live" tolerance of all beliefs as long as no one is harmed. Theocratic and cultural conservatives tend to see pluralism as civil amorality, a violation of God's laws that will destroy the moral fabric of society. Which governmental role would better serve a fairer pluralism, an intrusive government that prohibits discrimination through the force of law, or a neutral government that provides no protected status for any group? The issue of "special rights" versus "equal rights" illustrates these conflicting views. Pro-gay groups argue that anti-discrimination laws do not claim any particular right for LGBTs that everyone else does not already enjoy; orthodox Christians argue that civil pluralism is already invasive, a transgression by the State upon practicing one's religious belief in one's public life. The Constitution does give government the right to limit social actions for the public good, but it is not clear to what extent religious belief should determine what is "good." A great deal of controversy surrounds even the definitions used in the debate—what do the words "gay," "lesbian," "bisexual," "sexual orientation," "sexual identity," or "transgenderism" mean when theology, science, and politics are constantly redrawing the center and the boundaries of these terms? Laws must have reasons behind them, must be able to pass a "rationality review," but the parameters of the LGBT question are continuously evolving and expanding.

I would like to thank my colleagues, Tami Davidson, Linda Pratt, Stephen Hilliard, George Wolf, Lou Crompton, Bill Dick, Stephen Buhler, and Tracy Prince, for their encouragement and support. Elton Fukumoto helped me with constitutional issues, Alison Regan with pedagogical concerns, Judy Leveque with proofreading. A timely teaching grant from the William J. Fulbright Association allowed me to work on the book while teaching Queer Theory at the University of Lisbon, Portugal. I am grateful to Professors Miguel Tamen and Joao Figuerido, co-directors of the Theory Program there, for their collegiality, and to the Luso-American Educational Association, particularly Paulo Zagalo e Melo and Rita Bacelar, for their great hospitality and material aid during my stay in Portugal. I am especially indebted to Nancy Myers, without whose help this book would never have been completed.

The New Cold War

Recent events, like the easy passage of the anti-gay Defense of Marriage Act, the narrow defeat (50 to 49) of the pro-gay Employment NonDiscrimination Act, and a barrage of accusations and counteraccusations following Senate Majority Leader Trent Lott's (R-Miss) claim that homosexuality is comparable to alcoholism, sex addiction, and kleptomania (Lawrence 5A) illustrate how fundamentally divided Americans are over the issue of what freedoms and what limits can be justly applied to lesbian, gay, bisexual, and transgendered/transsexual people (LGBT). After thirty years of political activism and legal challenges, neither side has been able to dominate the debate; only 22 states have enacted a hate crimes law that includes sexual orientation, and only four extend protection to transgendered or transsexual persons. Various polls have shown that gay men and lesbians are still the least-liked groups in American society, that 70%–75% of heterosexual Americans believe that homosexuality is morally wrong (Schroedel 90), even though 60% support basic civil rights and fairness in housing and employment (Lewis and Rogers 123), but neither side can even agree on what constitutes "basic" rights and "fairness" in practice.

Among the many competing voices and agendas on either side, the general public hears everything from reasoned discourse and informed research to warlike hyperbole and demonizing stereotypes urging each side to see the other as an implacable enemy. Many religious groups have investigated the issue of sexual diversity, offering a principled condemnation or cautious approval in scholarly journals or church documents; others denounce homosexuality as a secular or demonic force that threatens Christianity itself. On his "Old Time Gospel Hour" television show, the Reverend Jerry Falwell described homosexuals as "brute beasts . . . part of a vile and satanic system [that] will one day be utterly annihilated (Robinson, "Homosexuality"). Randall Terry, founder of Operation Rescue, has claimed that "if the militant homosexuals succeed in their accursed agenda, God will curse and judge our nation. . . . The goal of the homosexual movement is to 'mainstream' unspeakable acts of evil. . . . Their cries for tolerance are really a demand for our surrender. They want us to surrender our values, our love for God's law, our faith, our families, the entire nation to their abhorrent agenda" ("Hostile Climate"). Former U.S. Congressman, William Dannemeyer, describes gays and lesbians as "the ultimate enemy" who will "plunge our people, and indeed the entire West, into a dark night of the soul" (Herman 64), while an anti-gay Oregon referendum won 43% of the state vote using a slogan reminiscent of the Cold War era, "Gays are the enemy within."

While many pro-gay activists work quietly within churches and main-stream political parties to increase tolerance for sexual minorities, some, embittered by physical and rhetorical attacks, belittle orthodox Christians as "the crazies," slick televangelists fleecing their followers for money and power, abetting gay bashing and covertly facilitating the AIDS epidemic (Rist 77; Goss 50, 54; Smith and Windes 108). Gay author Paul Monette labeled Roman Catholic officials "Nazis," and "the polish Pope and his diabolical sidekick, Cardinal Ratzinger, the Vatican's minister of Hate" (55). At a 1993 march, demonstrators threatened violence if legal protection for homosexuality was not extended, while others chanted "F_ _k the church, F_ _k the state, Hormones will decide our fate!" (Button et al. 1). Each side inhabits a different moral universe, avoiding the challenge of understanding how the other thinks about issues. Anti-gay groups dismiss pro-gay arguments as distorted reasoning made specious by sin. Pro-gay groups dismiss anti-gay arguments as unthinking prejudice or a rationalization for the desire to control others. Joe Dallas, the founder of Genesis Counseling, describes pro-gay religion as "a theology of lies," a "strong delusion" that requires not analysis but adamant opposition (206–207); Martin Duberman rejects anti-gay arguments because "to treat their insulting simplicities as legitimate arguments and to dignify their smarmy psyches with a rational probe feels like an exercise in self-hatred" (quoted in Smith and Windes 42). In a review of the rhetorical war, Ralph R. Smith warns:

For many gay activists, debates are futile and counterproductive spectacles. From their perspective, individuals opposed to gay civil equality cannot be argued out of their emotional anti-gay biases. . . . The attempt may harden prejudice. . . .

Some rhetoricians and social scientists are no more sanguine about public moral argument. Pearce, Littlejohn, and Alexander . . . assert that such arguments degenerate into reciprocated diatribe because "disputants lack a common moral frame with which to understand the issues." Sociologists . . . see opposing sides on gay issues as "worlds apart," making "any mutually agreeable resolution of policy, much less cultural consensus . . . almost unimaginable." (98)

To varying degrees, each side feels it is fighting for its way of life and that the other side represents the ruin of America.

The tenuous political position each side occupies is exacerbated by a patchwork of conflicting sex laws from state to state. Until 1961, all states outlawed consensual sodomy (generally defined as oral or anal sex); today only 15 criminalize it (ACLU, "Update"), though 45% of voters still support such laws (Lewis and Rogers 120). Campaigns are annually mounted by each side to convince state legislatures to shift positions, but finding good rationales for either policy is uniquely difficult because sodomy, as Walter Barnett argues, is the only class of sex acts judged criminal regardless of context. Rape is defined by the force involved, statutory rape by the partner's age. Pedophilia injures children. Necrophilia dishonors the dead. Prostitution is illegal, while promiscuity is not, because money is exchanged. Only sodomy laws penalize the sex act alone, in any and all circumstances, as intrinsically evil (81), but penalties vary widely because intrinsic qualities are difficult to demonstrate or prove: Kansas (6 months/$1,000), Missouri (1 year/$1,000), Oklahoma (10 years), Texas ($500), Alabama (1 year/$2,000), Florida (60 days/$500), Idaho (5 years to life), Louisiana (5 years/$2,000), Mississippi (10 years), North Carolina (10 years), Puerto Rico (10 years), South Carolina (5 years/$500), Utah (6 months/$1,000), Virginia (1–5 years), Massachusetts (20 years), Michigan (15 years) (ACLU, "Sodomy"; Rubin). Thirty-five other states impose no penalties.

These legal inconsistencies were judged constitutional by a 1986 United States Supreme Court ruling, *Bowers v. Hardwick*. Four years earlier, two Georgia policemen had appeared at 29-year-old Michael Hardwick's door with an unpaid traffic ticket. When they discovered him in bed with another man, the case shifted from traffic to a "crime against nature." Hardwick sued on the grounds that his right to privacy had been violated, and he expected to win (Millman 269). The Court had already set a precedent in a 1965 ruling, *Griswold v. Connecticut,* which recognized a constitutional right to privacy for married couples using contraceptive devices; until then, contraception, also viewed as an "unnatural" act in orthodox Christian theology, had been illegal in many states. In *Eisenstadt v. Baird,* the Court extended the same protection to unmarried couples, and it seemed only a matter of time before equal protection would be extended to same-sex couples. If a state could not prohibit non-procreative sex between husbands and wives, how could it prohibit other non-procreative forms of sexual expression, such as oral and anal sex (Barnett 52)? Justice Thurgood Marshall, in an allied case, *Olmstead v. United States,* had argued that privacy was worth protecting for it allowed each citizen to develop and put into practice religious beliefs in his/her daily life:

The makers of our Constitution undertook to secure conditions favorable to the pursuit of happiness. They recognized the significance of a man's spiritual nature, of his feelings and of his intellect. They knew that only a part of the pain, pleasure and satisfactions of life are to be found in material things. They sought to protect Americans in their beliefs, their thoughts, their emotions and their sensations. They conferred, as against the Government, the right to be let alone—the most comprehensive of rights and the right most valued by civilized man. (Barnett 59)

And the *Hardwick* case, as Kendall Thomas, Professor of Law at Columbia University, put it, "seemed to be the most private of privacy cases" (1437).

But by a 5–4 vote the Court upheld any state's power to criminalize whatever sexual activity it deemed depraved on behalf of its citizens. The right to privacy, Justice Byron White argued, is not absolute. The Court was also reluctant to invent new rights for specific groups: fundamental rights should be limited to those "deeply rooted in this Nation's history and tradition" (*Bowers v. Hardwick,* 478 U.S. 186 [1986]). America's sodomy laws were certainly "deeply rooted," having been written three centuries ago to outlaw various non-vaginal sex acts by both heterosexuals and homosexuals. Gay activists argued that the Court narrowly framed the case as an appeal for legalizing "homosexual sodomy" only. As Justice White said:

The issue presented is whether the Federal Constitution confers a fundamental right upon homosexuals to engage in sodomy and hence invalidates the laws of the many States that still make such conduct illegal and have done so for a very long time. (*Hardwick,* 478 U.S. 190)

In fact, the Georgia law was not so specific: "[a] person commits the offense of sodomy when he performs or submits to any sexual act involving the sex organs of one person and the mouth or anus of another" (Baird and Baird 101). Technically, sodomy was illegal no matter who performed it, but since Hardwick was gay, the case became, in the minds of the justices, a referendum on homosexuals only (Nan Hunter 541–542).

The Court was deeply split over the issue, with the deciding vote reluctantly cast by Justice Lewis F. Powell, Jr., who felt unhappy with either alternative, as John C. Jeffries, Jr. (University of Virginia Law School), argues:

Just as creating a new fundamental right went too far in one direction, flatly rejecting that claim went too far in the other. If, as the conservatives contended, consensual sodomy was not constitutionally protected, then presumably the states could regulate such acts as they pleased, including by criminal prosecution and punishment. Powell found this prospect barbaric. (109)

Personally, Powell despised sodomy laws, but he also feared that denying states the right to regulate sexual behavior "would entangle the Court in a continuing campaign to validate the gay 'lifestyle' in a variety of other contexts," such as employment, same-sex marriage, and adoption (108). He could find no "middle ground" and so voted for retaining the status quo.

As a result, *Bowers v. Hardwick* legalized an empty space where no constitutional guidelines exist for choosing liberty or imprisonment except for the political power of the groups involved. "Might makes right" when it comes to sexual orientation, since the Constitution does not mention protecting heterosexual behavior either, yet seldom are heterosexuals arrested for non-vaginal sexual behavior, even though it is widespread. Laumann et al.'s 1992 survey found that 60% of men and 41% of women with less than a high school education had experienced oral sex at least once in their lifetime, while the figure for both college educated men and women was 80% (105). In other surveys, 13% to 23% of women admitted to practicing anal sex "regularly" (Voeller 247–249). Yet heterosexuals are rarely arrested for "unnatural sex" unless rape or aggravated assault charges are also made (Law 189). Missouri law explicitly states that non-vaginal sex is a crime *only* for homosexuals. When Hardwick appealed his conviction, a married couple joined him as plaintiff, arguing that they too should have the right to engage in non-vaginal sex; but the District Court declined to add them to the case with the rationale that heterosexual couples were in no immediate danger of arrest since it is assumed that non-procreative sex is not fundamental to their natures. As a later court explained: "the act of homosexual sodomy 'defines the class' of gay men and lesbians," but the same act between opposite sex partners is only a diversion and so should not endanger their liberty (Nan Hunter 540–543; Halley, "Reasoning," 1734–1735). To LGBTs, this explanation targets not proscripted *behaviors* but proscripted *persons* for whom those behaviors are centrally meaningful (Nan Hunter 532).

Thus, sodomy is presumed to be socially destructive but only for non-heterosexuals. *Sex* is a metonym for *mind* (Halley, "Reasoning," 1747), not just a physical or emotional act but a manifestation of being, not something one *does* (that anyone can do) but something one *is*, influencing all areas of the self: emotional, cognitive, moral, and political (Foucault 43). As lesbian writer Pat Califia remembers, identifying her desire profoundly redefined her self:

Knowing I was a lesbian transformed the way I saw, heard, perceived the whole world. I became aware of a network of sensations and reactions that I had ignored my entire life. (Weeks 186)

For Califia, *liberated sex produced a liberated mind.* Anti-gay rights groups think along the same lines but reverse the polarity: *depraved sex produces a depraved mind.* When the Reverend Fred Phelps picketed a Kansas Bar Association meeting in opposition to a gay judge, Terry Bullock, he reasoned that

sodomite judges always vote their rectums! God has given every sodomite up "to a reprobate mind" Rom. 1:28. Which means that no fag can think right about anything. ("More Bible Commentary on Current Events")

Phelps is infamous for his bluntness, but St. Thomas Aquinas, the influential medieval Catholic theologian, reasoned similarly:

When the lower powers are strongly set on their objects, the result is that the higher faculties can no longer function, or do so only in a disordered way. Now, in the vice of sensuality the baser appetite, that is, lust, does strive most eagerly after its object of pleasure by a vehemence of passion and delectation [delight]. What comes of this is that sensuality runs a disorder through the nobler powers of reason and the will . . . it fathers a mental blindness. (Gilson 297)

Thus, sex either usurps mentality if not controlled by "higher" concerns (marriage, children, social order, God) or it frees mentality to see justice, politics, relationships, and spirituality in new ways. Phelps reasons that Bullock's judgments will be contaminated by the deceptions of gay desire. Gay activists hope that a gay judge *will* think differently, because his private behavior will help him see their "truth." Like the American communists of the 1950s, LGBTs are assumed to be "lost" to both conscience and community. Indulging a deviant desire that permeates their being shapes them mentally and spiritually so that they cannot "think straight" (Rubin 273, 306). Relying on this assumption, Colonel Ronald D. Ray, USMCR, recently argued that gay and lesbian soldiers presented a clear danger to our military because:

Even if homosexuals are not "turned" [blackmailed to commit treason] by foreign agents, evidence exists that homosexuals, as group or subculture, can and do turn against their country simply on account of the nature of homosexuality and its hostile attitude toward the existing moral order. (77)

It is ironic, but not surprising, that the most active anti-gay groups are commonly accused of being obsessed with sex too, abducted mentally and spiritually by an extremist way of thinking that penalizes dissent, so that they cannot, even if invited, "think queer." The strength of their convictions is regarded as proof of their mental disability. Marty Klein, in his Internet essay, "The Sex Lies of the Religious Right," sees no problem with pathologizing millions of Americans simply by connecting political orientation with private sexuality:

Clearly, the religious right and its cohorts are dreadfully frightened of their own eroticism. They struggle against their fleshly desires, but they cannot deny that their flesh desires. . . . Repelled by their own sexuality, they loathe and thus fear others' sexuality. And as a misplaced attempt to control their own eroticism, they try to control others'.

According to Klein, fundamentalists are not merely wrong; they have lost the capacity to see that they are wrong—the same accusation anti-gay rights groups make of LGBTs. Each side believes that changing public policy on sex will subvert an individual's ideology, conduct, and free will—the foundations of social order. Those who disagree with group politics can be written off as incompetent to judge the rightness or wrongness of their views.

Although LGBT groups and the Christian Coalition are both politically active and courted by liberals and conservatives respectively, centrists throw crumbs to each while letting them fight their internecine war (Button et al. 13). Bill Clinton's "Don't Ask, Don't Tell" policy illustrates how the activist margins can be effectively "contained" by the moderate middle. Introduced as a compromise between pro-gay and anti-gay groups, it benefitted neither while having the appearance of being a major event. Indeed, lesbian, gay, and bisexual (LBG) military personnel still face exposure and discharge (and the numbers of LGB discharges have increased 67% since 1993), while the religious right is dismayed to see tolerance of evil made official government policy (Gallagher and Bull 132; Haeberle 148; Galatowitsch).

Can a consensus be forged when each side discounts the other side's ability to think? And what role should schools play in this controversy? Prior prejudices—antisemitism, racism, sexism—seemed ideal subjects for educators because increased knowledge contradicts stereotypes and reduces the fear response behind hatred. But when the groups in question are identified by an abductive ideology based either on sex or religion, merely providing the basic information students need to join the debate, to eventually vote on the issue in an informed way, raises fears in parents that their children are either going to be "queered" or "reborn." Each side is tempted to regard education as a form of indoctrination. The result has generally meant blatant censorship of what can be said about Christianity or sexual diversity in the classroom. Although a few school systems have designed curricula to teach students about LGBTs in a fact-based way (Fairfax County in Virginia, Broward County in Florida, Houston in Texas, and San Francisco in California), many more are required by law either to ignore the issue altogether or issue vague condemnations (as in Alabama, Texas, Utah, Arizona, New York City, South Carolina) (Tenney 1600–1604, 1642–1643). At the same time, Christians feel discriminated against because teachers are allowed to include various secular and non-Christian books in their curricula, but the Bible cannot be one of them, as Ralph Reed, former Executive Director of the Christian Coalition, complains:

For example, when a group of students in Mobile, Alabama, decided in 1993 to include verses from the book of Ephesians in daily inspirational messages over the school intercom, attorneys for the school board muzzled them. The students explained that the Bible verses were no different than other readings they had included from Voltaire, Plato, and Thoreau—a source of inspiration and introspection. School board attorneys were not persuaded. The rights of the students to freedom of expression to read any passage went unquestioned until they included the Bible. (43)

Does instruction in Christianity constitute education or religious indoctrination? How does awareness of LGBTs affect students? Does it induce enlightened tolerance or moral apathy, a personal change or merely an intellectual change? Can schools ever guarantee students will not embrace what they learn? Should they have to? Activist groups who work to silence the other ironically find themselves reduced to invisibility in the one place students should be free to learn about the world. As James D'Entremont ruefully concludes:

Despite strong First Amendment protection for free speech at government-supported colleges and universities, both Left and Right have sought and obtained abridgments of speech on campus. The Right, which is quick to excoriate censorship rooted in [liberal] "political correctness," forgets its professed devotion to free speech when it comes to queer expression. . . . Many in the gay community, such as the angry crowd who shut down the information table of gay anti-abortion activists at the 1995 Boston Gay Pride Rally, see no contradiction in fighting fascist tendencies fascistically. (223–224, 227)

Silence is a poor alternative to debate because it denies students the opportunity to prepare themselves for the responsibilities and privileges of citizenship. Between 1974 and 1992, 33 anti-gay initiatives and referenda appeared on local ballots around the country, with victories evenly split between the two sides (Keen and Goldberg 6). Since then, the number of gay-related measures has been increasing annually, as Donald P. Haider-Markel reports:

In 1995 the National Gay and Lesbian Task Force (NGLTF) tracked 105 gay-related bills in the states. Only 16 states considered a total of 41 progay measures and 29 states considered 64 antigay measures. During the 1996 session there were 160 pieces of gay-related legislation of interest to the NGLTF. Only 25 states considered a total of 61 progay bills and 40 states considered the 99 antigay bills. In 1997 the amount of gay-related legislation in 49 states jumped to 248. Some 128 progay measures were considered in 38 states, while 120 antigay measures were considered in 44 states. . . . ("Lesbian" 300)

The most famous measure of the last decade was Colorado's 1992 Amendment Two, which would have denied gay men and lesbians any legal appeal to any government agency—local, state, or national—to defend themselves against discrimination based on sexual orientation. Such extreme measures would be unthinkable if applied to African Americans or Jews or women, but the amendment won by a margin of 53% to 47% partly because voters were inundated with fliers containing demonizing stereotypes and misinformation vilifying homosexuals as sexual predators of children (Gallagher and Bull 116). Without open and informed discussions in the classroom, will only false information become enshrined in law and perpetuate the conflict?

Ballot descriptions, by themselves, often can not give voters the information they need. While initiatives are quintessentially democratic (populist groups lacking representation in government are able to create new laws by persuading the public to agree with their cause), they also risk circumventing the checks and balances of the representative legislative process in favor of whichever special interest group can spend the most money or best exploit public fears. As law professor William E. Adams, Jr., has argued, ballot initiatives can create havoc merely by reducing complex issues to simplistic "yes or no" resolutions. Some amendments are so poorly written, ambiguous, long-winded, or numerous that voters misunderstand their intent and cast votes they later regret. Recent ballot descriptions in California and Oregon were written at the eighteenth-grade level, which meant that less than one-fifth of the voters had the ability to understand them (DuVivier 1195). In general, LGBTs lose at the polls but win in court: in 69 elections studied, 77% of anti-gay referenda won, while 84% of pro-gay rights initiatives failed. LGBTs have been more successful in the court, blocking repeals of existing anti-discrimination laws or preventing bans on laws protecting gay rights (Adams). But, in the end, this city-by-city internecine war exhausts time, resources, and good will without building consensus.

Classes should be open, inclusive, and respectful, allowing different students to value different things *whether or not students reach a conclusion about gay rights.* Freedom of speech is not about closure. Its value lies in opening up discussions so that they can incorporate ideas from both sides, so that students can understand how arguments and consensus-building work, not so that one side wins. The First Amendment protects the rights of students to receive accurate information and diverse points of view. In the 1967 decision, *Keyishian v. Board of Regents,* the Supreme Court ruled that "the role of education is to expose students to diverse viewpoints to teach them to assess competing ideas in preparation for their full participation in a democratic society." Lower court decisions since then have generally concurred, ruling that schools cannot ban or restrict speech merely because it conflicts with parents' or school officials' political views (Tenney

1625–1627). Schools can legitimately censor information if it is unrelated to the curriculum, but restrictions on curricular content are unconstitutional if they eliminate access to a particular idea or view, present only one side of a controversial issue, give inaccurate or misleading information, or compel students to hold a particular belief that precludes debate.

The gay rights debate affects the sexual and religious rights of all Americans, but how this status is to be negotiated and legislated teachers should leave to students. This textbook is designed to illustrate just how complex, interdisciplinary, irreconcilable, and yet unavoidable the gay rights debate is. Students learn best when they can synthesize diverse material on their own, to take what is known and imagine for themselves the unknown. This book is structured to give them that opportunity.

Group Affiliations and Post-Consensus Politics

The first obstacle to understanding the current debate on gay rights lies in oversimplifying each side's agenda and membership. Factions within pro-gay and anti-gay rights groups can be quite diverse, cutting across various ideological lines.

ANTI-GAY RIGHTS GROUPS

The political clout of the Christian Coalition has grown in recent years. While mainstream Protestant denominations have lost an estimated 25% of their membership over the last thirty years, evangelical membership has grown by 40% (Schapiro). In 1994, the Christian Coalition claimed to control 33% of the national vote, electing 38 out of 48 Republicans in the House of Representatives, and 8 senators. According to Congressional voting records, 165 Members of the House and 33 senators have supported the Christian Coalition at least 86% of the time ("TIAF"). The CR (Christian Right) is affiliated with large anti-gay groups: the Council for National Policy, the Institute for First Amendment Studies, National Empowerment Television (a 24-hour interactive satellite television network to coordinate local fundamentalist groups nationwide), the Christian Action Network, the American Family Association, Beverly LaHaye's Concerned Women for America, the Eagle Forum, Focus on the Family (which owns 1,550 radio stations worldwide), and the Reverend Lou Sheldon's Traditional Values Coalition, which is affiliated with 25,000 churches nationally. Religious broadcasting by the Christian Right is a $2 billion a year industry, controlling 1,485 full-time Christian radio stations and 336 full-time Christian TV stations (Porteous, *Jesus*, 18).

Although the CR is commonly viewed as a single religio-political entity with a consistent agenda, it is not a monolithic cadre of people who all think the same way. It includes believers from many of the 300 Christian sects that exist in America today, comprising roughly 20% of the U.S. population (Herman 12). Among the largest are the Evangelicals, who are broadly orthodox, though some are active in traditionally liberal causes (prison reform, civil rights legislation for ethnic minorities, health care reform, hunger relief, and Third World development) and so may dissent from the CR's positions against abortion, ordaining women, and evolution (Schmidt 16–17). Since the 1920s the term "evangelical" has covered many different kinds of Protestants who share the common aim of converting non-believers: they can be Baptists, Free Methodists, Pentecostals, Evangelical Presbyterians, Adventists and non-church-based Protestants who worship through televangelists—the fastest growing sector of the Evangelical movement. Not all Evangelicals insist that the Bible is an accurate description of earth or history: many believe that experience, tradition and reason must be applied when interpreting the Bible. However, CR leaders do tend to regard the Bible as "inerrant," true for all times, expressing with transcendent authority consistent and unchangeable values (Ammerman 5, 18; J.D. Hunter 44, 118). Literalists can be further divided into the fundamentalists (many of whom are Baptist) and the Pentecostals, but both fundamentalists and Pentecostals apply the Scriptures to social issues.

How strictly Scripture should apply varies even among conservative sects. In general, orthodox Christians oppose liberalizing dogma and favor shaping state law to reflect biblical law, but some evangelicals reject imposing Christian values on non-Christian citizens through state law; on the fringes lie splinter groups like Christian Reconstructionists, who advocate world rule by white, Anglo-Saxon/Germanic Christians and the death penalty for homosexuals as prescribed in the Bible (Robinson, "Christian"). Paul Weyrich, who helped found the Moral Majority, coined the umbrella phrase "cultural conservative" to include not only fundamentalists, evangelicals, pentecostalists, and Roman Catholics but Jews and secularists as well (6). James D'Entremont has recently argued that a more precise term for anti-gay rights Christians might be the "Theocratic Right": Christians who believe that state law should be consonant with Biblical Law. But since mainline and progressive churches also see correspondences between their religious beliefs and their political beliefs, this phrase cannot represent all of the diverse groups—religious and secular—who are opposed to gay rights.

Didi Herman, Professor of Law at Keele University, and Kathy Rudy, Professor of Women's Studies and Ethics at Duke University, further divide conservative Christians into premillennial dispensationalists and postmillennialists to highlight their differing views of what God expects of the faithful. More than 60% of Americans believe in the Second Coming of Christ to judge the world. Premillennialists predict that the world will descend into moral and social chaos (Revelations 21), the true believers will be raptured to heaven, the AntiChrist (Satan) will rule until Christ returns a second time to defeat him in a final battle (Armageddon). This will usher in a new millennium, a thousand-year reign of peace, justice, and Christian values. At the end of the millennium, Christ will destroy the world and transport the saved to heaven (Herman 13). Postmillennialists, on the other hand, believe that Christ will not return until Christianity has ruled the earth for one thousand years. Although many conservative Christians are postmillenialists, Christian Right leaders tend to be premillennialists and so typically warn the faithful of the coming battle against the AntiChrist's minions (LGBTs, abortionists, non-Christians, communists, etc.) (Herman 20; Rudy 56). Since Satan is a master of deception, he may disguise himself as a human being or a human institution that attempts to replace Christianity with a false system of values promising salvation. Historically, he has appeared as: ancient Rome, the Ottoman Empire, the Catholic Pope, communism, fascism, the United Nations, the European Common Market, Islam, multiculturalism, and, most recently, the "new world order" of secular governments and multinational corporations (Herman 21; Rudy 57). Gays and lesbians fit neatly into this list because the "gay agenda" presents itself as a substitute system of values. Since the AntiChrist is powerful and cunning, pro-gay groups are typically described as powerful co-conspirators working with the liberal elite to replace Christianity with a godless state-sponsored secularism that will destroy traditional social morality and order (Herman 24; Rudy 56).

PRO-GAY RIGHTS GROUPS

Just as diversity of beliefs, values, and ideology marks anti-gay rights groups, it is impossible to typify LGBTs. Although often condemned as atheists who "have rejected all moral sanctions and religious beliefs" (Ray 75), LGBTs are not only religious congregants but also priests and nuns, rabbis and ministers. A survey conducted in St. Louis found that 68% of homosexual men were Protestant, 27% Catholic, 5% Jewish, and 0% had no religious preference; among lesbians, 65% were Protestant, 22% Catholic, 9% Jewish, and 4% had no religious preference (Saghir and Robins 12–14). On the whole, LGBTs tend to vote Democratic but only half identify themselves as liberal. In a 1996 exit poll, the Voter News Service found that 66% of self-identified gay people voted for Bill Clinton, 25% for Bob Dole, 7% for Ross Perot, and 4% for other candidates. When asked about political ideology, 48% identified themselves as liberal, 35%

moderate, and 17% conservative (David Smith). As Karen Ocamb, the editor of *Lesbian News*, declared:

Not all lesbians are animal-loving, vegetarian Democrats. We acknowledge that there are authentic lesbian Republicans as well as Pro-Life, red-meat-eating, fur-wearing, re-born Christian lesbians who ought not feel excluded because of their lifestyle or point of view. (Wockner 75)

Nevertheless, political support for gay rights is stronger in certain groups than in others. Public opinion surveys have consistently shown a strong positive correlation between tolerance for LGBTs and years of formal education, a tendency to vote for the Democratic Party, affiliation with liberal and moderate elements within Catholicism, Protestantism, and especially Judaism, and being female rather than male. Opposition to gay rights occurs more frequently among voters with less formal education, strong partisanship for conservative philosophy and the Republican Party, affiliation with fundamentalist, "born again," and orthodox elements within Protestantism, Catholicism, and Judaism, and being male rather than female (Schroedel 90–91). Voters who identify "weakly" with the Republican party, however, tend to support banning job discrimination and allowing gays and lesbians in the military, as compared to "strong" Republicans who oppose pro-gay policies by 60% to 70% (Haeberle 152). Voters who label themselves Independent resemble Democrats when asked if they favor equal treatment in employment, but they resemble Republicans when asked about the morality and legalization of those relationships (Schroedel 112). In general, Americans support the concept of equal rights more than they favor specific laws to enforce equality; the perception that LGBTs are immoral seems to be the biggest obstacle to legal gains (Lewis and Rogers 139).

The debate about gay rights involves other political differences that are sometimes surprising. Because theocratically-inclined groups favor shaping public morals through state law written according to their interpretation of the Scriptures, they worry secular and libertarian conservatives who favor a less intrusive government and those evangelicals who regard politics as intrinsically secular and ungodly, threatening the purity of faith and personal spirituality (Herman 171, 187–188). According to orthodox Christian theologian Rousas John Rushdoony, constructing a truly theocratic State

means to ground the totality of our lives, thinking, institutions, and world, including church, state, and school on the Name of Christ the King, *under* His authority, power, law-word, and government . . . the state must serve the Lord. (Herman 190)

Such a scenario makes secular conservatives feel uneasy, as Mickey Edwards (Harvard School of Government) argues:

It's important to remember what conservatism is and what it isn't. . . . First, conservatism is decentralized power, not concentrated power. . . . Second, conservatism is maximized freedom, not lists of approved behaviors. . . . The essence of a free society, [the Founding Fathers] knew, was to protect against the tyranny of any faction of society, including a majority faction. A free society was based not on majority rule but on safeguards against the trampling of any individual's rights. . . . Third, conservatism is the philosophy of the rights of people against the rights of government. It is the philosophy of questioned authority, not worship of authority.

The late Barry Goldwater, longtime leader of the conservative wing of the Republican Party, rejected a theocracy as a "conservative" form of government and reasoned that welcoming gays into the military would strengthen America, since gays and lesbians have historically had good service records in every war since the American Revolution. Andrew Sullivan has argued that legalizing same-sex marriage would be in accord with traditional American values: reducing promiscuity, fostering a stable home life, and strengthening America's moral fiber (Nava and Dawidoff 104). Could the Republican Party split up on this issue? Would secular conservatives find allies among libertarian Democrats (who also oppose government interference, including anti-discrimination laws) to form an *ad hoc* party of their own (Corvino xxv)?

Both Democratic and Republican parties have disaggregated and fragmented since the 1960s, with members changing affiliations or forming their own independent advocacy groups to promote special interests to which they feel more committed (Weeks 35). A *Times-Mirror* survey conducted in July 1992 showed that 40% of America's 175,000 precincts currently have no Republican or Democratic precinct captain (Reed 109–110). The vocabulary of "left," "right," or "center" is less descriptive of the terrain of post-consensus politics than it used to be. Politics is marked by a plurality of subgroups that crisscross the left/right binary. Voters may band together not only because they belong to a certain economic class, a labor union, a "special interest" consumer or industry group, or a religion, but because they share a personal trait, such as race, ethnicity, gender, or sexuality. "Conventional politics" now shares the stage with "identity politics" (Button 4–5). The result is varied, sometimes unpredictable affiliations. Bill Maher, who hosts the television show *Politically Incorrect,* illustrates this tendency; naming himself a "true conservative" (i.e., a libertarian conservative), he favors abortion rights but opposes anti-cigarette laws, he is for gun control but against expanding government regulations, he approves of capital punishment but is against the killing of animals for sport. What this reflects is a fundamental characteristic of democracy: that people who *are* free to think independently *will* think independently, according to, but also in conflict with, whatever social, political or religious group they belong to.

To simplify usage, I will use the term "anti-gay rights" for groups, regardless of their political or religious affiliation, who are opposed to extending legal protections and privileges to LGBTs to approximate those enjoyed by heterosexuals. It is possible for people to oppose legislating a particular right, such as gay marriage, without necessarily being theocratic, conservative, or homophobic, especially if they are philosophically opposed to expanding the scope of government authority in general (Button et al. 9). But the issue of homophobia can be a tricky one. A conscious fear or hatred of LGBTs can be distinguished from a purely political opposition to expanded rights, but an unconscious homophobia may masquerade as a seemingly rational opposition. As Colleen R. Logan argues, it is not always easy to distinguish homophobia (an unacknowledged or unconscious conflict over which the individual has no control) from homoprejudice (an anti-LGBT bias resulting from cultural or ideological systems of belief, as well as faulty or incomplete information, which can be altered through education). What motivates a particular political position is not always clear.

I will also use the term "pro-gay rights," though it too does not adequately convey the different groups who, for various reasons, support increased legal protections for sexual minorities. Gay rights advocates may be conservative, liberal or centrist politically, militant or moderate, sharing only the common interest of legal protection. The gay rights movement is a collection of various advocacy groups with different histories, ideologies, goals and methods.

The first three organizations attempting to represent gays and lesbians were formed in the early 1950s: the Daughters of Bilitis, ONE, and the Mattachine Society. Naming themselves "homophile groups," they sought, through reasoned discourse and pleas for sympathy, moderate changes in the public perception of homosexuality and government policy. Dominated by white, middle-class gays and lesbians, they desired assimilation into and accommodation with mainstream heterosexual society. In 1969, after LGBTs rioted against police harassment outside the Stonewall Inn in Greenwich Village, many young activists abandoned the "apologetic tone" of the homophile groups and began expressing their anger at inequality, stressing "gay pride," pressing government through public demonstrations and legal challenges to outlaw discrimination. New coalitions were formed with other liberationist groups, particularly feminists and ethnic minorities, spawning a network of national organizations—the Gay Liberation Front, Radicalesbians, Third World Gay Revolution, and the National Black Lesbian and Gay Leadership Forum. Gay Liberationists rejected efforts to normalize homosexuality because it did not challenge the dominant sexual regime that reduces eros to a genital-centered, penetrative sexual norm (in which who penetrates whom determines identity). Positing all humans as innately bisexual and androgynous, Gay Liberation was also a gender revolution, for it attempted to overthrow the homo/hetero dichotomy intertwined with a sex-role system that views masculinity and femininity as mutually exclusive categories of gender identity. And since the sex-role system supported other social hierarchies, it was argued that sexual freedom for all would trigger a social revolution by undermining the power and privilege that supported sexism, racism and imperialism (Seidman 117).

Although Gay Liberation as a movement ended in the mid-1970s, social change organizations grew from perhaps 50 to 400. The AIDS crisis galvanized previously non-political LGBTs and produced many small, militant groups, often using confrontational methods, such as ACT-UP (AIDS Coalition to Unleash Power) and Queer Nation. But as America itself became more conservative in the 1980s, leftist activism declined, leaving a field of diverse groups: liberals formed the National Gay and Lesbian Task Force, Democrats created the National Stonewall Democratic Federation, centrists dominated The Human Rights Campaign and PFLAG (Parents and Friends of Lesbians and Gays), while conservatives founded the Log Cabin Republicans. As these groups became more established, they became more mainstream, relying less on countercultural activists and more on hired staffs to professionalize and bureaucratize ongoing negotiations with governments and institutions (Haider-Markel, "Creating," 247–251; Sherrill 270; Bull 231; D'Emilio 35; Blasius and Phelan 377–378). Throughout the short history of gay and lesbian social change movements, splinter groups have continually formed. Lesbians and gay men differ sharply about policy issues: lesbian feminists rate child care, rape, pornography, and sexism higher than gay men, who focus on sodomy laws and police harassment. While lesbians are more likely to believe that their sexuality is socially constructed, gay men usually favor a biological and inborn basis (see Chapter 7 for a full discussion of these terms) (Smith and Windes 140). In the late 1970s, women-only cultural events, institutions, and businesses sprang up as part of a separatist movement. But even within the "lesbian community," sharp divisions arise. In the early 1980s, an ideological battle occurred between cultural feminists, who condemned sado-masochism and pornography as male-identified desires, and radical feminists, who included such desires in lesbian eroticism. In the 1980s lesbians and gay men of color protested their invisibility in gay rights organizations (Seidman 122, 126). Thus, the "gay community," like the general population, is a mix of various groups and movements, espousing different ideologies (e.g., whether sexuality is fixed or fluid, biologically based or culturally constructed), different tactics (e.g., traditional lobbying versus confrontation), economic status (e.g., working class versus wealthy elite) and different goals (e.g., assimilation or separation).

Since the word "homosexual" has a sordid past in medical history, when it was associated with pathology, it may tempt readers to reduce otherwise complex LGB lives to the merely sexual. But there are times when it is an effective oppositional term for "heterosexual," and I will use it in such cases to delineate binary thinking. For brevity's sake, I will use the abbreviation

LGBT or the word "gay" (as in "gay rights," "gay bashing," or "anti-gay rights" groups) to stand for all of these groups if the issue in question can be applied to all; I will use "gay male" if I am referring specifically to gay men, and "LGB" if the research is not applicable to transgendered/transsexual persons.

TRANSGENDERED/TRANSSEXUAL PERSONS

Although gender identity and sexual orientation intersect (in that each is expressed in the terms of the other), transgenderism is thought to be largely independent of homosexuality. While sexual orientation is a question of which sex you find erotically attractive as a partner, gender identity is a question of how you see yourself psychically: man, woman, or some combination. It is possible that "how you see yourself" may be influenced to some degree by which sex you are attracted to (Stein 40), but in practice, if an individual is born anatomically female but feels like a man, and perhaps even sees her body as male, this person's sexual identity is considered to be male (Nangeroni). Transgender categories are:

- FTM individuals (female-to-male) are born female but see themselves as partly to fully masculine.
- MTF individuals (male-to-female) are born male but see themselves as partly to fully feminine.
- Intersexed individuals are born with some combination of male and female physiology, and there are roughly 80 combinations known. They may grow up accepting their mixed gender as natural. But often when a child is born with some combination of male *and* female sex organs (such as, testes and ovaries, penis and vagina, uterus and prostate, fallopian tubes and sperm transport ducts), doctors (often arbitrarily) usually alter the child surgically to fit a particular gender depending on how large the penis is; if it is judged too small, the penis (and testes) will be removed and a vagina constructed (if not already present); if the penis is large, all female organs will be removed. If the surgeon chooses wrongly, the child will grow up feeling like a man in a woman's body or a woman in a man's body. (Fausto-Sterling, "How," 221; Bill Stuart, "faq2TS")

What it "feels like" to be a man or a woman depends in part on how one's culture defines manliness or womanliness, and it may not correlate with genital anatomy or an identifiable gender (Stein 31). Most transgendered individuals do not choose to undergo "sex reassignment surgery," masculinizing or feminizing the body with sex hormones of the opposite sex, electrolysis or plastic surgery to conform to the gender that person identifies with, though such techniques can be very successful (Denny and Green 86–87). FTM transsexuals can be captains of the football team; some MTF transsexuals have become models in women's fashions.

In sexuality textbooks, transsexuals and transvestites are considered distinct groups. In its purest form, transvestitism means "cross-dressing," but psychologists distinguish between dressing for sexual stimulation (cross-dressing) and dressing for stress relief (transvestitism). Moreover, transvestites can include a wide range of styles and goals: they can be

fe/male impersonators, who dress as members of the opposite sex for a show; there are drag queens/kings, who dress with the intent to amuse or offend; there are shaman who cross-dress during religious/spiritual ceremonies; there are transvestites who dress only for an hour a week; there are transvestites who live almost full time as women or men. (Bill Stuart, "faq2TS")

In theory, transsexuals are generally certain from an early age that their anatomical sex and psychic gender are at odds, and they want to permanently alter their bodies to fit the image they have of themselves, while transvestites are typically heterosexual men who dress as women. In the real world, however, this distinction can often break down. Some transsexuals content themselves with cross-dressing; some transsexuals disparage cross-dressers as "men in skirts" or "chicks with dicks." Sexual orientation among transsexuals varies from heterosexual to homosexual or bisexual. Therapist Mildred Brown reports that drag queens account for only 5% of the gay male population, while 50% of the MTFs and 10% of the FTMs in her practice are married (Brown and Rounsley 15, 181; Nangeroni), though why such differences exist is unclear. Diversity exists within diversity. Labeled groups often contain individuals who exceed or unfix the label they are given or which they embrace.

Politically, transgendered and transsexual persons have not fared as well as lesbians and gay men, for they have been marginalized by both heterosexuals and homosexuals. Although centrally involved in the Stonewall riots and active in the sexual rights movement since the 1970s, TG/TS individuals have often been scorned or politely ignored by assimilationist gay and lesbian organizations working for acceptance by mainstream society. A few TG/TS organizations have sprung up—such as Transexual Menace, the International Conference on Transgender Law and Employment Policy, the American Educational Gender Information Service, FTM International, the Intersex Society of North America, and TGR! (Transgender Rights!)—but much less research has been done on transgender issues than on lesbian and gay issues, and so legal protections are far fewer (Bull 352).

Part One

Religious and Sexual Diversity

No culture that has ever embraced homosexuality has ever survived.
—*Rep. Steve Largent, U.S. Congress*

Among my people, gay is a special status.
—*Arizona Native American*

3

Religious Views:
Past and Present

Both pro-gay and anti-gay rights groups look to the past for corroboration of their present perspectives. Chief Justice of the Supreme Court, Warren Burger, cited "millennia of moral teaching" as a reason for denying Hardwick's appeal against Georgia's sodomy law (Halley, "Reasoning," 1751). Colonel Ronald D. Ray argues that gay men and lesbians should be excluded from military service because "for over 3,000 years, the Western world remained united in its condemnation of homosexuality as an abomination" (96). To provide counter evidence, anthropologist Gilbert Herdt cites ancient Greek documents, noting that the socially approved erotic unions between warriors of the Sacred Band of Thebes were praised by Plutarch for their military prowess: "An army consisting of lovers and their beloved ones, fighting at each other's side, although a mere handful, would overcome the whole world" (*Same* 69). History presents a complex picture of conflicting attitudes and rationales. In 1951 Ford and Beach reported that, of 76 societies outside of the U.S., 64% of them considered same-sex sexual relations normal or socially acceptable—at least for certain members of the community (130). A later study of 193 world cultures revealed that 28% left evidence suggesting they accepted male-male sexual relations, 14% rejected it, and 58% were neutral or left no evidence either way (McCary and McCary 254).

Of the 14% who rejected sexual diversity, the Zoroastrians were the most adamant, describing the devil as a homosexual who may be killed without legal consequences for the murderer (Stemmeler and Clark 9). Others include Orthodox Judaism, the ancient Assyrians, Persians, Mongols, Germans, Aztecs, Mbuti Pgymies, the Himalayan Lepcha, and the early Ashantis. Toleration of sexual diversity has also been long-lived, as suggested in the early legal codes of Mesopotamia (2375–1726 B.C.) and the records of the Albanians, Celts, Chinese, Japanese, Scandinavians, Egyptians, Hindus, Brazilians, Cathaginians, Gauls, Mayans, Syrians, Pakistanis, and the Sumerians. Late Paleolithic cave paintings depict male-male erotic connections from roughly 17,000 B.C. (Greenberg, 34, 124–183).

Images and stories about transgendered individuals occur in almost all cultures and mythologies. A 15,000-year-old cave painting in India shows a transgendered priest(ess) known as Hijra. Pakistan, Burma, Oman, Polynesia, Vietnam, Korea, Tahiti, South America, and Malaysia employed holy transgendered people (Bullough and Bullough 35–36; Greenberg 56–58). Some Buddhist divinities exhibited cross-gender behavior, and both Hinduism and Buddhism embrace the idea that reincarnation involves cross-sex rebirths (Helms 401). Non-religious transgendered persons (TGs) appeared in Kenya, Sudan, Ethiopia, Nubia, Ghana, Angola, Rhodesia, Madagascar, Senegal, and Uganda (Greenberg 61). In 1953, a Danish physician changed an ex-G.I. named George Jorgensen into Christine in the most widely publicized early sexual reassignment surgery. Since then, the number of postoperative transsexuals has grown into the tens of thousands, with many times that number in various stages of gender transition.

It is a common belief that sexual diversity received unqualified approval in ancient Rome and Greece, where love between men was praised as true love, for it included friendship, shared values, commitment, and even marriage (Churchill 76–77). But recent historical research presents a more complicated picture. Bernadette J. Brooten, Kraft-Hod Professor of Christian Studies at Brandeis University, has discovered that heated debates surrounded diverse sexualities for centuries in the ancient world, and that while certain male-male sexual relationships were socially acceptable under certain conditions, female-female sexual relationships were not. The ancients judged the value of sexual relationships on gendered terms: the active (insertive) role was considered appropriate behavior for men whether the penetrated partner was a man or a woman. Being penetrated was appropriate for a younger male, a woman, a lower class man, a foreigner, a prostitute, or a servant (*Love* 2–3). Women were presumed to be sexually passive, by nature receivers of semen, and so they were condemned as "monstrous, lawless, licentious, unnatural, and shameful" if they took on an active role with another woman (29).

The etiology (causative factors) of sexual orientation was also a highly contested issue. Ancient astrologers claimed that the configuration of Venus, Mars, and the Moon at one's birth determined orientation as well as the inclination to assume active or passive roles—which suggests that sexual diversity was regarded by some as "fated" and therefore not a moral issue (*Love* 115–141). Some Greek and Roman medical texts depicted same-sex relations as a "disease of the soul" to be treated with mind control or a clitoridectomy (144), but at the same time these texts employed biological terms (an enlarged clitoris for women, spermatic ducts misdirected to the anus instead of the penis for men). Several medical authorities blamed the individual for freely allowing lust to cause these physiological deformities, but, once established, they became an involuntary and lifelong condition that could be passed on to children (148–149, 156, 172), thus blurring the lines between choice and fate.

In the Islamic world, attitudes were also divided. As sociologist David F. Greenberg has pointed out, the Koran condemned same-sex couples but specified no punishment, and so they appeared—openly and often without censure—in many Middle East societies (13n.29). Some Moroccans, for instance, thought that a saintly man could transmit his holiness or virtue through sex with either men or women, and in Northern Morocco it was believed that a boy could not learn the Koran well unless his studies were accompanied by a sexual relationship with his male teacher (26–27). Public baths were popular meeting places for lesbians in Turkey, and in some Arab societies today lesbian relationships are acceptable for older single women. In Kenya, Muslim Mombasan women created open and extensive social networks of lesbian couples (178n.316, 182).

Sexual diversity was generally tolerated in pre-Christian Africa, Polynesia, China and Japan, especially among Samurai warriors for whom the erotic bond between men had been held in high esteem as "manly" since the Heian period (794–1185 A.D.) (Herdt, *Same*, 63–108; Greenberg 260). When Catholic missionary Father Francis Xavier first tried to convert Japanese Buddhists to Christianity, he was amazed to find same-sex relationships ubiquitous: "It is visible and public to all, including men and women, young and old, none of whom think much of it nor despise it as it seems to be a common habit indeed" (Bleys 28). In China, same-sex relationships had been socially acceptable for 2,000 years, as it was in Southeast Asia, India, Sub-Saharan Africa, New Zealand and Australia (29–32, 178). Spanish Conquistadors found LGBTs in Central and South America among the Mayans, Incas, and Aztecs, even though some sodomy laws were in place (Greenberg 165–166). James Wilson reported that the male *mahus* of Tahiti dressed and behaved like women, seeking "the courtship of men as women do, nay are more jealous of the men who cohabit with them, and always refuse to sleep with women," yet they were highly esteemed by their societies (78).

An equally wide variety of sexual attitudes were found among Native American societies. Sexual minorities were held in great contempt by the Papago, Cocopa, Chocktaw, Klamath, East Apaches, Creek, and Pima tribes. The Santee Dakotas exiled men who attempted to seduce other men; the Sinalwa of northwest Mexico viewed them with "horror." Other groups, like the Zunis and Mojaves, tolerated but teased sexually diverse individuals. And some, like the Winnebago and Koniag tribes, tolerated diversity until contact with European Christians (Greenberg 50, 52–54, 76, 79). Out of roughly 500 distinct tribes in North America, the Gay American Indian History Project found 133 which tolerated sexually diverse members (named "berdache" by European colonizers, a derogatory term), groups such as the Lakota, Cheyenne, Navajo and Mojave. Some believed that same-sex love or transgenderism was spiritually superior to heterosexuality because it was not tied to the economic rewards that children, as a labor/political force, brought to a married couple (Roscoe 217–222). Among the older Lakota tribes, lesbian and transgendered female members were valued as medicine women because it was thought that they had sacred ties to the God who had made them sexually unique. Gay and transgendered males in some Native American tribes became respected medicine men, shamans, artists, matchmakers, and storytellers. Among the Illinois and Nadowessi, gay/transgendered men served as advisors to tribe Councils; Koniag male TGs acted as civil judges; among the Oglala, Crows, Cheyennes, Navajo, Yokuts, Sioux, Fox and Sack tribes, they were given special roles in religious rituals (Greenberg 48–49).

Early European colonists were appalled that so many Native American tribes accepted sexual diversity. When French missionary Father P.F.X. Charlevoix visited the Iriquois tribe in 1744, he found the men were "unashamed to wear women's clothing and to practice all the occupations of women." Unsympathetic, he claimed that the Native Americans "pretend that this usage comes from their religion" when it was really only "effeminacy and lewdness" (Greenberg 40). But a number of Native American societies believed that LGBTs were fated by God to be sexually different. The Mojave Indians, for instance, thought that sexual diversity started in the womb, beyond the control of the individual. In southern Mexico the Zapotec Indians believed that God made such individuals for a special, spiritual purpose. Today, some Native American LGBTs use the phrase "Native Two-Spirit People," a term that focuses less on sexual acts and more on the belief that everyone has both a male and a female spirit within that may manifest itself in diverse ways (as lesbian, gay, bisexual, transgendered/ transsexual behavior). Greenberg argues that this theological construct accounts for why some two-spirit people married the same anatomical sex, and some the opposite anatomical sex (44). As Terry N. Tafoya explains:

To be male means seeing through the eyes of a male. To be female means seeing through the eyes of a female, but to be two-spirit means seeing through both sets of eyes, and therefore being able to see further, or more holistically, than someone who is only male or female. This concept suggests why the two-spirit person is often associated with power and spirituality—having this "double vision" gave a greater potential for one to exist on a more integrated level. In general, everyone was regarded as having a male and female element within—in some tribes, this is why wearing the hair in two braids was common, to signify the balance one should seek between those inner principles. (Cabaj and Stein 603–604)

Native Americans saw strong spiritual connections between individuals regardless of their differences, even while acknowledging that significant differences set them apart. As one Arizona Native American puts it:

Among my people, gay is a special status. . . . The more unique someone is, the more valuable they are, the more unique their vision, the more unique their gift, their perspective, everything they can offer is something that other people can't offer. . . . The thing that's different about where I come from, is that all human beings are respected because all human beings have potential, all human beings have value. (Walter Williams 229)

Clearly, a number of ancient religions found social and spiritual value in sexual diversity while others found only degradation and sin. Orthodox Christian theology rejects the idea that God created "evil" or "imperfection" because He is perfect in His oneness (Herman 71), as James B. De Young, Professor of New Testament Language and Literature at Western Seminary, argues: "There is only one God and one form of human sexual behavior that constitutes an acceptable union before God, namely, the marriage of a man and a woman" (16). Using Jeffrey Russell's research into historical conceptions of evil, Jonathan Dollimore theorizes that the extreme dichotomization of heterosexuality and homosexuality resulted from Christianity's dualistic thinking about God's moral nature. In many pre-Christian religions, good and evil were not viewed as absolute opposites but as closely conjoined aspects of one Supreme Being. God and the Devil were not separate beings, but often brothers working together; in some sects, the Devil was God's child. The God-Devil joined death and destruction indissolubly with life and fertility, creating infinite diversity. But the Hebrew/Christian tradition radically purified God of evil, shifting the blame for its existence onto individuals who defied God. Perversion (literally a "turning away" from the one, true path, becoming something estranged, other, and therefore evil) began with Lucifer, then Adam and Eve, who rebelled against God, logic, and proper desire (27, 145). Diversity became rebellion.

The growing visibility of gay Christians since the 1950s has caused some churches to reexamine the theological binarism behind their proscriptions of sexual diversity, though with mixed results. In 1963 the Quakers of England issued a statement that homosexuality was a condition no more unnatural or abnormal than left-handedness (Barnett 127). Some sects now perform ceremonies celebrating gay unions: Progressive Jewish congregations, some Baptist churches, the Unitarian Church, the United Church of

Christ, the Episcopal Church in Seattle, and all Metropolitan Community Churches (Nava and Dawidoff 80, 90; Marcus 135). In 1996 the Unitarians voted to endorse the legalization of same-sex marriages. Some Presbyterian congregations and the Episcopal Church ordain celibate gays and lesbians while still condemning the sexually active, drawing a moral distinction between condition and act (Crew; Toulouse 35). The Evangelical Lutheran Church recommends more openness towards gays and lesbians, but adds that homosexuality must still be judged "a departure from the biblical, heterosexual structure of God's creation" (Rudy 86).

Reasoning that spiritual services should be available to LGBTs whether or not official dogma is changed, some denominations, both independent and mainline, have formed affiliated groups for their LGBT members: Dignity (Roman Catholic), Integrity (Episcopal), Lutherans Concerned, Affirmation (United Methodist), American Baptists Concerned, the Brethren/ Mennonite Council for Lesbian and Gay Concerns, Friends of Lesbian and Gay Concerns (Quaker), Presbyterians for Lesbian and Gay Concerns, New Ways Ministry (Roman Catholic), Affirm (United Church of Canada), National Gay Pentecostal Alliance, United Church Coalition for Lesbian and Gay Concerns, and the Universal Fellowship of Metropolitan Community Churches (Scanzoni and Mollenkott 135). Catholic priests are allowed to officiate at services held by Dignity, a LGBT organization founded in 1969 with 83 chapters across the nation. Dignity's "statement of position and purpose" spells out a policy consistent with liberal interpretations of the New Testament:

We believe that gay, lesbian, bisexual, and transgender Catholics in our diversity are members of Christ's mystical body, numbered among the People of God. We have an inherent dignity because God created us, Christ died for us, and the Holy Spirit sanctified us in Baptism, making us temples of the Spirit, and channels through which God's love becomes visible. Because of this, it is our right, our privilege, and our duty to live the sacramental life of the Church, so that we might become more powerful instruments of God's love working among all people. We believe that gay, lesbian, bisexual and transgender persons can express their sexuality in a manner that is consonant with Christ's teaching. We believe that we can express our sexuality physically, in a unitive manner that is loving, life-giving, and life-affirming.

But the Vatican's position has been equivocal at best. In 1975, Pope Paul VI approved for publication, *Persona humana: Declaration of Certain Questions Pertaining to Sexual Ethics,* in which a distinction was drawn between people who have sex with the same sex but who are not innately homosexual and those who are instinctually or constitutionally homosexual:

In the pastoral field, these homosexuals must certainly be treated with understanding and sustained in the hope of overcoming their personal difficulties and their inability to fit into society. This culpability will be judged with prudence. But no pastoral method can be employed which would give moral justification to these acts on the grounds that they would be consonant with the condition of such people. For according to the objective moral order, homosexual relations are acts which lack an essential and indispensable finality. In Sacred Scripture they are condemned as serious depravity and even presented as the sad consequence of rejecting God. This judgment of Scripture does not of course permit us to conclude that all those who suffer from this anomaly are personally responsible for it, but it does attest to the fact that homosexual acts are intrinsically disordered and can in no case be approved of. (Congregation)

The Vatican was responding to scientific evidence that for some people sexual orientation may be an integral part of their emotional and sexual identity, and hence unchangeable (Sullivan, *Virtually*, 34). If the condition were innate, it might be morally neutral; *being* gay could be an anomaly of nature (caused by humankind's fallen state), but having same-sex sexual relations would still be a sin because it reinforces the anomaly by lacking "finality," that is, conception. *Persona humana* was seen by some gay Catholics as a hopeful sign. Optimism was reinforced by Cardinal Basil Hume's 1995 "Note on Church Teaching Concerning Homosexual People":

It is deplorable that homosexual persons have been and are the object of violence in speech or in action. Such treatment deserves condemnation from the church's pastors wherever it occurs. It reveals a kind of disregard for others which endangers the most fundamental principles of a healthy society. The intrinsic dignity of each person must always be respected in word, in action and in law. Nothing in the church's teaching can be said to support or sanction even implicitly the victimization of homosexual men and women. Furthermore, "homophobia" should have no place among Catholics.

A follow-up pastoral letter in 1997 from U.S. Bishops urged Catholic parents to love and accept their gay sons and lesbian daughters (Toulouse 35).

But Mark Jordan, Professor of Medieval History at Emory University, warns against optimistic expectations because none of these documents shows theological change. They reassert "natural law" arguments that "acts of homosexuality are disordered by their very nature," so unequivocal that it is "discoverable by human reason apart from divine revelation"; any sexual activity outside of heterosexual marriage is intrinsically evil; and the church's "unchanging principles" are universally applicable regardless of the quality of the relationship or the merit of the individuals involved. Moreover, Jordan argues, the "science" that the Vatican used is not that of the twentieth century but of the nineteenth, so plagued by prejudice and inadequate methodology that it has been largely repudiated by twentieth century research. While the Vatican admits that modern science has shown that "the human person is so profoundly affected by sexuality that it must be considered as one of the factors which give to each individual's life the principal traits that distinguish it," it dismisses scientific evidence suggesting the personal or psychological value of a same-sex sexuality. The assumption behind "natural law" is that a careful study of nature will corroborate it, but Jordan argues that the Vatican ignores careful studies that do not corroborate what orthodox theology thinks is true of nature (*Silence* 26–30). Finally, Jordan observes that a 1992 Vatican document recommended discrimination against homosexuals in employment as teachers or coaches, in housing, spousal benefits, and adoption or foster care, reasoning that the rights of homosexuals "can be legitimately limited for objectively disordered external conduct" in the same way that society limits the rights of "contagious or mentally ill persons" (41).

In spite of the church's theological inflexibility, some Catholics remain hopeful. Admittedly, *Persona humana* states that cultural changes in sexual attitudes should not affect moral standards: "principles and norms in no way owe their origin to a certain type of culture, but rather to knowledge of the divine law and of human nature" (Pilant 123). But, in practice, moral theology can be—and has been—amended in response to advances in science or changes in the cultural understanding of human nature because Catholic theologians do not rely exclusively on Scripture or literal readings to ascertain spiritual or moral truth. Roman Catholic priest C. Robert Nugent explains:

Catholicism uses four major sources for principles and guidance in ethical questions like homosexuality: scripture, tradition (theologians, church documents, official teachings, etc.), reason, and human experience. All are used in conjunction with one another. Scripture is a fundamental and primary authoritative Catholic source—but not the *only* source. Biblical witness is taken seriously, but not literally. An individual scriptural text must be understood in the larger context of the original language and culture, the various levels of meanings, and the texts' applications to contemporary realities in light of the role of the community's and its official leadership role in providing authoritative interpretations. (PFLAG)

Because of this interdisciplinary process (shared by many mainstream Protestant and Jewish sects), the Catholic Church has in the past adjusted its teachings in response to changes in scientific knowledge and cultural values. For eighteen centuries the Church, citing Leviticus, judged sex with a menstruating woman to be a mortal sin:

Do not have intercourse with a woman during her monthly period, because she is ritually unclean. (18:19)
If a man has intercourse with a woman during her monthly period, both of them are to be driven out of the community, because they have broken the regulations about ritual uncleanness. (20:18) *(Good News Bible)*

In ancient Israel, menstruation was thought to be unclean both spiritually and physically, and Jewish women were barred from religious services or any interaction with men until they had purified themselves. An extended version of Leviticus in *The Jerusalem Bible* (not included in Christian bibles) provides more detail on how menstrual uncleanness should be handled:

> When a woman has a discharge of blood, and blood flows from her body, this uncleanness of her monthly periods shall last for seven days.
> Anyone who touches her will be unclean until evening.
> Any bed she lies on in this state will be unclean; any seat she sits on will be unclean.
> Anyone who touches her bed must wash his clothing and wash himself and will be unclean until evening.
> Anyone who touches any seat she has sat on must wash his clothing and wash himself and will be unclean until evening. If there is anything on the bed or on the chair on which she sat, anyone who touches it will be unclean until evening.
> If a man sleeps with her, he will be affected by the uncleanness of her monthly periods. He shall be unclean for seven days. Any bed he lies on will be unclean. (Alexander Jones 150)

Although by modern standards such concern may seem odd, many ancient peoples believed that blood (whether menstrual or shed during birthing) damaged semen. The origin of this myth is unknown, but it may have resulted from an awareness that intercourse during menstruation seldom produced children, and since it was assumed by the ancients that semen alone contained all that was necessary to plant a child into a womb, it may have been reasoned that menstruation terminated the life of an unborn child. Wasting or killing seminal fluid therefore became a moral issue, and any man who ejaculated outside of a vagina was also considered unclean and had to observe similar precautions and rites (Gagnon 138).

This menstrual myth was finally disproved by late eighteenth century science, and by the late nineteenth century Catholic theologians began privately to question the Levitican prohibition, noting that after Jesus Christ was born, Mary attended a purification ritual to cleanse her of defiling birthing blood (Luke 2:22–24): could the very process that gave Jesus to the world be a sin (VanGemeren et al. 4:478)? After another century of further thought, in 1951, Pope Pius XII made the first approving reference to sex during menstruation as a morally acceptable way to avoid pregnancy ("the rhythm method"). Gay and lesbian theologians now make a similar argument: that loathing sexual diversity is just as outmoded as despising menstruation (Halsall, "Syllabus").

But theological changes are problematic because Christians cover a diverse field ideologically. Different issues get different responses. A recent poll asked Christians if they favored "gay marriages": only 13% of white evangelical Protestants, 27% of white non-evangelical Protestants, 31% of white Roman Catholics, and 25% of African American Christians said "yes" (Toulouse 33). At the same time, a 1992 Gallup Poll showed that

78% of the Catholics surveyed were in favor of gay/lesbian civil rights; 46% agreed that "sexual relations between gay or lesbian persons in committed relationships could be morally acceptable" (Roche); and 44% of Catholic priests agreed (Perry 59). Within the Catholic Church, conservatives and liberals vie for control. Conservatives created ORCM (the Orthodox Roman Catholic Movement) to oppose any liberalizing of church policy or practice. Some have joined Pat Robertson's Christian Coalition to form the Catholic Alliance "to stand together" against the "aggressive secularism of Western life." Ralph Reed predicts that if a coalition of 58 million Catholics and 24 million Evangelicals "support like-minded candidates, they can determine the outcome of almost any election in the nation" (14–16). In response, liberal Catholics organized the Interfaith Alliance, a faith-based group with 49 chapters in 23 states ("Catholic Clergy") with an online mission statement specifically targeting the Christian Coalition:

The Interfaith Alliance works to ensure that the religious traditions and heritage of all Americans are protected. We work towards a pluralistic society where people of all faiths—and those of no faith—are welcome; where no faith receives preferential treatment and our religious diversity is celebrated. ("Safeguarding Religious Liberty")

Orthodox Christians condemn moral tolerance as misguided and unbiblical, and they accuse gay-friendly churches of either self-deception or hypocrisy. Most offer tempered criticisms, but some are angered by what they see as an attack on the church itself. Brian Clowes, author of a massive Internet web site entitled "The Pro-Life Activist's Encyclopedia," describes gay-friendly congregations as

the pitiful spectacle of hardened sinners masquerading as Christians. Screaming Neofeminists, mega-abortionists, corrupt politicians, and simpering homosexuals desperately want to be a part of that which they so decisively reject. . . . Both Dignity, which embraces sodomy, and CFFC [Catholics for a Free Choice], which pushes abortion, know that the activities they are advocating are mortal sins in the eyes of the Catholic Church. Yet they try to confuse the faithful by spouting lies and misinformation. (115)

Clowes cannot reconcile Dignity's inclusive theology with the letter of Old Testament law. He cannot even conceive how it *is* a theology and so concludes that homosexuals must be consciously lying. Pastor Peter J. Peters of Colorado considers the problem in premillennial terms: not as individual self-deception but the worldwide deception of modern humanism:

Today's modern, state approved, tax exempt Christianity is quite different than the 1776 model. It has been made more refined and holy and is epitomized by such buzz words and phrases as: charity, forgiveness, meekness, gentleness, love thy neighbor, turn the other cheek, render unto Caesar, submit to authority, save souls, God is no respecter of persons, etc. Such words and phrases are in the scriptures, but the scriptures are distorted, twisted, improperly taught and misunderstood by most pulpits today.

The result has been a refined, palatable, goody goody religion that fits well within the plans of the one world Neo-Communist conspirators, is tenderly embraced by an effeminate world, and is socially accepted by a Christless, Lawless, Humanistic society.

The issue of whether dogma should evolve over time (as God's desires for humankind change or are better understood by each succeeding generation) or not (since God's desires are perfect and eternal, concisely stated by the ancient prophets, requiring no revision) is a longstanding debate within Judaism and Christianity. Revelation is the cornerstone of both. The belief that God spoke through the ancient prophets and demanded obedience makes the Judeo-Christian God an activist God, one who enters human history, directs events, and expects cooperation. But it is a matter of intense debate between sects about *how* God intrudes upon history and *what* constitutes cooperation: is it obedience to the letter of the divine law, or is it a continuing quest for a better understanding of the spirit of the law? Does God require piety from individuals only, or from governments too? Is revelation complete, or are more prophets to come? Is compromise even possible if the question of how to view LGBTs becomes a litmus test for religious commitment?

Cardinal Joseph Ratzinger has warned that little leeway is allowed on any serious moral question:

The Church's doctrine regarding this issue is thus based, not on isolated phrases for facile theological argument, but on the solid foundation of a constant biblical testimony. . . . It is likewise essential to recognize that the Scriptures are not properly understood when they are interpreted in a way which contradicts the Church's living Tradition. To be correct, the interpretation of Scripture must be in accord with that Tradition. (204–205)

In response, Revisionists point to John 16:12–13:

I have yet many things to say unto you, but ye cannot bear them now. Howbeit when he, the Spirit of truth, is come, he will guide you into all truth: for he shall not speak of himself; but whatsoever he shall hear, that shall he speak: and he will shew you things to come. (King James Version)

Theologian Raymond E. Brown believes that such oppositions within Christianity is not a failing but an advantage. The 300 Protestant sects that proliferated in the United States were produced by

diverse lines of development coming out of the New Testament diversities, and so biblical criticism should force the church to examine why it has chosen one line of

development rather than another. This may lead to a recognition that another
church has followed a different biblical line of development and thus preserved
another biblical value. That is not an affirmation of relativism but an encouragement to the churches to face ecumenism as an essential enrichment rather than a
grudging concession. (35)

Can disagreement be turned into enrichment in the gay rights debate as
well? In 1990 the World Council of Churches concluded that "God is calling us to rethink" sexuality (Robin Smith 3), but what will it take to do
this? Conservative scholar Thomas E. Schmidt warns:

. . . each new generation is not free to produce a new code of behavior, no matter
how enlightened it thinks itself. The inspiration of Scripture and the righteousness
stimulated by centuries of its influence suggests that biblical values are lasting values. We should resist tampering with the morality of the Bible unless a compelling
case is made. . . . God rarely speaks today in an audible voice. (19–20, 167)

How compelling need the case be? At what point does reverence for tradition become blindness, or nostalgia for a past that may never have existed?
Did the ancient prophets enjoy a pure, unambiguous view of human and
divine nature, superior to ours? Or does the present generation have something to contribute to an evolving spirituality? If twenty-first century politics can fuel theological change, it may be that a resolution of the gay rights
debate will reinvigorate Christianity with fresh insights into the boundary
between principle and love, Christian law and Christian charity. But it
could also threaten to divide religious groups even further if what is "lasting" about religious values cannot be satisfactorily defined.

4

Biblical Scholarship: Texts, Errors, and Methods

Did the original biblical texts specify that homosexuality is a sin? The answer to this question is enmeshed in complex, scholarly issues. The first English Bible, the King James Version (KJV), was written nearly 1600 years after Christ's death and over two millennia after Leviticus was composed. Such great temporal gaps seriously complicate translation, and much of modern biblical scholarship is devoted to examining how well and why James' scholars translated as they did. The KJV was derived from various foreign language texts, some of which were many generations of copies of copies, often by hands unknown, and numerous errors over the centuries had crept into variants. Even as early as the fourth century A.D., St. Jerome claimed that there were as many different versions of the Bible as there were manuscripts (Price 9). By the seventeenth century, it was impossible to know which ones were the most faithful to the original.

Errors could occur simply because of the way ancient Hebrew was written or spoken. The alphabet consisted of 22 letters, all of them consonants. Vowels were pronounced but not written down (Barthel 18). To conserve writing materials, the Jews did not separate words with spaces or punctuation, which sometimes makes it difficult to tell whether a certain consonant belongs to the preceding word or to the following word. In Hebrew the shift of a single consonant between words can deeply alter the meaning of a phrase (Price 18). Misspellings also occurred. Hebrew letters changed appearance over time, and when different parts of older and younger texts were combined (no Hebrew manuscript was dated until the ninth century A.D.), scribes sometimes mistook one letter for another. The confusion of the Hebraic letters English editors transliterated as *d* and *r* was very common, and scribes confused *b/k, b/m, b/n, g/w, g/y, w/z, w/y, w/r, k/n, m/s* as well, but nearly every letter in the alphabet was at one time mistaken for another (Price 134; VanGemeren 1:62).

Other errors can be attributed to copying practices. Hebraic texts were copied year after year for centuries, and overworked copiers could lose track of the material, repeating the same phrase twice or dropping a phrase altogether. For instance, as VanGemeren shows, Genesis 47:16 reads *w'tnh lkm bmqnykm* ("I will give you for your cattle") in the Hebrew Massoretic Text, while the *Septuagint* (the first Greek translation of the Old Testament, second century B.C.) reads *w'tnh lkm lhm bmqnykm* ("I will give you bread for your cattle"). VanGemeren reasons that the scribe may have skipped *lhm* (bread) not only because of nearby words with similar beginnings and endings, but because of the similar sound of *k* and *h* (1:62–63). To save time, a group of scribes might employ a reader who would dictate to them, but some Hebrew words, though spelled differently, sound almost identical, and various exchanges were made: thus "Hadoram" in II Chronicles 10:18 became "Adoram" in I Kings 12:18. Letters could be transposed, changing the meaning of a phrase: the Massoretic version of Deuteronomy 31:1 reads *wylk msh* ("and Moses went"), but the *Septuagint* renders it as *wykl msh* ("and Moses finished") (1:63).

Once an error became part of a biblical text, the next copier could duplicate it in all of his copies, perhaps adding some of his own (Price 23). Worn out manuscripts were destroyed (to keep them out of the hands of infidels), so subsequent scribes had no originals to go back to for comparison. Moreover, the Old Testament (OT) itself came from a large collection of diverse texts written by various Hebrew sects; centuries later, rabbis argued which ones should represent rabbinical thought. Some felt free to revise Biblical passages to make their meaning more accessible to contemporary readers, by replacing archaic Hebrew phrasing, adding material from parallel passages, and substituting euphemisms for vulgarities (VanGemeren 1:53, 57–58, 63). By Christ's lifetime, so many errors, revisions, additions and changes had crept into all OT texts, no one could say with certainty what the exact words of the original Scriptures were.

Six hundred years after Christ's birth the Massoretes, groups of Jewish families, launched an ambitious program to clean up the Hebrew Scriptures. By inserting vowels, punctuation and diacritical marks to suggest how a word should sound, they were, in effect, deciding how their Bible should be read and what it should mean. So influential was this work that all subsequent systems of Hebrew grammar were built upon the Massoretic system. But evidence suggests that some of their revisions were modernizations, not recuperations, of ancient Hebraic meaning (Price 29). By the 1500s a large number of Hebrew Bibles based on different manuscripts were available throughout Europe. No surviving manuscript of the complete Hebrew Old Testament—other than fragments—is older than the ninth century A.D. (Price 25–37). Scholars have no original to help them track down all the revisions, insertions, and deletions that subtly reworked the intent of the original authors. Ironically, the Dead Sea Scrolls, discovered in 1948, are the most complete, unedited, original manuscripts of Jewish religious writing today, yet even they are copies of copies made centuries after the original texts were written.

While OT texts were already regarded as sacred Scripture by the first and second centuries A.D., Paul's letters and the Gospels were not so revered until the eighth century (Boswell 92). Thus, early Christian copiers may have been less careful about preserving the exact wording of the original. By the fourth century, St. Jerome was "greatly disturbed by the evident corruptions" he found (Price 158). It is presently impossible to check for errors because we do not possess any of the original manuscripts of the New Testament. The oldest fragments date from the second century; the most complete passages survive in a fourth century manuscript (Lewis 15). Of the 4,500 known Greek manuscripts that comprise the New Testament (NT), many are fragmentary and difficult to read. As a rule, NT manuscripts resemble OT manuscripts, in that they were also written with no accent marks and no spaces or punctuation between words or sentences. Some words, like "God" and "Man" were abbreviated and marked, as in this passage from John 1:1–4:

> INTHEBEGINNINGWASTHEWORDANDTHE
> WORDWASWITHGDANDTHEWORDWASGD
> THESAMEWASINTHEBEGINNINGWITH
> GDALLTHINGSWEREMADETHROUGHHIM
> ANDWITHOUTHIMWASNOTANYTHING
> MADETHATHATHBEENMADEINHIMWAS
> LIFEANDTHELIFEWASTHELIGHTOFMN

In the King James Version of the Bible, the passage looks like this:

In the beginning was the Word, and the Word was with God, and the Word was God. The same was in the beginning with God. All things were made by him; and without him was not anything made that was made. In him was life; and the life was the light of men.

In his book, *The Ancestry of Our English Bible,* Professor Ira Maurice Price comments on the above passage:

This method of writing gave to subsequent scribes and copyists considerable liberty as to the divisions of words and sentences. In this very quotation one such variant occurs. In the margin of the Revised Version we find [an editor's comment]: "Or, was not anything made. That which hath been made was life in him; and the life, etc." But the text puts the period after "hath been made." This shows how the copyist, as soon as he abandoned the endless-chain method writing, could, by separating his words at different places, produce different meanings. Just this did occur in numerous places in the New Testament and gave rise to many of the variant readings collated from the different groups of manuscripts. (157)

For example, in the KJV Colossians 2:21, Paul advises his readers to "Touch not; taste not; handle not," warning against violations of the purity laws (touching women, eating or handling unclean things). But "touch," as Lewis points out, is not the beginning of this paragraph or this sentence in the original Hebrew. The KJV editors had inserted a break from the previous paragraph, which read:

Wherefore if ye be dead with Christ from the rudiments of the world, why, as though living in the world, are ye subject to ordinances?

In the original text, without the paragraph break, "touch not, taste not, handle not" clearly refers back to the "ordinances" of Jewish law. In other words, Paul may be saying just the opposite of the KJV translation: "why be subject to these outmoded rules of what you can touch, eat, or handle?" (Lewis 51–52).

Translating the Bible into English created a whole new set of problems. For centuries the Catholic Church had argued that the English language was incapable of rendering the subtle truths of Scripture (a comparable situation today would be translating the Bible into American slang, the language of the streets), that heretical interpretations would result (Lewis 18). Despite threats of imprisonment, English translations of the Latin Vulgate did appear, some pro-Catholic, others blatantly anti-Catholic (Lewis 25–26). By the seventeenth century, so many variants were circulating, some containing the errors of third- and fourth-generation translations, that King James I asked for a new, more authoritative edition. Fifty-four British churchmen, university professors, and lay scholars were selected, and, although they did try to follow the Hebrew and Greek texts in their possession, as much as 60% of the KJV incorporated earlier translations that had been previously condemned as corrupt and even heretical (May 26, 58; Lewis 21–22).

The KJV was criticized from the start. The Puritans, the Catholics, and the Presbyterians urged Parliament to demand a thorough review to correct both printer's errors and mistranslations. Dr. Hugh Broughton, a distinguished scholar in ancient languages and Hebrew theology, asked that all copies of it be burned (Price 275; Bruce 107). They were not, and subsequent scholars spent the next three centuries correcting thousands of errors (Lewis 30, 38–39). James' translators had not only used earlier English translations but non-English versions too—in German, French, Spanish, Latin, and Italian. The Greek NT text in their possession came not from the first century but several centuries later, a product of multiple recopying and errors (Bruce 127). The KJV translators knew of fewer than 25 late manuscripts of the NT; they did not have the Massoretic, nor any of the second century manuscripts that have since been found. While modern scholars have at their disposal 5,358 manuscripts and fragments, of which 800 are ancient Hebrew manuscripts, the KJV translators had only two texts from which to reconstruct the OT: the *Septuagint* and a corrupted copy of St. Jerome's fourth century work (Lewis 42).

James' translators were aware of the pitfalls and practices of Biblical translation, and perhaps because of their method of writing-by-committee, consulting all the variants before voting on the most likely translation, they did not claim to be making literal translations (Lewis 37). But they were also writers who felt passionately about truth, and in the KJV Preface, they defended their rewordings of the ancient texts:

. . . we have not tied our selves to an uniformity of phrasing, or to an identity of words, as some peradventure would wish that we had done, because they observe, that some learned men somewhere, have been as exact as they could that way. . . . For is the kingdom of God become words or syllables? why should we be in bondage to them if we may be free, use one precisely when we may use another no less fit, as commodiously? . . . Add hereunto, that niceness [exactness] in words was always counted the next step to trifling [insignificance]; and so was to be curious about names too: also that we cannot follow a better pattern for elocution than God himself; therefore he using divers words, in his holy writ, and indifferently for one thing in nature: we, if we will not be superstitious, may use the same liberty in our English versions out of Hebrew and Greek, for that copy or store that he hath given us. (KJV: I, xxvi)

All editors work with guiding principles that reflect interpretive policies, e.g., that an older reading is always superior to a newer one; that brevity is preferable to wordiness; that a compromise between different past readings is more prudent than choosing only one (Price 133). But translators can differ widely in how they view such freedom. Some try to be as literal as possible, producing sentences that, in English, are awkward and even puzzling. Others use contemporary phrases to simplify a complex passage or clarify a meaning their readers will recognize. The KJV Preface explicitly states this policy: "But we desire that the Scripture may speak like itself, as in the language of Canaan, that it may be understood even of the very vulgar" (KJV: I, xxvi). But how vulgar can a translation become before it suffers a loss of transcendent truth? When does freedom become license? Did seventeenth-century ideology, taste, and understanding reshape OT theology? "Niceness in words" may have seemed trivial to James' scholars, but today exactness of phrasing can form the basis for moral judgements, as I will show in the next chapter.

Modern Biblical scholars investigate and evaluate such linguistic-ideological intersections. F. F. Bruce, Rylands Professor of Biblical Criticism and Exegesis at the University of Manchester, argues that when the KJV translators changed words in order to avoid repetitions, they abused the original text. For example, in the opening verses of the fifth chapter of Romans, the KJV says:

we . . . *rejoice* in hope of the glory of God (2)
we *glory* in tribulations (3)
we also *joy* in God (11)

Bruce notes that the italicized verbs all were translations of the same Greek verb, which was repeated three times by Paul. Such a change may seem inconsequential, but it is often upon small inflections that interpretations are based. Bruce argues:

If the aim of translation should be the production of the same effect in the reader of the translation as the original wording produced in the reader of the original text, then there is much to be said in a passage like this for translating the same original word by the same word in English; for a good part of the effect intended by the original writer was produced by his deliberate repetition of one and the same word. . . . there are times when the recurrence of the same word is exactly what is required. The English language, for example, has a considerable range of words more or less synonymous with "horse"; but it is the repetition of "horse" that makes Richard III's cry so effective: "A horse! A horse! My kingdom for a horse!" (105)

This KJV practice of revision was apparently extensive: the Hebrew word *dabhar* (a "word" or "thing") was translated into 84 different English words; *sim* ("to place") into 59; *shubh* ("to turn back") into 60; *abhar* ("to pass over") into 48; and *tobh* ("good") into 41 (Lewis 49). How accurate were these substitutions? Jack Lewis, retired Professor of Bible Studies at Harding Graduate School of Religion, finds that some changes created distinctions that were not present in the earlier manuscripts:

"Ye thought evil . . . God meant it unto good" renders one Hebrew word in two ways (Gen. 50:20). Matthew 25:46 (cf. Matt. 19:16; Mark 10:17) has "everlasting punishment" and "life eternal" for the rendering of the same adjective; Matthew 21:23 and 28:18 have "authority" and "power" for the same word. . . . Matthew 18:33 has "compassion" and "pity"; and I Corinthians 12:4,5 have "diversities" and "differences."

In addition, the KJV translators collapsed separate Hebrew or Greek words into one English word, erasing differences intended by the author:

A distinction between "repentance" and "regret" (II Cor. 7:10) is not made, though the Greek [text] has two separate words. In II Corinthians 11:4 and Galatians 1:6

"another" which appears twice might be clarified by using "different" and "another." Two words, *morphe* and *schema,* are rendered "form" (Phil. 2:6–7) but should preferably be "form" and "fashion." (Lewis 49–51)

Did these changes lend clarity or distort meaning? In replacing the rhetorical rhythms of ancient Hebrew, did the seventeenth century verse of the KJV lose the subtle echoes and implied sentiments of the ancient prophets?

Some Hebraic words have no English counterparts, and so synonyms, circumlocutions, or editorial insertions may distort the original meaning. Lewis cites phrases that, when translated literally, convey no clear meaning in English:

> For who can eat, or who else can hasten *hereunto,* more than I? (Ecclesiastes 2:25)
> Dead *things* are formed from under the waters, and the inhabitants thereof. (Job 26:5)
> The noise thereof sheweth concerning it, the cattle also concerning the vapour. (Job 36:33)
> Woe to them that . . . stay on horses. (Isaiah 31:1)
> We do you to wit of the grace of God. (II Corinthians 8:1) (Lewis 53–54)

James' scholars admitted in the Preface that sometimes they had to make educated guesses about the meaning of words:

> There be many words in the Scriptures which be never found there but once, (having neither brother nor neighbour, as the Hebrews speak) so that we cannot be holpen by conference of places. Again, there be many rare names of certain birds, beasts, and precious stones, etc. concerning which the Hebrews themselves are so divided among themselves for judgment, that they may seem to have defined this or that, rather because they would say something, than because they were sure of that which they said. . . . (KJV: I, xxiv)

But how educated were their guesses? J. B. Smith, in his *Greek-English Concordance to the New Testament,* lists 100 different Greek words and particles that could not be rendered into English at all but were replaced by paraphrases or erroneous repetitions; since some were left untranslated more than once, the total number of textual gaps is closer to 1,000. Lewis reports that modern research has already corrected a "lengthy list" of inaccuracies in the KJV. In Genesis 12:19, the Pharoah of Egypt, tricked into believing that Abraham's wife was really his sister, discovers the truth and complains, "I might have taken her to me to wife," in the KJV; but in fact the Hebraic phrase should be translated as "I took her." In Mark 6:20 Herod "preserved" the apostle John, but the KJV changed it to "observed." In II Corinthians 2:17 Paul tells his audience, "For we are not as many, which corrupt the word of God"; the correct translation is "For we are not as many, which trade [or peddle] the Word of God." In light of so many errors, theologian Raymond E. Brown is right to warn us that: "Biblical critics must acknowledge that their interpretations of conveyed meaning range from certain, through probable and possible, to highly uncertain" (45–46, 27). Determining the integrity of translation requires careful scholarship as well as faith.

What, then, can be made of the KJV's condemnation of homosexuals? It has been known for years that neither ancient Hebrew nor ancient Aramaic nor ancient Greek had a word for gays, lesbians, or bisexuals (Petersen 188). The word "homosexual" was not coined until 1869 (by an Austro-Hungarian doctor, Karoly M. Benkert), it was not translated into English until 1912, and it did not appear in any English bible until 1946 (Brow). Historian Michel Foucault argued that the ancients did not think of people as belonging to a special sexual category requiring a name, for neither did they have a word denoting "heterosexual" or even "sexuality." Foucault reasoned that the ancients regarded sex as an act, not a definitive part of sexuality, the network of psychological, social, behavioral, and personal characteristics that make up one's identity. Bernadette Brooten has recently qualified Foucault's claims by citing several words that ancient Greek and Roman doctors used to refer to sexual categories they considered relatively stable and lifelong. However, these categories were judged on the basis of gender (women who acted like men, men who acted like women), and so "sexual orientation" was not a formal or useful concept, not even to the individuals involved. This conclusion seems to be supported by the fact that Brooten could find no evidence of a political organization, a community, a social group or a culture that self-consciously labeled itself by its sexual orientation (*Love* 17, 144).

Even if scholars have a word to base a translation on, they cannot always be sure how it was used in the distant past. An eleventh century Latin word, *sodomia,* evolved into "sodomy," but it was an unruly term: it could refer to anyone, of either gender, who had any kind of non-vaginal, non-missionary position sexual experience. In many medieval texts, between the fifth century and the seventeenth century, *sodomia* might refer to oral sex, anal sex, sex during menstruation, sex with a sterile man or barren woman, sex while standing up, "doggie-style" positions, sex with an uncircumcised man, sex with a child, masturbation, sex with animals, the use of mechanical instruments during sex, and same-sex relations (Boswell 93, 98; Jordan, *Invention,* 4; Nan Hunter 533–534; Halley, "Reasoning," 1755; De Young 152). Ironically, Michael Hardwick's act of fellatio would not have been punished as a crime in either Britain or America until 1885 when oral sex was added to the law (Goldstein 1784). Did James' translators know that *sodomia* was an unreliable term? Can we be certain they were thinking of only one particular meaning, the homosexual rather than the sterile man, or the menstruating woman, or the masturbator? Or did they, like the Supreme Court in 1986, focus the word's force onto a specific group?

Sometimes imprecision in translation is inescapable. When a word has multiple meanings, the translator must choose which seems right, but this can depend on how the translator understands the context in which the word appears, which is affected by grammar, poetic structure, the logic of the passage, the rhetorical effect of phrasing, and historical circumstances (Price 126). For instance, the KJV translated Galatians 3:4 as referring to the persecution of the Christians by the Jews: "Have ye suffered so many things in vain?" (Patrick et al. IV:729). Moises Silva, Professor of New Testament Studies at Westminster Theological Seminary, points out that the Greek verb for "suffer" can also mean "experience, in which case the context would suggest a positive idea, that is, the blessings brought about by the Spirit" (153). Words also accrue connotative meanings that can be historically and geographically specific. Proverbs 6:12–14 describes a person who goes about "with a corrupt speech, who winks with his eyes, signals with his feet, and motions with his finger, who plots evil with deceit in his heart." As Peter Cotterell argues, the winking of the eye is associated with playfulness, facetiousness, or a "knowing look" in today's culture, but to the ancient Israelites, it was associated with sin or maliciousness (in VanGemeren 1:135–136).

Language about sex, as Mark Jordan argues, can be even more figurative and elusive. "Sexual vocabulary is particularly rich in metaphors, ironies and allusions" that may only be intelligible within specific groups, such as a "Boston marriage" (a nineteenth-century lesbian couple) or a "Castro clone" (dressing to look alternative and buff):

This seems as true for medieval Latin as for modern English. Both use dozens of ways to speak about sexual things without speaking about them, to point without describing, to suggest without disclosing. . . . Although an uninformed hearer can make some guess at the meaning of "blow job," she is unlikely to make much sense of "French" or "Greek" without specific instruction. (*Invention* 7)

Because sexual language must be oblique to be proper, it can seldom be understood literally. The English phrase "lady killer," for instance, means not a lady who kills or a person who kills ladies (the literal reading) but rather a man who knows how to seduce women (the figurative reading). Would this term be evident to a non-English speaker living 3,000 years in the future with only a few surviving documents at hand, none of them a dictionary? Would he interpret it differently if he could hear the speaker's own voice, its pitch, stresses, coded gestures, and pacing? Translators may not know all the connotations different ancient Hebraic groups may have attached to the spoken word (Helminiak, *Bible*, 89). Since the ancients left us no dictionaries, biblical scholars look at how words were used in other Hebraic texts, compare them to related words in other languages (or in modern Hebrew), or trace how they had been translated into other languages (Aramaic, Syriac, Greek, Latin) at the time of their use. But this also means that modern translators must rely on ancient, unidentified translators to be reliable themselves, to have mastered not only vocabulary, grammar and syntax but the text's historical and social references, its use of proverbial sayings, figures of speech, symbol systems and mythologies—all in a time before cross cultural linguistics and anthropology became formal academic disciplines (Johnstone 130–131).

David F. Greenberg relates one such example of how biblical scholars work with controversial passages. The Gospel of Matthew (5:22) contains a possible reference to male same-sex relations, but a precise interpretation has so far eluded scholars because one word remains untranslatable:

> but I say unto you, That whosoever is angry with his brother without a cause, shall be in danger of the judgment: and whosoever shall say to his brother, *Raca,* shall be in danger of the council: but whosoever shall say, Thou fool, shall be in danger of hell fire. (KJV)

No one knows what *Raca* means. It has not been found in any other Greek text, and so scholars cannot compare its use here with its use elsewhere. Daniel Whitby, annotating an 1844 edition of the KJV, reasoned that *Raca* "signifies a vain, empty fellow" (Patrick et al. IV: 59). *Raca* seems to be insulting, but vanity is purely speculative. Other readings are possible too, as Greenberg argues:

> One intriguing possibility is that *raca* is actually the Hebrew word *rakha* (soft), and carries connotations of effeminacy and weakness. By implication, the phrase refers to passive effeminate male homosexuals. The case for this reading is strengthened when it is recalled that in Akkadian the syllable *raq* is used as a prefix to denote a woman's name or occupation. It appears in compounded form in the words for a woman, a particular kind of nun, and the female genitals. The Akkadian symbol derives from the Sumerogram for a woman. (211)

But do these other words in other languages define Matthew's use of *Raca* in a Greek text? William Johnstone, Professor of Hebrew and Semitic Languages at the University of Aberdeen, warns us:

> The problem is that we do not have nearly enough data to carry through the task. The relative dating of the biblical sources alone is fraught with uncertainty and, therefore, controversy. The attempt to eke out the Hebraic evidence by appeal to other languages of the same group adds much data, the relevance of which is, however, highly problematical: it assumes some kind of parallel development in the unfolding of meaning in the related languages. The application has at times been undisciplined and impressionistic, and, because of the vastness of the field, dictionary orientated, rather than a careful tracing of sense in the individual languages. (132–133)

Foreign words are often inducted into a language, but sometimes with change of meaning that can be unpredictable and unstable: the Portuguese word, *pinchar* ("to jump"), became "to pinch" in American English; the Aramaic word, *zahal* ("to crawl"), became *dehal* in Hebrew ("to be afraid"), as in Job 32:6, and *kitter* ("to surround") became *katter* ("to wait for"), as in Job 36:2. Changes were inevitable because while ancient Arabic had 28 letters in its alphabet and Ugaritic 30, Hebrew had only 22; so when words were exchanged, the larger number of consonants of Arabic and Ugaritic were funneled into the shorter Hebrew, producing identical-looking roots that were, in fact, not historically identical (Johnston 134–135). As Moises Silva argues, "there can be little question that a number of semantic loans in the New Testament remain unidentified" (90).

So was *Raca* a Hebrew word adopted by Greek writers to suit their meaning, or did Matthew alone use it, inserting it *as* a Hebrew word in an otherwise Greek text for a specific effect or association his readers could appreciate? When an author does something original with language (as good writers are apt to do), he/she may break with traditional meanings and usage, which challenges readers to think in new enriching ways, but which mystifies future readers who are not as familiar with the tropes, rhetorical strategies, or connotations of the time. As Greenberg suggests, *Raq* may be related to the Akkadian word for female genitals, but this doesn't necessarily imply homosexuality (in modern terms, calling a man a "pussy"). When heavyweight champion Mike Tyson told his opponent, Razor Ruddock, "I'm going to make you my girlfriend," he was declaring his physical superiority, not a sexual orientation (Sunstein 220). We may someday discover an ancient manuscript that also uses *Raca,* but until then we can only speculate (Silva 42).

How many more errors are left waiting to be discovered? And what effect might they have on moral theology? The next chapter discusses the recent work of revisionist theologians and historians whose research suggests that mistranslations, produced either by error, accident, ignorance, or a translator's cultural biases, are primarily responsible for Christianity's condemnation of sexual diversity. It is important to remember that their arguments are not the last word in Biblical scholarship, which has been ongoing for many centuries and shows no signs of abating now. Their speculations can be questioned further, amended, rebutted, contextualized, or replaced by other hypotheses in this debate. They cannot be lightly embraced, nor can they be lightly dismissed.

Neither should the objections to such revisionism by orthodox scholars be automatically discounted as mere intransigence or personal homophobia. Robert Gagnon, Assistant Professor of New Testament Studies at Pittsburgh Theological Seminary, complains that the label "homophobic" is "employed as part of an overall strategy of intimidation to forestall genuine debate and belittle vocal dissenters" (26). How biblical scholars approach linguistic ambiguities depends upon how they view the larger issue of revealed truth. On the whole, for Christians, revision is acceptable only when the evidence for it is "compelling," but what "compelling" means varies according to one's theology (Schmidt 18–20). Orthodox Christian scholars believe that the Bible means what it says, and it says what it means, because God spoke through the prophets and must have also guided myriad later translators. The passage II Timothy 3:16 claims that "all scripture is given by inspiration of God, and is profitable for doctrine, for reproof, for correction, for instruction in righteousness: that the man of God may be perfect, throughly furnished unto all good works" (KJV). This suggests to orthodox believers that the Bible was not intended to generate uncertainty or endless scholarly debates but to reveal the truth to guide the faithful through the perilous confusions of life. Progressive Christians see the Bible as an inspired text and a *living* text that changes as a better understanding of language, history and human nature evolves. Liberal scholars take linguistic ambiguities and divergent cultural ideologies as serious obstacles to making unqualified universal pronouncements, but they are also optimistic that as humankind grows, so will the Bible's contribution to a continuing exploration of spiritual truths (Tate 168–169; Countryman 37).

Ultimately, Christianity's position on homosexuality—while certainly not immune to bias—cannot be reduced simply to a prejudice that can be legislated away. It is a complex amalgam of scholarship, philosophy, mystery, and human experience, and it will take much more research and discussion to finally resolve it.

5

Textual Ambiguities and the Scriptures

Of the new revisionists who have reexamined Biblical pronouncements on sexuality, John Boswell, late Professor of History at Yale University, is the most cited in the gay rights debate. His book, *Christianity, Social Tolerance, and Homosexuality: Gay People in Western Europe from the Beginning of the Christian Era to the Fourteenth Century,* encouraged research on the history of homophobia, not as the product of bigoted individuals but the result of historical, cultural, and linguistic issues that require reexamination. Revered by gay advocates, reviled by the orthodox Christians, Boswell saw himself as neither prophet nor despoiler of the sacred. He considered his work provisional, an invitation for future inquiries, responses, criticisms, and corrections. Even though he judged Boswell's arguments ultimately "unconvincing," Richard B. Hays, reviewer for the *Journal of Religious Ethics,* concludes that, at the very least, Boswell

has shown that there is room for reasonable doubt about the meaning of biblical terms that have often been understood as references to homosexual persons or behavior; future lexicographical studies will have to take his work into account. (184)

J. Robert Wright, in a review-essay for *Anglican Theological Review,* also questions Boswell's conclusions, but Wright challenges his readers to embrace the spirit of inquiry, not partisanship:

It is my considered opinion of this case that its historical argumentation and methodology, although fascinating and provocative, are not convincing. Boswell has, I believe, done enough work to raise some serious questions about the clarity and unanimity of the generally received Christian tradition concerning homosexuality, but he has not succeeded in overthrowing or discrediting it. He has indeed, as he hoped, posted some landmarks where there were none before . . . Future studies will have to begin with his book and its reviews. (93)

THE OLD TESTAMENT

Among the Bible's 31,173 verses, less than a dozen OT passages address the issue of sex between men (none explicitly discusses lesbianism), and each, revisionists argue, turns on a problematic translation of key words.

The Meaning of *Qadheshim*

Four passages (Deuteronomy 23:17, I Kings 22:46, I Kings 14:24, and II Kings 23:7) originally used the Old Hebrew word *qadheshim* (or *kadeshim*), translated by KJV scholars through a metonymic substitution as "sodomite":

There shall be no whore of the daughters of Israel, nor a sodomite of the sons of Israel.

And the remnant of the sodomites, which remained in the days of his father Asa, he took out of the land.

And there were also sodomites in the land: and they did according to all the abominations of the nations which the LORD cast out before the children of Israel.

And he brake down the houses of the sodomites, that were by the house of the LORD, where the women wove hangings for the grove.

Boswell examined the use of *qadheshim* in other ancient texts where, literally, it meant a "hallowed" or "sacred" person, a religious prostitute who had sex with worshipers in Canaanite fertility rituals, reenacting the intercourse of the gods, Baal and Anath, who fertilize the earth (99; Batey 3). A number of ancient societies featured sex acts in their religious rituals as a natural pathway to the divine, stimulating the heavens/gods to produce rain and good crops (Helminiak, *Bible,* 46; Greenberg 93). Boswell was not the first to connect *quadeshim* to religious prostitution; as Dr. Symon Patrick, Lord Bishop of Ely and his associates noted in their 1844 annotated edition of the KJV, the word was referenced by a number of ancient writers to "sacred persons . . . both men and women" who were "consecrated whores" in non-Jewish religious services (I: 854).

Some scholars think that the male *qadheshim* serviced only female customers, not other males. Thomas E. Schmidt thinks "it would be nonsense in a fertility cult for males to mate" (92). But it is not clear if birth was expected, or if the act was merely symbolic of a spiritual communion, much as Holy Communion bridges the physical (eating bread) and the supernatural (receiving Jesus' spirit). Perhaps, male-male copulation expressed a different kind of relationship with the gods. James B. De Young argues that Deuteronomy 23:18 enlarges upon verse 17, and there *qadheshim* appears in both the feminine form of *qedesah* (female prostitute) and the masculine form of *qadesa,* or "dog," which De Young regards as a slur for "male prostitute" because of the sexual position likely taken. Although he admits that *qades* does not explicitly mean "homosexual" or "sodomite," *qades* "is broad enough in its use to include homosexual behavior." Gagnon speculates that *qades* must have been male prostitutes who serviced only other males since "women had no religious rights, or certainly far fewer rights than men" (40–42, 127). In rejecting a homosexual cult prostitute, he adds, the ancient Jews "were in effect repudiating a form of homosexual intercourse that was the most palatable in their cultural context." Surely, Gagnon reasons, they would have condemned even more severely sex between men who were not even priests (109). On the other hand, since the *qadheshim* was also a pagan priest in a rival religion (the dog was highly honored among the Egyptians as a symbol of one of their principal gods called Anubis; Patrick et al. I: 854), it is difficult to tell what the Jews were condemning, paganism or the pagan's sexual practices, or sexual practices regardless of religious affiliation. Perhaps, it was all three, but this passage does not make it clear.

Clarity can be hard to find because words are sometimes connected by indirect associations that readers outside of the culture may misunderstand. "Going postal" can be interpreted correctly only within a certain context limited to late twentieth-century America. Its metonymical, negative meaning of violent insanity has little to do with its primary reference to mail delivery. Revisionists desexualize the *qadheshim* by focusing on historical evidence to explain why the authors of Leviticus were so troubled by them. By the time Deuteronomy and Kings were written, some nomadic Jews had settled in Egypt and Canaan, marrying non-Jews and taking part in pagan religious practices (Patrick et al. I:487). Leviticus 18:3 and 6 warn them:

After the doings of the land of Egypt, wherein ye dwelt, shall ye not do: and after the doings of the land of Canaan, whither I bring you, shall ye not do; neither shall ye walk in their ordinances.

None of you shall approach to any that is near of kin to him, to uncover their nakedness: I am the LORD. (KJV)

Sex and religion are here allied in the metaphor of faithfulness and faithlessness. Jews were explicitly warned not to marry non-Jews, nor imitate their "doings" (customs), which tolerated or even encouraged prostitution and incestuous relations when whole families participated in ritual sex (Patrick et al. I: 488, 854). Those who converted from Judaism to the Canaanite religion were said to have gone "a whoring after Baal" (Batey 4).

Deuteronomy's injunction against any infiltration of paganism into Israel is also framed in terms of religious prostitution:

There shall be no whore of the daughters of Israel, nor a sodomite of the sons of Israel. Thou shalt not bring the hire of a whore, or the price of a dog, into the house of the LORD thy God for any vow: for even both these are abomination unto the LORD thy God. (KJV 23:17–18)

The prophet Hosea, condemning Jews who "sacrifice with harlots" (4:14), uses nuptial imagery here to describe God's promise that Israel would prosper if, like a good wife, it remains faithful (2:19–20). Contrary to the Canaanite emphasis on the fertile but transitory cycles of nature that encouraged liberal attitudes towards sex, Hosea offered Israel a marriage pledge to Yahweh that was eternal, unchangeable and strict. A linear view of history based on love replaced a cyclical view based on sex (Batey 6). Consequently, Boswell and Catholic theologian, Father Daniel A. Helminiak, concluded that it was the pagan religious practices of the *quadeshim* that the ancient Jews condemned, not homosexual love (*Bible* 100). Boswell further maintained that for centuries Christian scholars who worked with this passage did not think *qadheshim* referred to homosexuality (99). But Gagnon counters this argument too: if what makes the *quadeshim* forbidden is Canaanite idolatry, not homosexuality, why are so many other Canaanite practices not rejected by Deuteronomy and Leviticus (131)?

The Meaning of *Toevah*

The only statements in the OT where same-sex sexual acts seem specified are in Leviticus:

Thou shalt not lie with mankind, as with womankind: it is abomination. (KJV 18:22)
    If a man also lie with mankind, as he lieth with a woman, both of them have committed an abomination; they shall surely be put to death; their blood shall be upon them. (KJV 20:13)

The Hebrew version of Leviticus 18:22 literally reads, "You shall not sleep the sleep of a woman with a man," and Jewish moralists debated for a millenium about what "the sleep of a woman" meant and who qualified as "a man" (Boswell 101n.34). Could it be any man, married or unmarried, a stranger off the streets (a whoremonger)? Boswell's research centered on the translation of the Hebrew word *toevah*, which the KJV editors rendered as "abomination." Three factors affect how scholars interpret these passages: context, history and semantics.

"Abomination" is a particularly forceful word in English, suggesting a serious moral offense. But the original Hebrew word in this passage was *toevah*, for which there was no corresponding seventeenth-century English equivalent. In ancient Hebrew texts, *toevah* referred to the "unclean" practices used in pagan fertility religions, and so James' scholars may have been thinking of "impurity." Boswell argued that the Hebrew idea of "uncleanness" was not the same as our ideas of impurity, sexual or otherwise. He cited a second century rabbinical commentator, Bar Kapparah, who defined *toevah* as "you go astray because of it"—in other words, it is not intrinsically evil, but it could lead to negative consequences later (Alpert 65). This definition could explain why, in Deuteronomy 23:10, involuntary ejaculation during sleep rendered men unclean for religious ceremonies (Scanzoni and Mollenkott 65).

Boswell tracked down *toevah* in other texts and found it was often part of a common phrase, "*toevah ha-goyim*," "the uncleanness of the Gentiles," which he considered an ethnic contamination, not a moral judgement. The author of Leviticus could have chosen the Hebrew word *zimah*, which Boswell argues did explicitly denote a sin condemned by God (100; Helminiak, *Bible*, 52), which suggested to Boswell that *toevah* simply meant that a particular behavior was not a Jewish thing to do. As we might say today, "it isn't kosher." Certain animals, for instance, were thought to be "clean"—not in the modern sense of being "sanitary" (the ancients did not understand disease in this way) or moral: they were "appropriate" and so could be eaten by Jews. Other animals, like pigs, camels, lobsters, and shrimp, were thought to be unclean and therefore taboo. Israel's hated enemies, the Greeks and the Romans, regularly ate pigs, lobsters and shrimp, which may explain why the Jews avoided them. In 1844, Patrick et al. arrived at the same conclusion:

> . . . the main drift and scope of [the dietary law] was, that the Israelites might be separated from all other nations in the world by a diet peculiar to themselves, which kept them from such a familiar conversation, as otherwise they might have had with the gentiles; and consequently from learning their idolatrous customs. And I do not see why I should not add, most of the creatures, which are reckoned *unclean,* were such as were in high esteem and sacred among the heathen. (I:441)

Leviticus also says that getting tattooed, planting two different kinds of seeds in the same field, and cursing one's parents were all *toevah ha-goyim*. From this evidence, Saul Olyan reads "abomination" as merely the "violation of a socially constructed boundary" (quoted in Brooten, *Love*, 62). The passage 1 Kings 14:24 suggests as much:

> And there were also sodomites [*quadeshim*] in the land: and they did according to all the abominations of the nations which the LORD cast out before the children of Israel. (KJV)

For Boswell, the vehemence of "cast out" did not necessarily signify a moral judgement. At the Vatican today, for instance, tourists wearing "inappropriate" clothing (women in shorts or with uncovered hair) are asked to leave the cathedral, but dress is not considered a sin. As

Associate Professor of Theology at Drew University, Darrel J. Doughty, reports, the first century debate about circumcision also "stirred up passions of ferocious intensity" in much the same way that the gay rights debate does today, but circumcision was not considered a moral issue (Scanzoni and Mollenkott 139). Boswell believed that the early Christians rejected—after a long debate—selected Leviticus laws (e.g., required circumcision, dietary restrictions, ritual purifications), because they were seen as relics of Jewish nationalism, not Christian spirituality. The Apostle Paul urged other Christians against "giving heed to Jewish fables, and commandments of men, that turn from the truth," for "unto the pure all things are pure: but unto them that are defiled and unbelieving is nothing pure; but even their mind and conscience is defiled" (Titus 1:14–15; Boswell 103, 104). What this implies is that uncleanness is in the mind of the beholder, not necessarily in the thing itself. Can the same be said for homosexuality?

Boswell's interpretation may be further supported by the Reverend Helminiak's studies of the OT between 300 and 150 B.C.E. At that time, more and more Jews were living outside of Palestine and no longer read Hebrew; they read Greek, which was the language of the outer Roman Empire. A translation of the Holy Scriptures into Greek was prepared called the *Septuagint,* in which *toevah* in Leviticus 18:22 was translated as *bdelygma,* which in Greek means "ritual impurity." The Greek translator could have chosen the word *anomia,* which specifically meant a violation of God's law, a sin, but he did not. Helminiak concludes from this that male-male sexual relations were not considered a sin, only culturally inappropriate behavior (*Bible* 52–53), and that Jesus agreed:

Jesus knew the difference. He is very clear that being a good person and keeping the requirements of the Jewish Purity Law are not the same thing. He is also very clear that the only thing that matters is being a good person. One of the reasons that Jesus was killed was because he challenged the real importance of the [Jewish Purity] Law. (*Bible* 56)

In Matthew 15:10–11, Jesus calls upon the multitude and says:

. . . Hear, and understand: not that which goeth into the mouth defileth a man; but that which cometh out of the mouth, this defileth a man. (KJV)

When told that the Pharisees, who enforced dietary restrictions and ritual washings, had overheard him and were offended, Jesus replied:

. . . Every plant, which my heavenly Father hath not planted, shall be rooted up. Let them alone: they be blind leaders of the blind. And if the blind lead the blind, both shall fall into the ditch. (KJV 15:13–14)

Following dietary restrictions, ritual washings, fabric taboos, Helminiak interprets, were only outward shows. What really mattered to Jesus was inward goodness. The Pharisee rituals were not good or bad in themselves, except as they could help people appreciate spiritual values. By Christ's time these rituals had become hindrances, mechanical preoccupations that had lost sight of transcendent meaning. The early followers of Christ quickly abolished the Purity requirement of circumcision, rejecting a central requirement of Jewish culture (Helminiak, *Bible,* 56, 58). "In doing so," Tobias Haller adds, Jesus

freed us from the [Hebraic Purity] Law, and left us only that rule of conduct: Love others as yourself, and do as you would be done by. Homosexual relationships that are loving, faithful, and mutually supportive appear to meet this test. If that is enough for Jesus, it is enough for me.

Helminiak has also argued that Leviticus 18:22 may not refer to sexuality at all because it uses the word *zakar,* which, in Leviticus 1:3 and 3:1, relates to animal sacrifices (*zakar* signifies an animal used as an idol, a pagan symbol) and in Isaiah 57:3–13 is used to scold the Israelites for practicing pagan idolatry. Helminiak concludes that an accurate translation of Leviticus 18:23 ("Neither shalt thou lie with any beast to defile thyself therewith") is: "You shall not serve animals or images representing strange gods; this is detestable" ("Jewish"). The Reverend Samuel Kader reasons along similar lines when examining the Levitican word for "woman": "If a man also lie with mankind, as he lieth with a woman, both of them have committed an abomination." Kader notes that the original Hebrew word for "woman" was *ishshah,* which could mean "any woman," but it could also mean "a harlot," a woman of the streets. Thus, Kader reads this line as: "If a man lies with a man as he would a harlot," he cannot enter the temple. Using another man as if he were a harlot, a person of no consequence, for whom he feels nothing but lust, is *toevah,* something Gentiles do in their fertility rituals where sex is nothing more than a bartering tool for good harvests (49–51).

Revisionists like Boswell and Helminiak argue that, although a sentence of execution implies moral condemnation, its position in Leviticus suggests otherwise, for it is placed among other prohibitions that are merely culturally-bound taboos. Leviticus forbids the eating of raw meat, getting tattooed, having sexual intercourse with a menstruating woman, planting two different kinds of seed in the same field, interweaving linen and wool in a single garment, or mixing different breeds of cattle. According to Paul Halsall and Thomas M. Thurston, they were an attempt to glorify the pure perfection of God by recognizing the orderly pattern of the Universe (in which animals, foods, and behavior can be—and should be—separated into discrete categories) and urging Jews to imitate that pattern. To symbolize divine order, Jews could wear cotton or wool but not a mixture of both, eat milk or meat but not from the same dish; women wore women's clothes, men men's clothes, etc. ("Moral"). Saul Olyan speculates that the Jews considered anal sex unclean because it mixed substances—semen and excrement—and it wasted male seed, which many of the ancients believed contained fully formed human beings in it, making sodomy equivalent to murder (since semen is not involved in sex between women, Brooten reasons this is why Leviticus does not condemn lesbianism) (*Love* 62). But orthodox scholar Robert Gagnon wonders why there is no corresponding prohibition against heterosexual anal intercourse too. The true abomination, he reasons, must not be focused on the mixing of semen and excrement but the intercourse of two men in violation of God's created order of two opposite sexes (135–136). As for why the OT never forbids sex between women, Gagnon speculates:

Possibly lesbianism was unknown to the Israelites and/or Canaanites (it goes unmentioned in other legal materials from the ancient Near East) so there was no need to legislate it out of existence. . . . In a society dominated by men and with a high view of chastity it might have been impossible for a sustained lesbian relationship to develop. (145)

On the other hand, it is possible that the OT and other ancient legal documents do not condemn sex between women because it was not regarded as evil or even as sex (since it lacked the only valorized sexual substance, semen).

Progressive Christians question whether they are required to follow the cultural codes of Leviticus because subsequent biblical passages contradict or reject the hard line they take. The author of the Book of Ruth attacked Leviticus for its strict laws (in 23:3) which would have excluded King David from high office because his grandmother, Ruth, was a Moabite woman. David was not excluded and became a hero for the Jews. But such nitpicking generally does not settle the issue. Liberal Christians argue that even in its lawgiving the Bible is not monolithic (like the Jewish people, it includes liberal, centrist, and conservative views) and certain parts may be qualified by others (Halsall, "Background"); orthodox Christians argue that the Bible is unified because "the same unchanging God inspires the whole" even if individual parts seem diverse (Schmidt 20–21). Each side can find corroborating evidence for their beliefs.

Do modern Christians enjoy the same privilege to disagree with Leviticus as the early Christians did? Rabbi Jacob Milgrom has argued that the Leviticus prohibition of same-sex sexual relations "is addressed only to Jews. Non-Jews are affected only if they reside in the Holy Land, but not elsewhere." Leviticus itself defines holiness as Israel's separate status as a "chosen" group when God says to His people: "I the LORD am holy, and have severed you from other people, that ye should be mine" (KJV 20:26). And it has been a longstanding teaching of Christianity since the Council of Jerusalem (49 A.D.) that the rules of Jewish rituals do not automatically bind Christians, that Christians have the right to examine, modify, or abandon whatever seems outmoded or inconsistent with Christ's teachings. Sometimes, such corrections take a long time. Leviticus 25:44–46, for instance, condones slavery, as does Ephesians 6:5–9, Colossians 3:22 to 4:1, 1 Peter 2:18, and the epistle of Philemon. When the Southern States fought in the Civil War, pro-slavery preachers cited the Bible as God's official approval of slavery (Helminiak, *Bible*, 30; Nava and Dawidoff 110). For one hundred years Vatican theologians argued over the passage, until 1965 when an official condemnation of slavery as unchristian was included in the Vatican's Pastoral Constitution (Halsall, "Syllabus").

Other OT judgements have fallen into disrepute on their own over time. In the books of David, Samuel, and Deuteronomy, it is written that a man may have more than one wife—Solomon had 700 wives and 300 concubines—a practice no Christian follows any more, or can afford to. In Exodus, Deuteronomy, and Leviticus, it is said that a father can sell his children into slavery to get out of debt. Today's Christians can keep the children and declare bankruptcy. Deuteronomy 23:1 bans any man whose testicles or penis has been injured, crushed or cut off, from holding governmental or religious offices (this tended to exclude foreigners from positions of power, since eunuchs were products of Roman or Greek culture). Deuteronomy 23:2 requires that a bastard child be banned from the temple "even to his tenth generation," a phrase that meant *never* for the ancient Hebrews (Patrick et al. I:850). Exodus 22:25 and Psalm 15 condemn charging interest for loaned money; Ezekiel 18:13 even compares interest charges to adultery, robbery, idolatry, and bribery, infractions worthy of death (Corvino 14). Adulterers and prostitutes could be executed (Leviticus 20:10 and 21:9), so too the child who curses his father or his mother (20:9), anyone who blasphemes the name of God, or who works on the Sabbath (24:16; 23:30). In I Samuel 15 God commanded Samuel to attack the town of Amalek and "kill both man and woman, child and infant," an act we now regard as genocide (Countryman 12). No biblical scholar supports these punishments today, blames children for their illegitimacy, or considers injured genitalia a sin.

A prohibition of cross-dressing appears in the Book of Deuteronomy 22:5: "The woman shall not wear that which pertaineth unto a man, neither shall a man put on a woman's garment: for all that do so are abomination unto the LORD thy God" (KJV). Gagnon reasons that since God created two different sexes, a man with long hair feminizes himself against God's plan (235). Pro-transgender activists, Sharon Stuart and Tom Heitz, argue that the ancients lived by gender display rules that are not universal. "Proper" Jewish women could not appear in public with uncovered hair;

such behavior was considered "outrageous" and caused their families such great shame that forfeiture of fortune and divorce could result (Batey 23n.4). Men were forbidden from rounding the corners of the hair on their heads or shaving off the corners of their beards (Leviticus 19:27). In I Corinthians 11:14 St. Paul claimed that long hair on men and short hair on women was unnatural. If Paul based his claim upon Leviticus, he may have not understood its historical specificity: in their 1844 annotations to the KJV, Bishop Patrick et al. interpret Leviticus 19:27 as a warning to Jews "not to cut their hair equal, behind and before; as the worshippers of the stars and planets [astrologers], particularly the Arabians, did." Indeed, circular cuts were popular among various Gentile groups the Israelis regarded as heathen. The guidelines on beards outlawed the style worn by "idolatrous priests" (I:501). What is passed down through the generations as "natural" may, when examined, arise from historical contexts irrelevant today.

Orthodox scholars, however, are more cautious about qualifying biblical injunctions simply because they do not accord with contemporary moral attitudes. They may agree with liberal scholars that it is important to distinguish between moral law and ancient custom, but such distinctions are not easy to draw. Gagnon contends that purity and morality are often allied in sexual matters because purity systems functioned as safeguards against moral transgressions (126). If, as Bar Kapparah says, "you go astray because of it," impurity can have moral consequences. This may be why the Levitican prohibition against same-sex intercourse is placed near prohibitions against adultery, incest, and bestiality, which were regarded as sins (Gagnon 129). De Young rejects Boswell's argument that the death penalty does not measure the gravity of an offense because, for the ancient Jews, anything that prevented procreation was an attack on the holy character of the family. Since procreation reflected God's nature, homosexuality was also a rejection of God, and therefore the worst of sins (55). Gagnon adds that *toevah* refers in Leviticus 18:22 and 26–30 to sexual acts that "put the entire nation at risk of God's consuming wrath, God's departure from the midst of the people, and expulsion of the people from the land of Canaan." Such drastic consequences suggest to Gagnon that *toevah* does not simply mean "ceremonically unclean" but rather "inherently evil" (118). De Young also disagrees with Boswell that Paul always used *anomia* for "violations of the law" and *bdelygma* for "violations of ritual purity" because 1) any idolatry qualifies as both, and 2) *toevah* was translated both ways: into *anomia* in the *Septuagint's* Jeremiah 16:18, into *bdelygma* in Ezekiel, and into *anomia* six other times, all of them in Ezekiel (52, 65–67). Is this a translation error or a editorial revision unique to Ezekiel? Were there occasions when the Jews perceived no difference between ritual violations and moral violations? Did all three words denote sin?

Although admitting that Christians were freed from Jewish dietary restrictions and cultural rituals (such as the washing of the hands, mentioned in Matthew 15:2), Lynne C. Boughton argues that both Jesus and his followers conformed to the traditional Jewish Sabbath rituals mandated by the Torah (such as the cleansing of the lepers, mentioned in Matthew 8:4). Acts 15:1–29 may have exempted Gentile converts from circumcision, but it clearly prohibits unchastity, which, for Boughton, logically includes homosexuality (147–148).

David Bradshaw (University of Kentucky Philosophy Department) admits that some biblical commandments are clearly cultural and intended only for Jews, while others, like the prohibition of murder (Genesis 9:6), are universally applicable because

they purport to make explicit a standard that, in some sense, is already given in the nature of things; thus Cain, for example, was at fault for his murder of Abel, although there was at that time no explicit commandment against murder.

To which of these two classes do the commandments against homosexuality belong? One important clue is the fact that the people of Sodom and Gomorrah were held accountable for their homosexual acts, despite the fact that they were non-Jews and lived long before the time of Leviticus. . . . The commandments against homosexuality are simply one aspect of a broader sexual ethic rooted in the creation account in Genesis. As such, they are binding upon the entire human race. (20–21)

The implication here is that the placement of a biblical passage may not always be a reliable indicator of its status as a universal truth or cultural attitude. De Young also argues that Paul's words are meant to be taken as moral injunctions because they parallel Leviticus 18:20: Paul may even have been thinking of Leviticus as he was writing (50–54). De Young follows traditional editing practices by looking for parallels between biblical passages to infer meaning, using each to support the other.

Boughton and De Young also critique Boswell by using his own methods against him. While admitting that Boswell is correct in noting that *toevah* appears in texts that condemn idolatry, De Young argues that the verb form, *ta'ab*, occurs often in passages that are not ceremonial and so has an ethical sense (48). Furthermore, De Young collapses the meanings of *toevah* and *zimah*: both denote sin (50). Boughton argues that it is misleading to suggest that *toevah* "conveys only a sense of cultural/ritual contamination" (144). He observes that food taboos usually employed the Hebrew word *sheqets,* which is translated as "filthy" or "unclean." Even when *toevah* was used, it referred to the food eaten, not to the eater, such as in Deuteronomy 14:3: "Thou shalt not eat any abominable thing" (KJV). To Boughton, certain foods were *toevah* because they produced revulsion, a natural reaction against them; the act of eating repulsive food contradicted the fundamental nature of the eater. Same-sex sex, therefore, constitutes a "denial of a person's sexual physiology" and "is a violation of a much more fundamental or moral law because, though it may be in accord with a person's desires, it rejects a person's God-given gender" (146). Boughton maintains that Boswell's approach fails to consider the places in the Hebrew Torah and Prophets where *toevah* is used to describe acts such as incest, bestiality, and adultery. Perhaps, *toevah* signified different levels of seriousness in different contexts—these passages may simply be saying that incest, bestiality, and adultery, besides being immoral, also violate purity laws—but conclusive evidence for this argument has yet to be found.

Certainly, orthodox Christians vary as to how strictly they apply Levitican rules. Most do not abide by the food, clothing or menstrual restrictions, but they will cite Leviticus when it comes to sexual diversity. It is with this inconsistency that gay rights polemicists often attempt to "catch" their opponents in a contradiction: why retain the Jewish proscription against same-sex sexual relations as "universal" while the others are set aside as "cultural"? The Reverend Mel White, who had been closely associated with the Christian Coalition for twenty years until he came out of the closet, argues:

> even the *Fundamentalist Journal* admits that this Code condemns 'idolatrous practices' and 'ceremonial uncleanness,' and concludes: "We are not bound by these commands today."
> And yet R. J. Rushdoony, a Bible "expert" admired and quoted by leaders of the religious right, is clearly on record that Leviticus should be taken literally, at least when it condemns men who lie with other men. Rushdoony is not a literalist. He is a selective literalist, choosing to interpret literally only those texts that suit his predetermined purposes. . . . "God in His law," Rushdoony writes, "requires the death penalty for homosexuals". . . .
> My old friends from the religious right say they take the Bible seriously, and I believe them. But I must ask, why do they go on denying the historic, cultural, and linguistic evidence (and modern scientific discoveries) that would help them understand the meanings of those passages for our times? (238–239)

White accuses Rushdoony of hypocrisy, of allowing prejudice to influence how he interprets the Bible. But is Rushdoony's failing a personal homophobia, or a theological disagreement resulting from a different way of thinking about what constitutes persuasive evidence and how much modern sensibilities should count? When does selective literalism become prejudice? Pro-gay scholars are also selectively literal when they accept the Bible's prohibition against murder but not against homosexuality for they experience their sexuality as good. Orthodox Christians do eat pork and shellfish, in violation of Leviticus, but without the "natural revulsion" that signals a transgression of God's law, and many *do* experience negative reactions to homosexuality, which they interpret as a morally significant reaction validating Leviticus' injunction (Gagnon 120). Is the repulsion they feel based on an objective moral structure (as Boughton argues) or a culturally produced homoprejudice (as Boswell argued)? If this point could be settled, we might better understand how binding Leviticus should be for modern readers, but whose self-validating interpretive strategy or life experience will be used? We are back at the same issue that divides progressive and orthodox Christians in the first place. If different theologies shape the way different Christians read the Bible *and* non-biblical supporting evidence, then radically different interpretations (of the Bible and of the reader's own emotional reactions) are not only possible; they will all find some kind of validation.

What can we know about Rushdoony's inner thoughts? He may be deliberately distorting the Scriptures to rationalize a hatred of gays and lesbians, or he may feel morally justified in selecting which Biblical passages take precedence because he believes that his search for Scriptural truth is guided by God. White and Rushdoony do not share the same perspective on how relevant historic, cultural, and linguistic evidence should be for how one reads the Bible or how reads oneself. White is moved by compassion for the persecution of LGBTs that he has witnessed, but Rushdoony may look upon White's invitation to revise Biblical principles as a satanic temptation to rationalize immorality. He may even regard historic, cultural, and linguistic scholarship as a product of fundamentalism's enemies—secularism, humanism, and modernism. Each man relies on faith to support the integrity of his own perspectives. Since the Christian God is often seen as an activist God, involved in human history and responsive to prayer, many believers trust that God *will* help guide them to understand the Bible. But is faith all that is needed to avoid error or self-deception? Jesus criticized the Pharisees for mistaking blindness for faith (Matthew 15:14), but there are two difficult challenges here: to see one's own blindness *when one is blind,* and to preserve faith even while *changing one's mind.* Orthodox Christians caution that human beings can deceive themselves; progressives warn that the fear of change risks perpetuating already established deceptions. Can criteria be developed to help Christians avoid either pitfall?

The Story of Sodom

The destruction of the city of Sodom for its homosexual sins is the most famous, and most commonly quoted, biblical story in the gay rights debate. On his television program, The 700 Club, Pat Robertson argued: "If the world accepts homosexuality as its norm and if it moves the entire world in that regard, the whole world is then going to be sitting like Sodom and Gomorrah before a Holy God. And when the wrath of God comes on this earth, we will all be guilty and we will all suffer for it" ("Stupid"). The Vatican's Cardinal Ratzinger also refers to Sodom to justify the condemnation of homosexuality, as does the Catholic Church's 1992 *Catechism* (Jordan, *Silence,* 76). But revisionist scholars contend that the story of Sodom is not about homosexuality. English speakers call anal intercourse "sodomy"

because theologians 1500 years later adopted the word *sodomia* as a categorical name for various forms of non-vaginal, non-procreative sex performed by either heterosexuals or homosexuals, only one of which was anal
sex (Jordan, *Invention,* 29). Over the years, the popular (though not the
legal or the ecclesiastical) understanding of "sodomy" evolved until, in
modern times, it is popularly used to mean only anal sex.

Genesis 19:1–11 reports that God sent down two angels to warn Abraham's nephew, Lot, of the forthcoming destruction of the city. The angels
arrived "at even," and the city dwellers of Sodom attempted to "know" the
angels:

But before they lay down, the men of the city, even the men of Sodom, compassed
the house round, both old and young, all the people from every quarter: and they
called unto Lot, and said unto him, Where are the men which came in to thee this
night? bring them out unto us, that we may know them. And Lot went out at the
door unto them, and shut the door after him, and said, I pray you, brethren, do not
so wickedly. Behold now, I have two daughters which have not known man; let me,
I pray you, bring them out unto you, and do ye to them as is good in your eyes: only
unto these men do nothing; for therefore came they under the shadow of my roof.
And they said, Stand back. And they said again, This one fellow came in to sojourn,
and he will needs be a judge: now will we deal worse with thee, than with them.
And they pressed sore upon the man, even Lot, and came near to break the door.
But the men put forth their hand, and pulled Lot into the house to them, and shut
to the door. And they smote the men that were at the door of the house with blindness, both small and great: so that they wearied themselves to find the door. (KJV)

Since the angels took the form of men, medieval Catholic theologians
assumed that the Sodomites' sin was homosexuality (Jordan, *Invention,* 34).

Revisionist scholars argue that the original Hebrew text does not specify
homosexuality as the Sodomites' crime but rather that they were unjust,
mean, and inhospitable to visitors (McNeill 43–50; Boswell 93). References
in other OT books do not specify homosexuality (Boswell 95–96; Jordan,
Invention, 30–37; Kader 35). As Ezekiel 16:49–50 says:

Behold, this was the iniquity of thy sister Sodom, pride, fulness of bread, and abun-
dance of idleness was in her and in her daughters, neither did she strengthen the
hand of the poor and needy. And they were haughty, and committed abomination
before me: therefore I took them away as I saw good. (KJV)

Isaiah 1:10 and 3:9, Jeremiah 23:14, and Ezekiel 16:48–49 as well as various rabbinic commentaries, mention Sodom's sins of injustice, oppression,
insolence, pride, partiality, adultery, lies and encouraging evildoers—but
not same-sex sexual relations (Eron 31). When Jesus Christ refers to it in
Matthew 10:5–15, he cites inhospitality, not homosexuality (Helminiak,
Bible, 40). Although De Young questions how inhospitality could be so

wicked, Geslin argues it was a serious breach of Jewish custom, as it was for the ancient Greeks. Moreover, Sodom lay in desert country, where robbers, wild animals, and dehydration were a constant threat. In their commentary to an 1844 edition of the KJV, Symon Patrick et al. note that the phrase "at even" suggests the angels "had been with Abraham in the heat of the day," so Lot would have been required by both custom and morality to provide them with rest (I:82–83).

Traditional readings of this story focus on the Sodomites' expressed desire "to know" Lot's guests, which suggests carnal knowledge (De Young 33). Revisionists counter that the Hebrew verb, *yada* (also spelled *yadha,* "to know"), used twice in this passage, occurs 943 times in the Old Testament but refers to sex only 10 times (Boswell 94). James Hall adds that the word chosen to translate *yada* into Greek for the *Septuagint* means "to make the acquaintance of" with no sexual connotation (Hall). The Reverend Samuel Kader of the Grace Institute Bible College argues that if the Genesis author had wanted to specify sexual intercourse, he would have used the word *shakab* (23). Kader focuses on verse 6, which says:

. . . the men of the city, even the men of Sodom, compassed the house round, both old and young, all the people from every quarter.

The Hebrew word translated as "men" was, Kader notes, '*enowsh,*' which meant "a mortal," a human being of either sex:

The Bible is *not* talking about a crowd of homosexual men. It is talking about a crowd comprised of every human being who lives in this city: the men, the women, the children, *all* the people, verse four says, from every quarter. Every citizen is present. (25)

Could the whole population of Sodom—men, women, and children—be homosexual? The issue here, Kader concludes, is not sex.

Orthodox scholars reject this interpretation. Boughton admits that "*yada* is rarely used in the Hebrew Scriptures to refer to genital activity and that the Prophets do not specify homosexual conduct as one of Sodom's sins," but because Lot offers his two daughters to the crowd, and specifically describes them as virgins, context here suggests that *yada* must mean "carnal knowledge." The two daughters will act as sexual substitutes for what must be same-sex desires (142). Did Lot correctly read the crowd's mind, or was he trying to throw them off by offering sex in exchange for violence? Boughton reasons that Christians can favor the former view even though later biblical writers do not specify it because:

Prophetic writings rarely recapitulate events or actions described in older sacred texts. Instead they remind audiences that the obvious sins and punishments associated with the name of a historical person or community result from the less readily recognised sins that a later generation shares. (143)

Thomas Schmidt adds that since "the Jews were a modest people who often used figures of speech or other kinds of code for sexually explicit subject matter," later writers may have used inhospitality as a euphemism for anal rape (88). Boughton assures us that the word "sodom" could stand in later times for a general climate of luxuriousness and self-indulgence, which anal sex symbolized. A later prophet may talk of inhospitality, but his readers would see its implied connection to a host of other sins, including homosexuality. And De Young notes that Sodom's sin of pride could be taken to mean homosexuality since the two terms were linked in later rabbinical writings:

> . . . Sirach [180 B.C.] interprets the sin of Sodom as pride, but he appears to allude to homosexuality also. Since there was no available term that could specifically refer to this vice, he employed broader terms, for example, *bdelygma,* which in Leviticus 18 and 20 explicitly refers to homosexuality. (80)

Biblical scholars traditionally look for parallels between passages to infer meaning, and each side finds evidence since figurative connections can go in many directions. If pride is a turning away from God, then revisionists can argue that nearly every sin could be alluded to under a "broad" term like *bdelygma.* Kader cites verse 2:6 in Peter, which says that God destroyed the city of Sodom "and made them an example of what is going to happen to the ungodly." The Greek word for "ungodly" is *asebes,* literally "without worship." Later writers may have focused on inhospitality not to infer a specific sexual sin but to point to a much more pervasive failing: the sodomites were a people who did not worship God, an offense referred to in Deuteronomy 32:17 ("They sacrificed unto devils, not to God" KJV) (Kader 27, 35).

J. Robert Wright takes a more provisional attitude, at first arguing that the majority of patristic (early Christian theological) commentaries on Sodom stress the sexual licentiousness of the town's citizens, and so the most likely sin "consisted in the violation of hospitality *by* homosexual conduct" (83). But, Wright adds,

> All this does not absolutely prove that Boswell is wrong, but it certainly does not convince us that he is right. . . . Published now by the *Centre National de la Recherche Scientifique* in Paris and called *Biblica Patristica: Index des citations et allusions bibliques dan la litterature patristique* . . . these volumes present computer-format references to every known mention of every scriptural verse in each patristic author covered. . . . Maybe the consensus of patristic interpretation of Genesis will support Boswell's view, maybe his claims will stand up once these 157 patristic references to the Genesis passage (and others still to come in subse-

quent volumes) are checked, but until someone has done this it would seem unwise to accept his assertions as if they were documented. (83–84)

THE NEW TESTAMENT

In all of the New Testament, only the apostle Paul seems to condemn homosexuality, and he does it in three passages (in Romans 1:26–27, I Corinthians 6:9–10, and I Timothy 1:10). In Romans, Paul writes:

Wherefore God also gave them up to uncleanness through the lusts of their own hearts, to dishonour their own bodies between themselves: who changed the truth of God into a lie, and worshipped and served the creature more than the Creator, who is blessed for ever. Amen. For this cause God gave them up unto vile affections: for even their women did change the natural use into that which is against nature: And likewise also the men, leaving the natural use of the woman, burned in their lust one toward another; men with men working that which is unseemly, and receiving in themselves that recompense of their error which was meet. (KJV)

The Reverend Dan Geslin interprets this passage as condemning sexual activities that are idolatrous, in which sex is worshiped and placed above love of God, a charge, he points out, that is equally applicable to heterosexuals as to homosexuals. John Boswell takes a more linguistic approach, arguing that later editors mistranslated the phrase *para physiken* as "against nature." *Physis* is a Greek word for nature, the root of the English "physics," but Boswell claims that other Greek texts written during Paul's time, which the KJV scholars did not know as well as modern scholars, did not use *para physiken* to mean "against nature," that is, as something in conflict with divine law or "natural law." Both Boswell and Halsall maintain that the concept of natural law did not fully develop until 1,000 years later when Aquinas theorized that certain sexual acts could be condemned as "unnatural" because they contravened God's laws, which were embodied in the design of nature. For Paul, Boswell argues, "nature" was not a question of universal law but rather a personal or group characteristic: e.g., Jews are Jews "by nature," just as Gentiles are Gentiles "by nature," or "by birth." For a Jew to act like a Gentile was against his nature. Nature may not have been a moral force for Paul but a custom, so habitual as to be automatic, "second nature," as we might say today (Boswell 110; Halsall, "Boswell"). But did King James' translators see the difference?

Boswell's critics read the passage differently. Gagnon thinks Paul refers to nature not as the way things are usually done but as "the material shape of the created order" which, upon reflection, reveals "the nature of God and God's will" (256–257). De Young reports that "*physis* occurs in profuse quantity throughout secular Greek writings," changing meaning in different times and contexts, such as: pertaining to origin (birth and growth), nature or character, the regular order of nature, a philosophical order, a creature, or a species. De Young finds no suggestion of "what is natural to me" or "orientation," except perhaps in "nature or character," but, he adds, "this usage points to what results from origin or growth and includes the instinct of animals. No one applies it to the source of homosexual desires" (147–148). Although Richard B. Hays admits that Paul offers no explicit reflection on the concept of "nature," Hays maintains that Paul identifies "nature" with the created order:

The understanding of "nature" in this conventional language does not rest on empirical observation of what actually exists; instead, it appeals to an intuitive conception of what ought to be, of the world as designed by God. Those who indulge in sexual practices *para physin* are defying the creator and demonstrating their own alienation from him. (194)

Hays reports that while Paul's contemporaries, the Greek Stoic philosophers, did not characteristically speak of nature as a divinely ordered Law, they did sometimes think of it as an ideal norm or as right reason, which could involve a moral dimension. In general, the Stoics praised *kata physin* (natural) and condemned *para physin* (unnatural). However, considerable debate surrounded the question in ancient Greece, as William R. Schoedel, retired Professor of Classics and Religious Studies at the University of Illinois, has demonstrated. For if natural inclinations are also moral ones, then the impulse of the strong to rule the weak would be ethically acceptable. Self-interest is abundantly clear in nature and in our inclinations, but Christian ethics require us to be altruistic when another person's need arises (45).

Thus, the word "nature" can have two fundamentally different meanings depending upon context. In 1 Corinthians 11:14 Paul uses "unnatural" to condemn long hair for men, which he characterizes as *atimia*. King James' scholars translated *atimia* as "degrading," but Helminiak argues that in Paul's time *atimia* meant "not highly valued," or "not respected"–socially inappropriate but not a sin (Helminiak, *Bible*, 64, 71–72). Is long hair degrading? Helminiak asks rhetorically. More to the point, are there different kinds of degradation—aesthetic, cultural, moral–and which one was Paul referring to? Schmidt thinks Paul does imply moral degradation:

While it is fair to note that in Paul's context, social disgrace in the realm of sexuality was not always the direct result of sinful behavior (as the case of menstruation shows), we must apply such a distinction carefully. The language of social disgrace may imply sinful behavior. . . . In 1 Corinthians 15:43 Paul writes of the body being "sown in dishonor [*atimia*]" before it is "raised in glory." Surely this implies more than death as social disgrace: death is the penalty for sin. (75)

Does *atimia* refer to sin in both passages (homosexuality and long hair)? Or is Paul saying that, as a result of Original Sin, all bodies—gay and straight—born into this world partake in its dishonored or "fallen" state, as Christine Gudorf argues (134)? Can we accept the interpretation (Schmidt's "surely this implies") of one passage as definitive for another? William Schoedel says no:

. . . when writers of the period appeal to nature as a guide, they are referring *(a)* to the biologically and/or culturally determined character of individuals or groups . . . or *(b)* to what ought to be in the light of the universal order of things. . . . When an appeal to nature involves moral judgements (as in Cor. 11), it is clear that we are dealing with nature as a normative conception that has in view the universal order of things [since God created two different sexes, they should look and behave differently]. It is true, of course, that here Paul's view of nature will seem to us to fall back not on nature but on custom. What this means, however, is that from our point of view Paul mistakes custom for nature, not that he uses the term "nature" in the sense of custom. What can be readily agreed to is that nature in Paul's world plays no overarching role comparable to that found in the Greco-Roman philosophical tradition. But he had apparently read enough in Hellenistic Jewish materials to recognize that the appeal to nature could at times serve to illuminate what he took to be the will of God. (59)

The question is: is this one of those times? Were the forceful connotations of *para physiken* morally negative or culturally negative? Were the acts evil or merely less than ideal? Did these Greek words convey the same meaning to Paul's Semitic mind (Silva 58)?

Boswell and Helminiak approach this passage by focusing on the prefix *para,* claiming that it is usually not used in ancient Greek texts to mean "un-" or "anti-" but rather "beside," "more than," or "over and above." In modern English a "paralegal," for instance, is not someone who stands in opposition to attorneys but who is trained to assist attorneys by working "alongside" ("parallel") them in a subordinated role. Boswell concludes that *para physiken* could therefore mean "extraordinary," "surprising," "out of the routine," or "unusual." Thus, it could refer to any sexual experience that did not result in children: oral sex, heterosexual anal sex, sex during a woman's period, sex with a barren women, sex while standing up, sex with an uncircumcised man, and same-sex sexual relations—anything that was not the standard way of having sex, that is, missionary position, procreative sex (Boswell 111–112; Helminiak, *Bible,* 62–69). Hays admits that Boswell is correct for a large number of his citations but insists that a small number of ancient texts do use *para* to mean "against" or "contrary to" (196), as in the phrases *para to dikaion* ("contrary to what is just"), *paranomia* ("lawlessness"), and *paraptoma* ("false step, sin") (198). Hays concedes that *para physin* is not in itself a moral judgement, but it can be accented as such by the context in which it appears. For instance, in Romans 1:11:21, 24, Paul compares the union of Gentile nations and Israel in Christianity as grafting a wild olive branch to a domesticated olive tree, which is *para physin,* an artificial but amoral act, while in Romans 1:26 Paul does provide a moral context for sexual behavior that shifts the meaning to "unnatural" in an immoral way (199). Consequently, though he believes that Paul's judgement condemns unnatural sex, Hays warns that

the expression "contrary to nature" probably did not carry for Paul and his readers the vehement connotation of "monstrous abomination" which it subsequently acquired in Western thought about homosexuality. Consequently, this phrase should certainly not be adduced as if it were a biblical warrant for the frantic homophobia which sometimes prevails in modern society. (199)

James De Young disagrees, arguing that if the grafting of an olive tree is Paul's metaphor for God's grafting the Gentiles (who are wild by nature) onto the cultivated Jews, then Paul is adapting the Greek concept of a secular nature to the Judeo-Christian idea of nature corresponding to God's will. Whoever strays from God's plan sins (155–156). Gagnon concurs, arguing that since Original Sin perverted human passion, we cannot rely alone on how we feel to show us how to behave but rather "the bodily design" of gender, which has spiritual meaning. He cites Plato's *Laws* for support: "when male unites with female for procreation, the pleasure experienced is held to be in accordance with nature (*kata physin*), but contrary to nature (*para physin*) when male mates with male or female with female." Unnatural pleasures are evil because they are experienced not for the sake of procreation but for themselves, which removes them from control; rather than generating families, they destabilize the family unit (just as homosexuality, incest, or adultery would). This must be why Paul's passage refers to the moral and social chaos Gentiles had brought upon themselves: passions that are contrary to nature undermine social order (164–178, 391): the foundation argument for sodomy laws.

Scholars also argue about mistranslations of Paul that have occurred in the twentieth century. In the 1946 and 1952 publications of the Revised Standard Edition Bible, I Corinthians 6:9–10 is translated as:

Do not be deceived; neither the immoral, nor idolaters, nor adulterers, nor effeminate [*malakoi*], nor homosexual offenders [*arsenokoitai*], nor thieves, nor the greedy, nor drunkards, nor revilers, nor robbers will inherit the kingdom of God.

The original Greek words, *malakoi* and *arsenokoitai,* had been translated as "effeminate" and "abusers of themselves with mankind" in the King James Version:

Be not deceived: neither fornicators, nor idolators, nor adulterers, nor effeminate, nor abusers of themselves with mankind, nor thieves, nor covetous, nor drunkards, nor revilers, nor extortioners, shall inherit the kingdom of God.

The difference here is that the modern edition uses the first word to determine the translation of the second word, producing the more specific "homosexual offenders." Without spaces or punctuation between words in ancient texts, editors combined "effeminacy" and "sexual activity among men." But a nagging suspicion led a committee of scholars to reverse the decision in 1989, translating each word separately as "boy prostitutes" (effeminate because of their youth) and "practicing homosexuals." Then, at the last minute, the committee changed its mind again and published the passage as "male prostitutes" and "sodomites" (Scanzoni and Mollenkott 75–76).

Boswell went back to the original Greek texts and reasoned that *malakoi* literally meant "soft": in Luke 7:25 and Matthew 11:8, it described "soft robes," the expensive clothing worn by courtiers in kings' palaces (106; Patrick et al. IV: 270). When modifying a personal noun, *malakoi* could mean "gentle disposition," "weak-willed," "indolent," "spineless," a fondness for expensive clothes or food, long hair, gluttony, indulgence in too much heterosexual sex, or indulgence in homosexual sex (Scanzoni and Mollenkott 78; Kader 73; Martin). The Greek word for "effeminate" is *malthakos,* but it did not necessarily imply homosexuality: rather, it meant a lack of masculine vigor. In Plutarch's *Dialogue on Love, malthakos* refers to an aging, enervated heterosexual love (Greenberg 212). This meaning of "effeminate" may have been known to King James' translators, because later that century the English poet, John Milton, used it to condemn heterosexual males who ignored their proper duties as men by spending all their time seducing women (Scanzoni and Mollenkott 78). In this sense, an "effeminate man" was a "ladies man."

Boswell and Helminiak maintain that *malakoi* was never used in ancient Greek texts to designate or condemn gay people as a group, while it often occurred in reference to heterosexual persons or heterosexual activity (Boswell 106–107; Helminiak, *Bible,* 85–89; Brow). James' scholars may have translated *malakoi* as "effeminate" because it was situated next to the word for "adulterers," implying that both words were about sex. Indeed, according to Boswell, *malakoi* was sometimes translated as "masturbators" until "homosexual" replaced it in the modern edition, perhaps because fewer people today regard masturbation as a capital offense (107). But orthodox scholars can also point to other ancient texts to support contrary conclusions. Lambert Dolphin argues that *arsenokoitai* and *malakoi* belong together because they refer to the active partner and the passive partner in anal intercourse. Boughton adds that *malakoi* designated the adoption of a passive, feminine role in physical relations, citing two of the most famous ancient Greek writers, Aristotle and Plato. Gagnon notes that Philo, a first century Jewish writer, uses *malakia* twice in a discussion of homosexual behavior (308).

A similar controversy exists over *arsenokoitai.* The word did not appear in any text prior to Paul's use, nor was it used again for two hundred years; this was not unusual for Paul, who used 179 words seen nowhere else in pre-Christian Greek literature (Schmidt 95; De Young 195). It seems to be a compound of the roots *arsen,* meaning "man" or "male," and *koitai,* meaning "beds," usually the marriage bed, from which the English word "coitus" is derived. Revisionist Paul Thomas Cahill speculates that Paul is talking about promiscuous males who cheat on their wives in the marriage bed, despoiling the site of legitimate sex. The KJV does use such a phrase in Hebrews 13:4: "Marriage is honourable in all, and the bed undefiled: but whoremongers and adulterers God will judge." Other revisionist historians have found evidence that *arsenokoitai* meant "male prostitute" well into the fourth century, but it was also used to refer to abusive sexual practices, cult prostitutes, child molesters, perverts, murdering one's parents, kidnapping, abuse of slaves, or public pornographic displays (Boswell 107; Kader 73; Helminiak, *Bible,* 86, 90; Geslin). Were any of these other meanings in Paul's mind when he used this word?

Neuhaus and Boughton find Boswell's argument "unconvincing" when he attributes *arsenokoitai* to cult prostitutes in order to move the sin from sex to idolatry. Neuhaus reasons that homosexual acts are wrong not because they are associated with idolatrous cults but because they are themselves a form of idolatry, a turning away from God's plan for the two sexes (56). Boughton's argument is three-pronged. First, if Paul had meant a male cult prostitute, he would probably have chosen the Greek word *pornos,* since he refers to female prostitutes in 1 Cor 6:15–16 as *porne.* Second, Boswell cites no evidence to support his claim that other Greek texts used *arsenokoitai* to refer to idolatry. Third, the etymology of the word focuses on sex acts, not religion:

The first part of the compound, *arsen-* means "male." Unlike the stem *anthropo-* which refers inclusively to "mankind," the stem *arsen-* specifically designates the male gender. The second part of the compound, the verbal *koita-* is derived from the verb *keimai.* Although *keimai* means "to lie outstretched" in a reflexive way or passive sense, *koita-* indicates in biblical Greek the active male role of impregnating or "seeding."

. . . Could, as Boswell suggests, the *arsenokoitai* be male temple prostitutes whose active role involved servicing women as well as men? As David F. Wright has noted, among the more familiar Greek words that involve *-koites,* the first part of the compound is the object, not the subject of the verbal. (149–150)

Boughton reasons that if *arsenokoitai* followed the same grammar as other compound words using *koitai* (e.g., *doulokoites,* "lying with slaves," or *chamaikoites,* "lying on the ground"), and if its use in Paul's time retained its etymological origins, then it would denote "one who sleeps with men." Since *koite* became a euphemism among Hellenised Jews for "the emission of seed," Boughton assembles these elements to translate *arsenokoitai* as "seeding men," a man who treats other men carnally as if they were women. Boughton presumes that *arsenokoitai* followed the same grammatical construction of other words, and that its original meaning was preserved over the centuries, but we do not know if Paul was conscious of *koite's* euphemistic meaning among Hellenised Jews, or if he was deliberately using it here. It is also unsettled whether William L. Petersen is correct when he reasons that *arsenokoitai* could euphemistically signify the act of "male seeding" while literally referring to male prostitutes, not homosexuals in general (189).

Jesus' silence on the subject of homosexuality has been a contentious topic in the gay rights debate. Orthodox Christian Lambert Dolphin reasons that since the only form of sexual behavior Jesus actually endorsed was marriage (Hebrews 13:4), Christians can assume that anything else, including homosexuality, was forbidden. Dolphin speculates that either Jesus did not think it was necessary to condemn male-male sexual relations because Judaism had already forbidden them, or that "gay lifestyles" were unknown in the Israel of his day. Revisionists counter that it may have been true that the ancients did not practice a "gay lifestyle" as found in America today, but same-sex sexual relations, whether in isolation or firmly placed within social or kinship structures, were common in the ancient world (Herdt, *Same*, 63), so both Jesus and his audiences would likely have known about them. It is possible that, since the Hebrews had no word for homosexuality, it might have been included in a broader category of sin, such as "fornicators."

Gagnon argues that Jesus' silence implies acceptance of the Hebraic tradition condemning same-sex relations. First, Jesus would have said so: "Jesus was not shy about expressing his disapproval of the conventions of his day." Second, if he disagreed with the Torah, he would have at least qualified his statement in Matthew 5:17–18: "Think not that I am come to destroy the law, or the prophets; I am come not to destroy but to fulfill" (KJV). Finally, in Mark 7:21–23, Jesus mentions the sins of sexual immoralities (*porneiai*), adulteries, and licentiousness. "No first-century Jew," Gagnon argues,

could have spoken of *porneiai* (plural) without having in mind the list of forbidden sexual offenses in Leviticus 18 and 20 (incest, adultery, same-sex intercourse, bestiality). The statement underscores that sexual behavior does matter. If Jesus made this remark, he undoubtedly would have understood homosexual behavior to be included among the list of offenses. (191–192)

But silence can go either way. Jesus may have been silent because he did not read *toevah* and *qedashim* in Leviticus as condemning homosexuality. Gagnon relies on his translation of the contested passage in Leviticus to resolve a contested passage in Mark. Moreover, Gagnon admits that other biblical scholars doubt Mark was accurately quoting Jesus because it is corroborated by only one independent source, and it occurs in the context of a private setting when Mark sometimes embellished his reports with material from other traditions, in this case ancient Greek vice lists, which included *porneiai* without reference to Leviticus (192). This does not necessarily disprove Gagnon's argument, but it does show how biblical interpretation often relies on supporting interpretations that are themselves problematic.

Pro-gay arguments also make assumptions. Elizabeth Stuart believes that Matthew's account of Jesus and the Roman centurion's servant (8:5–13) indirectly suggests that Jesus was tolerant of same-sex relationships. The centurion asks Jesus to cure his servant, who lies sick inside the house, and Jesus agrees, praising the centurion for his faith. Matthew chose the Greek word *pais* to refer to the servant, a word used in Hellenistic culture to refer to a male slave lover. Since it was common for Roman soldiers to make lovers of their orderlies, Jesus' silence on the matter could suggest "that Jesus was not interested in whether this centurion was having sexual relations with his slave" (160).

Since neither side has direct evidence for what Jesus thought about sexual diversity, progressives take the long view, arguing that, overall in sexual matters, the Bible stresses mutual respect, caring and responsible sharing in a loving relationship. They conclude that since this is the spirit (if not always the letter) of the Holy Scriptures, then being an anti-gay Christian is a contradiction in terms:

Paul insisted on faith and love as the things that really matter in Christ. But by misunderstanding Paul's argument, people unwittingly rely on tastes and customs instead of the word of God. They argue about what's dirty or clean, dispute who's pure and impure, and pit heterosexual against homosexual. Thus, they divide and splinter the church over what does not matter in Christ. In God's name they foment hatred and fuel oppression and disrupt society at large. They commit a grave injustice. . . .

Such oppression is the very sin of which the people of Sodom were guilty. Such behavior is what the Bible truly condemns over and over again. So those who oppress homosexuals because of the supposed "sin of Sodom" may themselves be the real "sodomites," as the Bible understands it. (Helminiak, *Bible*, 41, 83)

Other theologians use a "consensus" reading to apply Biblical wisdom to modern times when LGBTs are a more visible, definable group than in ancient times. The Baptist Reverend Dr. William R. Stayton adds:

There is nothing in the Bible or in my own theology that would lead me to believe that God regards homosexuality as sin. God is interested in our relationships with ourselves, others, the things in our lives, and with God (MAT 23:36–40). There is nothing in the mind of God that could be against a loving, sexual relationship, freely entered into, without coercion, among sincere adults whether gay, bisexual or straight. . . . (PFLAG)

Episcopal Bishop John S. Spong, one of the most visible of pro-gay religious leaders, adds:

Some argue that since homosexual behavior is "unnatural" it is contrary to the order of creation. Behind this pronouncement are stereotypical definitions of masculinity and femininity that reflect rigid gender categories of patriarchal society. There is nothing unnatural about any shared love, even between two of the same gender, if that experience calls both partners to a fuller state of being. Contemporary research is uncovering new facts that are producing a rising conviction that homosexuality, far from being a sickness, sin, perversion or unnatural act, is a healthy, natural and affirming form of human sexuality for some people. (PFLAG)

Literalist and orthodox Christians see such statements as dangerously diluting the stern but just and timeless guidance of the Bible. The corrosive action of sin in the world corrupts not only nature but humankind's ability to reason, to perceive evil as evil, to know ourselves and our own self-deceits. Life is full of false gods and false promises, imperfect because of our fallen state. Joe Dallas, the founder of Genesis Counseling, describes biblical revisions as "a theology of lies":

The pro-gay theology is a strong delusion—a seductive accommodation tailor-made to suit the Christian who struggles against homosexual temptations and is considering a compromise. Some who call themselves gay Christians may be truly deceived into accepting it; others might be in simple rebellion. What compels them to believe a lie we cannot say. What we *can* say is that they are wrong—dead wrong. (206–207)

For Dallas, the literal truth of Scripture is absolute; it cannot be diluted by "warm and fuzzy" appeals to human notions of harmony and good will. He rejects the contention that the Gospels are more authoritative than the OT, or that Jesus' emphasis on love supersedes the OT's emphasis on law, as does Gagnon, who argues:

One of the main reasons why proponents of same-sex intercourse often think that they can enlist Jesus in their cause is that they labor under a popular misconception; namely that Jesus was far more tolerant on sexual matters than his Jewish contemporaries. The reverse conclusion is likely to be closer to the truth. On matters relating to sexual ethics Jesus often adopted stricter, not more lenient, demands than most other Jews of his time. (196–197)

Jesus forbade divorce and remarriage for both husbands and wives (Matthew 5:31–32) and warned that the mere desire for adultery was already sin (5:27–28). Like Gagnon, Dallas also rejects the argument that Jesus' silence on the subject of homosexuality implies approval since Jesus did not mention other sexual variations, such as pedophilia or sadomasochism, yet we can assume that he condemned them. Most important,

Dallas argues, gay Christians denigrate the authority of the Bible by mis-taking their own standards of fairness for God's. Why would God make a human being homosexual and then require lifelong chastity and atonement? Because, Dallas answers, God requires obedience and self-denial from everyone in some way, and he cites what he sees as an analogous situation:

When David and his armies brought the ark of God from Judah to Jerusalem, they had been given specific instructions by God regarding its maintenance and trans-portation (1 Samuel 6:1–8). One rule was clear: after it was prepared for travel, the ark—"a holy thing"—*was not to be touched* (Numbers 4:15). But during the trip to Jerusalem the cart that was transporting the ark began to shake, and one of the driv-ers (Uzzah) with the best of intentions grabbed the ark to steady it. . . . He was struck dead on the spot (2 Samuel 6:7). (34–35)

Such a punishment may seem unfair by modern, humanistic standards, which judge the morality of behavior by the intent behind it, but Dallas believes that God operates by His own rules, which may not match our understanding of justice. Revising the Bible is equal to rejecting it (172).

In response, progressive Christians, such as Christopher Camp, believe that literalists are committing "a grievous sin of their own. The apostle Paul condemns going against one's own nature, which is another way of saying, 'To thine own self be true'" (Davis). Orthodox Christians reply, if all God asks of the faithful is their obedience, they should give it. Is this all God asks? Progressives see a God who encourages growth in wisdom and self-governance; relying on unquestioned judgements from the patriarchs of the past strikes them as safe but stagnant, succumbing to the sin of pride by believing that one group is more righteous than all others. To the orthodox Christians, destiny is divinely fixed because God is fixed in His perfection.

Must belief in perfection exclude dissent and diversity? Even perfection is a controversial concept. The Levitican rabbis who prohibited the wearing of two different kinds of cloth saw divine perfection in a changeless unity, one perfect design reflecting one perfect God. Native Americans who wear two braids in their hair see divine perfection in a duality embodied in the "double vision" that two-spirit people enjoy. Orthodox Christians believe that the ancient prophets got it right the first time. Progressives invite Chris-tians to become prophets again, to continue the quest for the meaning of life that the ancient prophets began, to give voice to the divine living in our own time. As Wilem A. VanGemeren, Professor of Old Testament and Semitic Languages at Trinity Evangelical Divinity School, and general edi-tor of *New International Dictionary of Old Testament Theology & Exege-sis,* concludes:

. . . each generation can and must interact with the Bible. On the one hand, it has received the legacy of past interpreters. On the other hand, it can make a contribution by interacting honestly with the cultural changes. To this end, we affirm that while the traditional interpretations of the Bible are important and appropriate, the Bible itself opens up perspectives that may challenge past interpretations and invites the traveler to journey into exciting, but not always known, landscapes of literary and linguistic possibilities. This journey requires interpretation—a detailed and nuanced assessment of the exegetical possibilities of the text, and an openness to the text as well as to one's self. In between these two horizons (text and self), the text presents a message of God afresh to a new generation. (1:7)

VanGemeren cites St. Augustine for a useful interpretive strategy to accomplish this task:

If a literal reading fosters neither the love of God nor the love of neighbor, then one must choose the spiritual interpretation that does. Multiple readings are not dangerous so long as none of them contradicts the rule of faith, hope, and love. (1:19)

If Augustine was right, the gay rights debate may serve as a touchstone for a broader and enriching reconsideration of human relations, and perhaps even the nature of God, but by the same token this connection complicates the debate enormously.

6

The Theological Meaning of Sex

In the Middle Ages Christian scholars explicated Biblical pronouncements by constructing theories about the nature of God and sex to privilege procreative, vaginal sex as ordained intercourse, in the double sense that it is validated by God and, like the priesthood, it provides a direct connection to God by participating in the creation of new life. All the other forms of sexual behavior were condemned as "*sodomia,*" unnatural because they diverged from this life-giving path to the divine.

But what do the terms "natural" and "unnatural" really mean? Different societies and religions have had different ideas about what actions are congruent with the perceived order of nature. Theoretically, any sex act that is anatomically feasible is "natural" (Barnett 29). Orthodox Judeo-Christian attitudes favored the missionary position as natural because it expressed the dominant nature of men, but this view was not shared by all ancient cultures. Among the several thousand portrayals of sexual intercourse left by ancient civilizations, the missionary position is extremely rare. The most common depiction in the ancient art of Greece, Rome, Peru, India, China, Japan, and Mesopotamia places the female above the male (Kinsey, *Male,* 373). Perhaps these artists believed they were representing the male's strength by having the woman be supported by him. Perhaps expressing dominance was not their goal, or not the goal of sex. Or perhaps reading the metaphorical significance of "who's on top?" is more problematic than medieval theologians imagined.

Both pagans and Christians based their arguments about "natural" or "unnatural" sex on the assumption that sexual diversity did not exist in the animal kingdom, even though at the time this claim was becoming controversial. Some, like Plutarch, the Roman jurist Ulpian, and the medical writer Soranos denied that same-sex animals ever copulated. But same-sex sexual behavior, including pair-bonding, was observed in animal species even in Ulpian's time. Aristotle, Pliny the Elder, and Claudius Aelian noted female-female mating among various birds. Surveying the conflicting opinions, Brooten concludes: "before, during, and after Paul's time, the jury was out concerning whether animals practiced same-sex mating" (Brooten, *Love* 270n.10, 330, 274). Nevertheless, homosexuals could be condemned from both perspectives: either as inventing a behavior not found in animals, or imitating (and sinking down to the level of) animal behavior (Boswell 309).

St. Thomas Aquinas, the most influential theologian in the Catholic Church's history, contended that naturalness need not be argued strictly from animal nature but from human nature, which exceeds animal nature, operating by its own rules which nonprocreative sex violates. Any sexual act could be judged unnatural if it was intended to prevent procreation, was mired in animality, or induced such intense pleasure that it threatened the soul's rational order (Jordan, *Invention,* 156). Sex had the power to corrupt judgement so that even heretical thinking would seem natural and self-evident. Even vaginal intercourse between husband and wife could be morally wrong if it compromised their spiritual natures; one of the consequences of Original Sin is that married couples must constantly be on guard against sex because of its intensity.

A theology of what constituted proper heterosexual sex was constructed over the centuries, focusing on a spiritual transaction analogized by anatomical structure: the joining of opposites, the experience of the human "other" (a spouse) in order to be opened further to the entry of the divine "Other." In producing children, human beings imitate and become partners with God-the-creator. As Joseph Cardinal Ratzinger, writing for the Vatican, declared in a 1986 letter to Catholic bishops:

Human beings, therefore, are nothing less than the work of God himself; and in the complementarity of the sexes, they are called to reflect the inner unity of the Creator. They do this in a striking way in their co-operation with him in the transmission of life by a mutual donation of the self to the other . . . To choose someone of the same sex for one's sexual activity is to annul the rich symbolism and meaning, not to mention the goals, of the Creator's sexual design. (Quoted in Elizabeth Stuart 75)

This transcendental view was also common among the ancient pagans, who often gendered their gods and read godliness in the metaphor of gender. The

Babylonian God, Marduk, had his consort, Ishtar, and in Egypt Osiris possessed the goddess, Isis. The Greek god, Ares, was joined with Aphrodite, and Zeus united with Hera (Batey 1–2). Married love represented this ideal fusion. As historian Richard Batey reports:

The "one flesh" concept in the first century was a symbol of unity intelligible to both Jew and Greek and was employed to express religious and philosophical meanings. The rabbinic consensus concerning the creation of Man was that God originally made a single person in his own image and afterward divided him into two complementary parts—male and female. The reunion of man and woman into "one flesh" constitutes a permanent blending which restores the original wholeness of Man and brings peace and satisfaction. (32)

As Batey explains, Philo, the most influential Jewish theologian on early Christian thinking, believed that only heterosexual relations in marriage signified this unity,

in which both partners shared the same experiences of suffering and pleasure; even more, they thought the same thing. Philo utilized the "one flesh" concept as a literary device to communicate the ideal unity of Mind, the male quality, and Sense perception, the female principle. Mind left God the Father and Wisdom, the Mother of all things, and cleaved to Sense becoming one flesh and one experience with her. . . . For Philo the identity of two persons has allegorical significance for revealing the nature of the abstract unity existing between Mind and Sense. The unity ideally should result in Mind, as the superior force, assimilating unto itself the faculty of Sense. . . . The character of the union was to be mutual, complete, and permanent with the male quality assuming the dominant role. (32–33)

Here mental abduction is viewed as a blessing. St. Paul's instructions in I Corinthians 7 suggest that he regarded the union as so powerful that even a pagan spouse would be converted to Christianity. Perfect unity erases difference even in thinking.

Early Christians viewed human marriage as symbolic of not only the unity between Christ and his Church but of all the binaries that structure the world. Thus, Eric Fuchs reasons that the "impurity of homosexual intercourse" lies

in the refusal of differences and the triumph of non-differentiation i.e. disorder. Now sexual difference . . . crowns the creative action of God: the creation of the world culminates in the creation of man as man-and-woman. The couple thus experiences in their flesh the order of differentiation which structures the world. . . . [Hence] sexuality should be lived out by the man and woman as the very meaning of all differentiation, that is, recognized as a call to a relationship that is organized and creative, like a call to arms against the constant threat of disorder and chaos, whose most insidious form is the confusion of the sexes. (Quoted in Scruton 309)

Only by integrating otherness with self can the lure of chaos be resisted. Homosexuality, then, is not just about sex; it is about understanding the nature of God and the universe and whether believers accept or reject the distinctions that give human beings a valued place in that universe. For orthodox Christians, redefining sexuality threatens religion itself. To honor the creator of gender differences is to live within those differences.

But unity and difference were unstable terms even for the ancients. The idea that the two sexes originally existed as a single being appears in Plato's *Symposium* to explain the spiritual power of sexual union: "Thus anciently is mutual love ingrained in mankind, reassembling our early estate and endeavoring to combine two in one and heal the human sore" (Batey 33). But another version of sexual origins exists that includes same-sex couples. The Greek playwright Aristophanes related the legend that, at the beginning of time, there were three different kinds of unified beings: a man and a woman, two women, and two men. Opposite-sex and same-sex couples resulted as each human being sought his/her original partner (Brooten, "Paul's Views," 65). Difference here was not anatomical but ontological; each gender could achieve full being because there were different kinds of othernesses to be integrated in sexual union.

Judaism and Christianity added sin to the psychic wound of separation by tracing eroticism back to Adam and Eve, whose disobedience separated them from God. Once they had fallen from innocence, Adam and Eve felt ashamed of their naked bodies and the inordinate sexual desire elicited upon seeing the other's genitals, which became the very mark of incompleteness, alienation, and transgression. The genital romance is thus two-sided: a promised union that requires an isolation to be overcome, an insistent lack that even a lifetime of coupling cannot completely fill. Desire and lack are indissolubly joined, each feeding the other, both the result of sin. "All sex is a form of longing," sociologist William Simon notes, "even as it happens" (139). Only marriage and children keep this addictive cycle in check by subsuming it to a higher good, the joining of humankind with God through procreation. Philo interpreted this to mean that a man without children was "rightly worthy of death by those who obey the law" because he "does his best to render cities desolate and uninhabited by destroying the means of procreation" (Brooten, "Paul's Views," 73). Indeed, Philo condemned both celibates and husbands who refused to divorce their barren wives and marry fertile ones: "Those who woo women who have been shown to be barren with other husbands are simply mounting them in the manner of pigs or goats and should be listed among the impious as enemies of God" (Koppelman 47). Without procreation, sex is degrading, a perspective which led some medieval theologians to argue that adultery, rape, and incest were more acceptable than masturbation, homosexuality, or contraception because the former were still open to conception (Rudy 114).

Modern "new natural lawyers" try to avoid such reductive conclusions by integrating theological and psychological discourses. John Finnis, Professor of Law and Legal Philosophy at Oxford University and the most quoted of the new natural lawyers, explains why only married vaginal sex is a fundamental good, and all other acts, no matter who performs them or for what reason, are bad:

The union of the reproductive organs of husband and wife really unites them biologically (and their biological reality is part of, not merely an instrument of, their *personal* reality); reproduction is one function and so, in respect of that function, the spouses are indeed one reality, and their sexual union therefore can *actualize* and allow them to *experience* their real *common good—their marriage* with the two goods, parenthood and friendship . . . [even if] their capacity for biological parenthood will not be fulfilled by that act of genital union. But the common good of friends who are not and cannot be married (for example, man and man, man and boy, woman and woman) has nothing to do with their having children by each other, and their reproductive organs cannot make them a biological (and therefore personal) unit. So their sexual acts together cannot do what they may hope and imagine. Because their activation of one or even each of their reproductive organs cannot be an actualizing and experiencing of the *marital* good—as marital intercourse (intercourse between spouses in a marital way) can, even between spouses who *happen* to be sterile—it can do no more than provide each partner with an individual gratification. . . . whatever the generous hopes and dreams and thoughts of *giving* with which some same-sex partners may surround their sexual acts, those acts cannot express or do more than is expressed or done if two strangers engage in such activity to give each other pleasure, or a prostitute pleasures a client to give him pleasure in return for money, or (say) a man masturbates to give himself pleasure and a fantasy of more human relationships after a grueling day on the assembly line. (26, 28–29)

Finnis builds upon the old natural law tradition, eclecticly integrating concepts from biology, psychology, and theology. Moral behavior is not only righteous but rational and psychologically beneficial because the goals of God, biology and love match. All these added layers are meant to prove one thing: only one kind of intercourse ennobles us with its divinity, all others betray us with false happiness through illusionary thinking.

Pro-gay theorists have responded to Finnis' argument in several ways, some on logical and theological grounds, some on empirical grounds. Michael J. Perry, Professor of Law at Northwestern University, asks why the commitment of a man and woman should necessarily disparage the quality of same-sex commitments (48). Stephen Macedo, Professor of Constitutional Law and Politics at Syracuse University, sees a logical inconsistency in Finnis' idea that the union of the reproductive organs of husband and wife "really unites them biologically" *even when* conception is impossible, but the union of homosexuals cannot achieve such a unity *because* conception is impossible: "Is not exactly the same thing true of sterile couples?" ("Homosexuality," 278). Both Perry and Macedo argue that Finnis applies different rules to the sexual orientation he discredits, and he assumes that only one specific kind of biological connection can be both personal and spiritual, no matter what the intention or the experience of same-sex lovers is. As we will see in Chapter 9, there are homosexual couples, in lifelong, monogamous, faithful and deeply loving relationships, who report experiencing their lovemaking as joining them physically and spiritually. Finnis dismisses their experience as an "illusion" but provides no evidence that this is true.

Finnis relies on anatomical difference to posit a truly biological union whether children are produced or not, but he has yet to specify what that union is apart from the fact that two different sexes participate in it. Since two sexes were created by God, he argues that heterosexual intercourse fulfills a godly goal. But gay and lesbian couples would not be possible without the two sexes either, and it could be countered that same-sex contact creates a spiritual connection and fulfills a godly goal of its own, a different one that Finnis cannot see. He discredits the subjective reports of gay couples as illusory, not because he has found evidence that they are false but because the "singleness" of their unions is not suggested metaphorically by same-sex anatomy. His argument is *a priori* and deductive, selecting and defining evidence by how it accords with the operating theory that since God is a perfect unity, singleness must be intrinsically good and diversity is intrinsically evil. The argument is compelling as long as our assumptions of what constitute perfection are unchallenged. Suppose, for instance, divine perfection does not lie in singularity but rather in diversity, an infinite and creative perfection that surpasses human categories. Finnis' approach is impervious to this challenge because divine nature cannot be observed directly, and so he relies on earthly models to suggest the unknown metaphorically. But could same-sex couples stand as another earthly model for a spiritual good? No, orthodox theologians argue, because at the heart of Christian theology is Original Sin, the fall of Adam and Eve, and since a fallen Nature is no longer perfect, it cannot fully reveal a reliable correspondence between creation and the Creator. Indeed, sexual diversity is viewed *as* a product of Original Sin, a conclusion several Christian writers (St. Paul, Richard Hays, Marva J. Dawn, Thomas Schmidt, Joe Dallas) propose. Thus, Finnis can view the observable world as an example of God's goodness *and* humankind's wickedness, as a suggestive metaphor (validating what heterosexuals "hope and imagine" their unions accomplish) *and* as an unreliable metaphor (invalidating what homosexuals "hope and imagine" their unions accomplish).

Finnis discounts science as irrelevant to spiritual values, but has he already crossed the line between the two when he concludes that gay couples are psychologically damaged human beings? At times he seems to be arguing that anatomy counts (he judges oral or anal sex between husbands and wives to be inferior), at times that intention counts (husbands and wives who seek individual gratification in vaginal sex debase the act), but ultimately he hopes that both anatomy and intention are each intrinsic parts of the other: only vaginal sex elicits the right motives, and only the right motives redeem vaginal sex. But does he demonstrate that this is true? Does he shift between metaphysical discourse and scientific discourse to answer such objections or to avoid them? Can he avoid dealing with opposing evidence from the real-life experiences by LGBTs simply because theology defines what is true? We are once again back to St. Matthew's unanswered question: how does one see one's own blindness *when one is blind* (15:14)?

New natural lawyers Robert P. George (Associate Professor of Politics at Princeton University) and Gerard V. Bradley (Professor of Law at Notre Dame University) argue that LGBT experiences are irrelevant because unmarried people are incapable of recognizing the intrinsic goodness of marital sex:

They cannot imagine . . . why spouses would perform marital acts, not (or not merely) as a means to, or of, procreation, pleasure, expressing feeling, and the like, but above all, and decisively, for the sake of marriage itself, understood as actualized in such acts.

Intrinsic value cannot, strictly speaking, be demonstrated. . . . Hence, if the intrinsic value of marriage, knowledge, or any other basic human good is to be affirmed, it must be grasped in noninferential acts of understanding. Such acts require imaginative reflection on data provided by inclination and experience. . . . Nor can it be attained except with strenuous efforts of imagination, by people who, due to personal or cultural circumstances, have little acquaintance with actual marriages thus understood. (307)

Marriage, like revealed religious truth, must be experienced and believed in before it becomes compelling: it cannot be refuted or verified through reason or evidence (Law 198). Gays and lesbians cannot, therefore, understand how their experiences distort perceptions and abduct judgement. Natural law is apparent only to those who already live within its domain and according to its rules. Those who question it are already outside its beneficial effects: a theological catch-22.

Pro-gay theorists can use the same argument against George and Bradley, as heterosexuals who have never experienced what it is like to be homosexual. Pat Califia believes that the genital romance of heterosexuality is a defense against knowing what sexual dissidents know:

The third layer of queer hatred says same-sex activity is ridiculous, a parody of heterosexuality, an awkward attempt to achieve pleasure that will forever elude us because our bodies don't fit together. . . . [But] so much happens when two women simply sit next to each other and hold hands! The very air between them fills up with the color of potential intimacy! I got one five-minute close-dancing lesson from another girl in junior high school, and the smell of her hairspray and the feel of our breasts rubbing against each other was enough lesbian sex to get me through the next five years of no contact at all with other female bodies. But what can we expect from a group of people who, by and large, cannot deal with the revolutionary things they could experience during vanilla penis-in-vagina sex? It seems to me that heterosexual culture has devoted a great deal of energy to guaranteeing that a penis plus a vagina will always equal zero—no social change, no insight, no shared understanding, and above all, no switching of intimate apparel. ("Identity" 98–99)

Just as George and Bradley view homosexual sex as a hollow parody of heterosexual sex, Califia views heterosexual sex as a parody of itself: what was once a liberatory act has been so purified of nonreproductive, illogical, and divergent desires that it is now monochromatic and stagnant. From Califia's perspective, heterosexuals who condemn gays and lesbians for enjoying their sexualities are prisoners of their own straight-jacketing idealism. Both marginalize the other. As sociologist Steven Seidman argues: "A binary sex system, whether compulsively heterosexual or not, creates rigid psychological and social boundaries that inevitably give rise to systems of dominance and hierarchy—certain feelings, desires, acts, identities, and social formations are excluded, marginalized, and made inferior" (149).

Even if both sides can agree that marital sex is an ideal, why must it be the only good? Why should less-than-"perfection" become its polar opposite? LGBTs suspect that such a leap of logic is not merely the result of binary thinking about the two sexes but of prejudice, especially when Finnis equates a loving gay couple's intimacy with casual sex between strangers or between a prostitute and her client. Why is sex treated as an all-or-nothing issue when so many other moral issues in Christianity have gradations of value? Centrist moral theologians Philip Keane and Vincent Venovesi, S. J., have suggested that loving monogamous homosexual relationships may be viewed, not as inherently good, but as better than promiscuity; to this Kathy Rudy adds that we could consider homosexuality "morally equivalent to the use of birth control" (73). But George and Bradley categorically condemn all non-procreative sex acts as intrinsically grave wrongs because they damage the acting person as a dynamic unity of body, mind, and spirit: "To treat one's own body, or the body of another, as a pleasure-inducing machine, for example, or as a mere instrument of procreation, is to alienate one part of the self, namely, one's consciously experiencing (and desiring) self, from another, namely one's bodily self" (314). As Andrew Koppelman has argued, such a view is based on the old scholastic natural law theory that human faculties should only be used in ways that "realize their natural powers." But this rationale logically should lead us to condemn chewing sugarless gum because the organ designed to receive sustenance is being used only for pleasure; it is not realizing its full potential (53). George and Bradley do not present evidence that gay couples (or straight couples engaging in non-procreative sex) reduce themselves to mere machines; non-procreative acts are, *by definition, not by demonstration,* psychologically and spiritually damaging. One such example is Roger Scruton's argument about masturbation by married couples:

Consider the woman who plays with her clitoris during the act of coition. Such a person affronts her lover with the obscene display of her body, and, in perceiving her thus, the lover perceives his own irrelevance. She becomes disgusting to him, and his desire may be extinguished. The woman's desire is satisfied at the expense of her lover's, and no real union can be achieved between them. (319)

Although such an argument makes analogical sense (the woman uses her body instrumentally for herself, and so the couple has not become "one flesh"), it is not obvious that disgust is a necessary response simply because a woman has more than one source of pleasure. Couples often do not give and take pleasure in perfect equality, perfect simultaneity, or perfect self-lessness. Many lovers know by experience that different occasions create different patterns of interaction. Theology offers perfection as humankind's proper aim, but why must perfection be so minimalist?

Using anatomy as an analogy for persons runs the risk of becoming reductionistic. In the 1967 edition of the *New Catholic Encyclopedia,* the Reverend John F. Harvey expressed the church's position in the psychoanalytic term "narcissism" because gay lovers are the same sex:

All true love is a going-out of oneself, a self-giving; but, all unconsciously, homosexual love is bent back upon the self in a closed circle, a sterile love of self, disguised in apparent love for another. What seems like ideal love to the homosexual must be shown to be narcissism. (119)

The Greek myth of Narcissus, from which Sigmund Freud borrowed the name, does involve a young man who falls in love with a male image, but it is not another man's; it is his own. The argument that loving someone of the same sex is narcissistic has not been substantiated, and the implication that shared characteristics determine how a relationship works is simplistic. Would it be narcissistic to fall in love with someone from the same race, neighborhood, or religion? Heterosexual couples often attribute their success to "things in common" without incurring the charge of narcissism. The implication here is that gender constitutes so much of the individual that little else is of value to a relationship. Psychological studies suggest that sufficient differences exist between people of the same gender to make a relationship just as challenging, other-directed, and enriching as heterosexual relationships (Barnett 3; Weithman, "Natural Law," 238). But natural law arguments have yet to address this evidence.

What the gay rights debate needs is a new way to conceive of gendered persons without reducing them to simplistic binaries based on anatomical difference. Moral philosopher Roger Scruton inadvertently illustrates the shortcomings of binary thinking when he theorizes heterosexual sex:

the opening of the self to the mystery of another gender, thereby taking responsibility for an experience which one does not wholly understand, is a feature of sexual maturity, and one of the fundamental motives tending towards commitment. . . . For the homosexual, who knows intimately in himself the generality that he finds in the other, there may be a diminished sense of risk. The move out of the self may be less adventurous, the help of the other less required. In an important sense it is open to the homosexual to make himself less vulnerable and to offer, because he needs, less support. (307)

Because no barrier divides same-sex couples, Scruton believes that homosexuals find only a desire "already intimately known" and therefore less enriching, more cheaply purchased. Indeed, Scruton is worried that if modern civilization continues to minimize gender differences, eventually a "decline in the sentiment of sex" will rob even heterosexual sex of mystery and romance (309). If difference disappears, so will desire, as if only gender counts. Even when centrist Catholic theologian Michael Novak tries to avoid pathologizing gays or reducing relationships to sin, he cannot escape the assumption of the oppositeness of the opposite sex:

What is at stake in the argument over homosexuality is the value we place upon sexuality. . . . Overt homosexual acts, even in the context of permanent commitment and perfect mutuality, do not symbolize this Catholic sense of earthiness and harmony [as found in the union of opposites]. . . . They represent, at best, the overflow of friendship through sexual demonstrativeness. (Malloy 230)

The result, Novak concludes, is a false happiness—not real love but merely intense friendship—that cannot bestow that "transcendent unity and peace" which comes when two who are different become one.

But are the two sexes so different that their union surpasses understanding? Traditionally, males have been assumed to be aggressive, extroverted, action-oriented individuals who pursue and impregnate women with rigid, penetrating sex organs. Women have been assumed to be passive, introverted, emotion-oriented individuals who coyly encourage pursuit in order to be impregnated in their soft, penetrable sex organs. Males assert themselves publically through culture, social groups, and institutions; thus, sex is only a partial aspect of their selves, while women's lives are organized entirely around sex, as wives and mothers and caretakers of men (Simmel 107–111). As Helen Haste has argued, seeing analogies between anatomy and psyche enables us to think about ourselves as subjective beings because subjectivity is difficult to define on its own terms (11). Anatomy gives visible shape to mental features by finding similarities between apparently unrelated things, and since sexual anatomy is binarized, thinking about gender is binarized too, dehumanizing both through stereotyping (McNeill 131–133). In today's popular discourse, men are from Mars, women are from Venus. But research suggests that such a dualism is arbitrary because it works as a continual feedback loop, reinforcing and reproducing itself until all human characteristics are lined up on either side, exclusively belonging to one or the other sex, a difference that is more conventional than real (Butler, "Imitation"; Bornstein; Bullough and Bullough). Psychological studies show that, overall, men and women share all human characteristics, to varying degrees in different individuals, and there are no single personality features that are the exclusive property of just one gender.

Gender ideology has contaminated sexology since its inception in the late nineteenth century when Karl Heinrich Ulrichs, Richard von Krafft-Ebing, and Havelock Ellis represented homosexuals as gender dysphoric, as women who wanted to be men and men who wanted to be women. For much of the twentieth century, gendered markers accumulated to the point of absurdity, as Colleen Lamos notes of a 1961 mass-marketed paperback by Carlson Wade entitled *The Troubled Sex*, which offered clues to the American public on how to "detect" a lesbian:

"The aggressive lesbians of the masculine kind" have wide shoulders and narrow hips, "more than the usual amount of hair," a "sultry," "sharp" voice, "thick fingers," and ankles, "strong, sturdy, and rather bony" arms, and a "short, thick" neck; the lesbian "walks with a broad gait, and is somewhat ape-like in appearance." Her clothing is "mannish". . . . "In warm climates, lesbians often wear Bermuda shorts." Like the men they wish to be, "Lesbians have an attraction toward dogs. . . . Lesbians do not scare easily from such things as mice, bugs, or snakes. Many can ride horses."

Wade hardly mentions femme lesbians at all, depicting them only as "innocent girls" who are not really homosexual but were seduced into "the strange practice of lesbian love" by their "male" butch partner (Lamos 92).

What, then, can be perceived of homosexuality if gender ideology sees only a reversed heterosexuality, an incomprehensible strangeness, or an unfulfilling sameness? Has the genital romance been replaced with a genital idolatry? Getting beyond inadequate descriptors presents a formidable theological challenge for both pro-gay and anti-gay churches and theologians. Even sympathetic Christians like Edward Malloy are handicapped by their own discourse, by the way they imagine and conceptualize what sex means:

[the question is] whether homosexual love-making can effectively symbolize the kind of completeness and harmony that is part of the Christian vision of creation and reconciliation. . . . Christians have yet to discover what it is that is symbol-ized by the homosexual partnership. Until they do and until they are convinced that it is compatible with Christian values, they will beg off celebrating the bond. (Mal-loy 231)

But what is it "that is symbolized by the homosexual partnership" when gendered descriptors are no longer applicable to theologizing sex? As Kathy Rudy puts it:

Part of the reason that Christians have had a difficult time discussing sex (both het-erosexual as well as homosexual) is because we intuit that something important—something almost beyond words—happens during sexual activity. . . . Lacking the language to discuss these connections, we allow ourselves . . . to be captured by legalistic formulas prescribing narrow conditions for legitimate sex. (xii)

Finnis' legalisms fill the bill. He cannot describe how spirituality operates in sexual relationships without resorting to polysyllabic abstractions based on narrowly interpreted physical metaphors.

This is, by no means, a heterosexual theorist's problem only. In his review of sexology books in the last century, Jeffrey Weeks found them nearly uni-versal in using hydraulic metaphors to describe male desire, as if it were

an unbridled almost uncontrollable force (a "volcano", as Krafft-Ebing graphically put it, that "burns down and lays waste all around it; . . . an abyss that devours all honour, substance and health). . . . (81)

The disadvantage of visualizing male desire as an irresistible force has pro-foundly affected our debate about sexuality, for, by implication, it relegates marriage to serving as a necessary containment, a civilizing of brute instinct, protecting society from the violence of male desire (Weeks 102). Secular social thinkers like George F. Gilder still argue that, from a suppos-edly scientific socio-biological perspective, men are inherently violent and aggressive, while women are intrinsically passive, and that female sexuality acts essentially as a wet blanket, domesticating and civilizing men by sub-ordinating sex to family values (35). Conservative Phyllis Schlafly employs this view in her book, *The Power of the Positive Woman,* to warn her women readers that feminism by itself cannot keep men in line:

A married man . . . is spurred by the claims of family to channel his otherwise dis-ruptive male aggressions into his performance as a provider for wife and children. (Quoted in Weeks 42)

As Weeks notes, the pro-family policies of the Religious Right build upon this hydraulic metaphor to argue that only a containing family structure based on fixed gender roles can hold back a destructive flood of desire:

In the New Right vision of social order the family has a policing role. It ensures care-fully demarcated spheres between men and women, adults and children. It regulates sexual relations and sexual knowledge. It enforces discipline and proper respect for authority. It is a harbour of moral responsibility and the work ethic. This is con-trasted to the ostensible moral chaos that exists outside. (43)

Is this why the stereotype of the promiscuous, subversive, anti-family homo-sexual has such appeal for the Christian Right? If male desire is opposed to social order and "family values," then gay men (conceived as "sexual preda-tors") and lesbians (conceived as "mannish" women and therefore partaking in unruly male desire) represent a violent revolt against proper containment and a wholesale surrender to moral and sexual chaos. The gay "lifestyle" is typically imagined as a building flood that will unleash anti-establishment, atheistic, and social lawlessness (Herman 80). Professor Sylvia A. Law (New York University Law School) argues that orthodox churches and traditional-ists in general consider homosexuality a threat not because they are squeam-ish about sex but because it challenges the very nucleus of social and kinship relations established by fixed gender roles in marriage. Queer rebels in the early 1970s established new kinds of partnerships, communities, sexual codes and utopian dreams of a non-hierarchical society. In "A Gay Manifesto (1969–1970)" Carl Wittman spoke for the Radical Left when he argued:

We have to define for ourselves a new pluralistic, role free social structure for our-selves. It must contain both the freedom and physical space for people to live alone, live together for a while, live together for a long time, either as couples or in larger numbers; and the ability to flow easily from one of these states to another as our needs change. Liberation for gay people is defining for ourselves how and with whom we live, instead of measuring our relationship in comparison to straight ones, with straight values. (Blasius and Phelan 383)

To rethink sexual relations, some gay and bisexual men increased the num-ber of sexual contacts, having sex with hundreds of partners a year. Sexual experimentation was seen as an integral part of developing a new con-sciousness and a new ideology. They became sexual outlaws, defining them-selves against the straight culture. As sociologist Steven Seidman reported:

Casual sex [is] viewed as a primary community building force in gay life. Through casual sex, gay men were said to experience heightened feelings of brotherhood and male solidarity. . . . Barriers of age, class, education and sometimes race were said to be weakened as individuals circulated in this system of sexual exchange; compe-tition and rivalry between men might give way to bonds of affection and kinship. (Rudy 76)

Once desire was freed from the constraints of marriage and reproduction, radical LGBTs theorized, sexual freedom would lead to a social revolution, as if sex had a essential truth that could be discovered and harnessed (Weeks 55), a truth that promised revolutionary changes in all the social relations that have suppressed it. In 1972 a New York group of Black and Latino gay men called Third World Gay Revolution issued a political manifesto that challenged the very traditional gender roles of the procreative family that it rested on:

We want the abolition of the institution of the bourgeois family. . . . All oppressions originate within the nuclear family structure. Homosexuality is a threat to this family structure and therefore to capitalism. The mother is an instrument of reproduction and teaches the necessary values of capitalist society, i.e., racism, sexism, etc. from infancy on. The father physically enforces (upon the mother and children) the behavior necessary in a capitalist system: intelligence and competitiveness in young boys and passivity in young girls. Further, it is every child's right to develop in a non-sexist, non-racist, non-possessive atmosphere which is the responsibility of all people, including gays, to create. (Rofes 17)

If, as new natural lawyers have argued, heterosexual coupling validates the order of differentiation that structures the world (Scruton 309), then radical gays and lesbians hoped to restructure the world by voiding the distinctions that separated the sexes, races, and nations. But they inadvertently bought into the notion that male desire contained within it the seeds of destruction for the containment marriage offered. This provided leaders of the Christian Right with powerful propaganda material, powerful not only because of its shock value but because it accorded so nicely with the orthodox view of gender.

Did the sexual revolution succeed in giving us a new conception of what it means to be gay? A considerable debate within the gay community centers on this very question. While much good came out of the 1970s—the egalitarian nature of gay relationships and politics, the building of gay communities and alliances with other liberation groups, the questioning of conventional wisdom—many LGBTs were still thinking in terms of a deviance from the norm, a norm that was not theirs. The alternative to politicizing deviance is the assimilationist idea that gays and lesbians are like everybody else; they merely practice a different "life-style" within a pluralistic society (Miller 52). Books such as Kath Weston's *Families We Choose,* Laura Benkov's *Reinventing the Family,* and Phyllis Burke's *Family Values: A Lesbian Mother Fights for Her Son,* represent a quest for order, permanence, and binding ties "as the natural extension of gay liberation" because, in theory at least, they too challenge the denigration of homosexuality (Rudy 69). Some LGBTs, however, worry that the push for gay marriage or gay adoption or gays in the military will only dilute their uniqueness, conventionalizing sexual difference until it is regarded as merely an unimportant variation of the norm (Rudy 82). Mainstreaming gays may only create a policing policy that excludes or discounts anyone who does not fit the "long term monogamous, adult-to-adult, intraracial, intragenerational, romantic sexual and intimate values" borrowed from heterosexual ideals—such as career, family, home, security, hobbies and anniversaries (Seidman 150, 173). Ironically, both assimilationist and separatist perspectives validate the orthodox gendered view of sexuality: that family ties constrain the destructive potential of desire. Many LGBTs still find themselves talking about relationships and roles and expectations in heterosexual terms—the queen, the butch, the femme, the "top" or "bottom" partner—even though they do not accept these categories as definitive. If all desire is described as gendered, then a homosexual identity becomes merely a copy of the heterosexual. The gay couple who lives like a married couple may be monogamous, comfortable, and neighborly, but do they really help us conceptualize what it means to be gay?

Can a "different" sexual identity remain unique, a "single reality" that actualizes "the good" of a sexual union, as Finnis would put it, when it is accepted in heterosexual terms that denigrate nonheterosexual behavior? Or is there room enough in these terms to construct difference? Has the butch lesbian who dresses like a man really left behind heterosexist notions of what it means to be a woman who pursues other women? Or is she subverting the whole notion of masculinity by parodying it, using it for her own purposes, making the signifiers of masculinity "lesbian"? Has the leatherman dressed like a cop or the effeminate queen discovered or constructed a gay identity, or are both recycling straight culture's immobilized notions of gender? On the other hand, would abandoning these sexual stylizations leave gays and lesbians without distinguishing marks? Would the best society be one where everyone leaves gender display behind to "just be themselves"? Or is "being ourselves" always a matter of adopting some outward display because subjectivity without bodily display is indefinable? Are we all, in a sense, dressing in drag?

AIDS reinforced the heterosexual paradigm by becoming a tangible metaphor for the intrinsic dirtiness of the sex instinct, whether straight or gay. The orthodox view of sexual desire, going back at least as far as Martin Luther who specified it, compares the desire to copulate with the impulse for fecal evacuation, an association tied up as much in anatomical location as in sin. As Jeffrey Weeks reasons:

[S]exuality was essentially male, with the woman just a hallowed receptacle: "the temple built over a sewer." A more respectable view was that sexuality represented the "instinct of reproduction," a more appealing theory in that it did reflect one result, at least, of heterosexual copulation, and could offer an explanation of women's sexuality as a product of "maternal instinct." (83)

Without procreation to ennoble it, sex is dirty, even for heterosexuals. The romantic triumph of "two in one flesh" is always undercut by the necessity of employing corrupted flesh and the metaphorical mingling of sex organs with eliminatory organs. If LGBTs are perceived as reveling in dirt, the dirty little secret hiding in the heterosexual closet is also revealed. Is homophobia, then, the displaced unease heterosexuals feel about their own sexual instincts?

The analogical potential of anatomy not only infers an intrinsic dirtiness in sex; it also suggests that the fundamental otherness of women invites abuse. As Bernadette Brooten points out, throughout ancient and medieval Europe, "coitus was culturally conceived of as penetration, rather than, for example, as the vagina swallowing or engulfing the penis" (*Love* 157.n43). Women were defined by their role in coitus, to be penetrated, to be used and controlled. Sociologist Georg Simmel observed that the relationship is fundamentally unequal both physically and socially because the woman needs the man more than he needs her, since his sexuality, in the form of aggression, can be expressed in the public sphere, while her sexuality, in the form of conception, is hidden in the privacy of home (103). As Susan Brownmiller argues, such asymmetry suggests that all heterosexual intercourse bears a metaphorical resemblance to rape:

Man's structural capacity to rape and woman's corresponding structural vulnerability are as basic to the physiology of both our sexes as the primal act of sex itself. Had it not been for this accident of biology, an accommodation requiring the locking together of two separate parts, penis into vagina, there would be neither copulation nor rape as we know it. . . . By anatomical fiat—that inescapable construction of their genital organs—the human male was a natural predator and the human female served as his natural prey. (13–14, 16)

Andrea Dworkin extends this reading to explain how the social and economic subordination of women throughout the ages was also anatomically-based:

Intercourse is commonly written about and comprehended as a form of possession or an act of possession in which, during which, because of which, a man inhabits a woman, physically covering her and overwhelming her and at the same time penetrating her; and this physical relation to her—over her and inside her—is his possession of her. He has her, or, when he is done, he has had her. By thrusting into her, he takes her over. His thrusting into her is taken to be her capitulation to him as a conqueror; it is a physical surrender of herself to him; he occupies and rules her, expresses his elemental dominance over her, by his possession of her in the fuck.

For Dworkin, the word "fuck," denoting both sexual intercourse and assaultive violence, betrays the negative implications of the genital romance. This is not necessarily a matter of what the man wants or intends consciously, Dworkin notes: "The act itself, without more, is the possession" (63). Thus, while otherness may invite Finnis' romantic notions of mystery and completion, it can also invite Dworkin's fear of domination and exploitation. Analogies drawn from anatomy support both traditional notions of marriage and traditional forms of oppression. In the second century Clement of Alexandria observed that a woman's body was made "soft" by nature in order to nurture the husband's seed. From this, he concluded that wives must be subservient to their husbands, shut themselves up in their houses, and avoid unnecessary contact with any nonrelatives. If her husband behaved abusively toward her, she had to endure it and had no option to leave (Brooten, *Love,* 327). Significantly, in the same century, Artemidoros of Daldis noted that sexual relationships between women featured a striking difference that set them apart from heterosexual relationships he had observed, and which marked them as socially dangerous in his mind: they were "unnatural" because the shape of their genitals did not suggest or require the subordination of one partner to the other. By its egalitarianism, lesbianism abandoned the hierarchy of dominance that gave men their authority and society its structure—reason enough to condemn it as "monstrous, lawless, licentious, unnatural, and shameful" in an age that tolerated or even celebrated same-sex unions as long as they were between social unequals: men and boys, servants, lower class males, foreigners, and prostitutes (*Love* 184, 29, 216).

The theological denigration of women extends far back into Judeo-Christian history. Numbers 30:2–8 claims that a man can make a vow to God on his own and be bound by it, but a woman must obtain her father's or husband's approval, a qualification that diminishes women as moral and spiritual beings (Ochshorn 146). When God's messengers are threatened by the people of Sodom, Lot offers his virgin daughters to the mob for assault and possibly murder. Jesus valued both sexes equally, but in I Corinthians 11:8, Paul reinvoked OT admonitions that marriage was not supposed to be a relationship between equals: "Indeed, man was not made from woman, but woman from man. Neither was man created for the sake of woman, but woman for the sake of man" (Brooten, *Love,* 275). Medieval theologians depicted women as not only spiritually inferior to men but as the embodiment of what men had to repress in themselves, a concupiscence that threatened to destroy the social order. As Rosemary Radford Ruether, Professor of Applied Theology at the Garrett-Evangelical Theological Seminary, argues:

While allowing woman baptism, patriarchal theology stressed her "greater aptness" for sin and her lesser spirituality. As an "inferior mix," woman can never as fully represent the image of God as man, who is seen as representing the rational and spiritual part of the self. . . . Aquinas concludes that woman, although defective and misbegotten in her individual nature, nevertheless belongs to the overall "perfection" of nature because of her role in procreation. It is for this and this alone that a separate female member of the human species has been created by God; for any form of spiritual help, man is better served by a companion of the same sex than by woman. (94, 96)

Christianity has yet to reconcile its idealization of marriage with its concomitant disparagement of women (Elizabeth Stuart 109–110). What is the "mystery" which Woman brings to marital intercourse that is so uplifting if she also represents what Man must deny or control because so dangerous? Why does her gender disqualify her for the priesthood, while men, whose desire needs marriage to be contained, monopolize the church hierarchy? The Apostle Paul seems to attribute women's inferiority to an essential weakness:

But I suffer not a woman to teach, nor to usurp authority over the man, but to be in silence. For Adam was first formed, then Eve. And Adam was not deceived, but the women being deceived was in the transgression. (KJV I Timothy 2:11–15)

Created first, the male possessed greater self control, a superior spirituality, which is perhaps why Satan realized that he had to tempt the woman first in order to get at the man: only with her cooperation could he overcome Adam's self-control. When Pat Robertson told *The Washington Post* in 1992—

the feminist agenda is not about equal rights for women. It is about a socialist, anti-family political movement that encourages women to leave their husbands, kill their children, practice witchcraft, destroy capitalism and become lesbian. ("TIAF")

—he was expressing binary thinking that has haunted the genital romance for millennia: with dominance comes a marginalizing hierarchy in which anyone who "gets fucked" is inferior and ripe for rebellion if not strictly controlled.

The myth of the genital romance cannot answer central questions in the gay rights debate. What is "gay desire," and how may it be conceived without turning gay males into women or lesbians into men? Is gender the only way sexual relations can be explained? If, as Aquinas reasoned, human nature exceeds mere physicality, can any bodily metaphor for spiritually fulfilling sexual relations suffice, or are they all too "dirty," "fucked up," and "mired in animality"? Can the meaning of anal, oral or digital sex be theorized on their own terms? What is the purpose of a lesbian or gay life when it is the excess that gender metaphors cannot account for? The first anti-gay Roman law, passed by Christian emperors Constantius and Constans on 16 December 342, expressed mystification at what same-sex love could mean to the participants:

When a man marries [and is] about to offer [himself] to men in a womanly fashion, what does he wish, when sex has lost its significance; when the crime is one which is not profitable to know; when Venus is changed into another form; when love is sought and not found? (McNeill 76)

Aquinas could not answer this question either. He confessed that he could not understand why some people preferred sex with the same sex over sex with the opposite gender (Jordan, *Invention,* 155).

Mystery no longer suffices as a rationale to applaud or condemn. When a group of Protestant churches filed an amicus brief during *Bowers v. Hardwick,* they included a statement that acknowledged both the ambiguities of natural law and the caution that should follow:

To the extent that there is any consensus concerning alternative forms of sexual expression, heterosexual or homosexual, it is that private sexual conduct is a matter fundamentally committed to individual moral choice. Because we do not understand the full mystery of human sexuality, and because we are unwilling to condemn that which we do not understand, we believe as a matter of ethics that characterizing consensual sodomy as immoral is unwise. (Quoted in Law 215)

As long as the moral argument against sexual diversity is comprised of circular arguments and slippery anatomical metaphors, court decisions will vary according to the subjective standards of individual judges. In some cases, this works against LGBTs, but in other cases it benefits them, as Janet E. Halley, Associate Professor of Law at Stanford University, points out:

In significant equal protection cases challenging discrimination against gay men and lesbians, courts have begun to apply rational basis review in a way that requires the government to articulate its reasons for anti-gay policies, and that requires judges to decide whether those reasons are reasonable. In Dusty Pruitt's challenge to her discharge from the Army, the Ninth Circuit required the defendant to state nontautological [non-circular] reasons for its anti-gay policies. In Keith Meinhold's suit alleging unconstitutional discrimination by the Navy, the court held that "[t]he Department of Defense's justifications for its policy banning gays and lesbians from military service are based on cultural myths and false stereotypes" and fail rationality review. ("Reasoning" 1728–1729)

States have long relied on ambiguous analogies about natural law and gender stereotypes to enforce their sex laws, but rationality review puts this technique in jeopardy, preferring evidence over metaphor, the nuts and bolts of real gay lives over the genital romance. Ironically, *Bowers v. Hardwick,* while at first seeming to protect the arbitrary power of states to define depravity without evidence, has in fact made states vulnerable by failing to set a standard for sex legislation.

Clearly, natural law needs to be rethought, but procreation alone seems too narrow a base and anatomy to broad. The Bible asserts that God

"created human beings male and female and told them to 'fill the earth'"
with children. Now that this goal has been achieved and the earth is full,
indeed crowded, what spiritual value lies in the 99.9% of heterosexual sex
acts that do not produce children? How do non-procreative acts serve society or God? Does infertility rob sex of its meaning? There are some literalists who think it does. During the Springfield, Missouri, Bias Crime Ordinance debate of 1994, anti-gay fliers claimed that *all* non-procreative
individuals threaten the future of society (Witt and McCorkle 101). But
even St. Paul's condemnation of non-vaginal sexual acts makes no mention
of procreation as a rationale: he is concerned with what turns people away
from God and the social order (Brooten, *Love*, 252). So the religious questions should really be: does homosexuality enhance or obstruct one's relationship with God? Are there different spiritual paths for different physical
unions? Aquinas wrestled with a similar question in his time—whether vir-
ginity was unnatural because it violated God's command to multiply—and
reasoned:

The needs of the human race are, therefore, sufficiently taken care of when some
take up the work of carnal generation; others abstain from it and have leisure for
contemplation of divine things in view of the welfare and adornment of the entire
human family. The same principle holds in an army; some protect the supplies, some
give signals, some go into battle, and in this way the total obligation is on the group
and could not be borne by one. (Gilson 296–297)

Not every individual is responsible for all the needs of the human race, and
each has his or her own unique gifts to contribute to society. Bearing children may be only one of many ways to enhance spirituality through a sexed
body. If Aquinas was right about human nature surpassing animal nature,
requiring unique methods of fulfillment, then restricting ourselves to the
minimal, reproductive use of our bodies may only impoverish us spiritually.

Part Two

Science and Uncertainty

My father had a problem . . . with alcoholism. Other people have sex addiction. Other people are kleptomaniacs. I mean, there are all kinds of problems and addictions and difficulties and experiences of this kind that are wrong. But you should try to work with that person to learn to control that problem.
—*Senate Majority Leader Trent Lott, R-Miss, explaining his view on homosexuality, 15 June 1998*

Psychologists, psychiatrists and other mental health professionals agree that homosexuality is not an illness, mental disorder or an emotional problem.
—*American Psychological Association, July 1998*

7

The Etiology
of Homosexuality:
Biology and/or Culture?

Biologists have suspected since the late 1800s that sexual orientation may be innate. Theories about instincts, drives, unconscious impulses, hormones, interhemispheric brain function, and evolutionary aims were proposed by various scientists, including Darwin, Krafft-Ebing, Freud and Ellis. In 1936 Magnus Hirschfeld noted that both male and female sexual orientations tend to run in families (gay men have more gay brothers and lesbians have more lesbian sisters than heterosexuals do), and recent research has borne this out (Pillard 233). Contemporary science has focused on genes and brain function to explain why, but this work is controversial both for its methodology and its relevance to moral or political values. Even as biologists are formulating deterministic models for sexual behavior, cultural anthropologists and sociologists, observing disparate social groups worldwide, argue that sexuality may be as much a product of history, culture, and ideology as it is of nature.

The nature/nurture debate has a number of implications, not the least of which is the simplistic binary itself. Is it even possible to decide which aspects of sexuality are innate and which parts are learned when biological systems are so responsive to environmental conditions and when the hypotheses science tests contain concepts that are themselves socially constructed? If sexuality is a cultural product, its expression may be part of a larger system of meaning science cannot reduce to a manageable focus. We may find ourselves caught in a paradox: deciding the origin of sexuality may require us first to admit that we cannot observe how biology or culture works independent of the terms each imposes upon our observations (Allen 243).

BIOLOGICAL RESEARCH

Animal Studies

"The world is, indeed, teeming with homosexual, bisexual, and transgendered creatures of every stripe and feather," reports biologist Bruce Bagemihl, author of *Biological Exuberance, Animal Homosexuality and Natural Diversity*, but sexual diversity in the animal kingdom has only recently been systematically studied (9) because it was traditionally regarded as a byproduct of living in cages, mere sex play, or as dominance behavior (Pillard 233). As Bagemihl notes:

Homosexuality is not generally the result of animals "deprived" of heterosexual mating opportunities—this can be seen quite clearly in the behavior of individuals toward members of the *opposite* sex in skewed or segregated populations (in both the wild and captivity). Potential heterosexual partners are often ignored or even actively refused in such situations—they are rarely inundated with attentions as would be expected if animals were being excluded from participation in opposite-sex matings. . . . Female Japanese Macaques and Hanuman Langurs engaging in homosexual activities usually disregard males entirely and may actually threaten or attack them if they make sexual overtures. (142)

Sexual diversity has been found in every geographical location and in every major animal group, including monkeys, dogs, cats, rats, goats, horses, elephants, mice, lions, baboons, apes, and porpoises. It is exhibited not only genitally but socially, ranging from fellatio, cunnilingus, anal intercourse, and mutual masturbation to courtship, shows of affection, pair-bonding, and same-sex parenting (12). Male orangutans copulate anally, male dolphins pair off and masturbate against each other, avoiding females even in courting season, and male squirrel monkeys and common chimpanzees engage in full mouth-to-mouth kisses (16). Male stumptail macaques perform mutual fellatio in a "69" position, while a number of other primate species swallow their partner's semen (20). Female primate same-sex behavior takes the form of mutual grooming, cunnilingus, masturbation, mounting, and rubbing. Many of these same-sex partnerships are monogamous, occur in roughly the same percentages among males and females, and occasionally same-sex "threesomes" will form (21–22). In a review of the research, Bagemihl estimates that one-fifth of all mammal and bird interactions that include courtship, sexual relations or pair-bonding are same-sex. In general, such activity does not elicit hostile behavior from heterosexual members of the same species. Indeed, some same-sex couples (such as gorillas, big horn sheep, savanna baboons, and red deer) enjoy high status in their groups (36, 54–55).

What can such research contribute to the gay rights debate? While same-sex *behavior* in animals can be observed, it may not necessarily represent a homosexual *identity* or an *orientation* as human beings experience it. Vernon A. Rosario argues that animal studies tell "nothing about how animals *conceptualize* their erotic attractions or identities" (4). Does a bull experience same-sex relations differently than his opposite-sex relations? Does it experience these differences as consonant with an identity? Or are these human terms simply not applicable to animals? It is tempting to think simplistically about sex as an animal instinct. But we humans can be moved by multiple factors: unconscious associations, culturally defined models of beauty, a partner's social status or wealth, love, anger, fear, loneliness, and gratitude. We display an enormous repertoire of sexual behaviors, only some of which are linked to reproduction. Sex can be intensely interpersonal, focusing on aspects of a partner that may not be sexual. William Simon, Professor of Sociology at the University of Houston, argues that

the complexity of motivations in sexual behavior reminds us that the desire for sex is rarely, if ever, in the exclusive control of "sexual desire" . . . other animals may hunger; only the human experiences and is shaped by an awareness of what others desire of us. We are rarely only what others desire of us, but we never fully escape the fact of their desiring. (72, 139)

Genetic Studies

The largest genetic study to date, by psychiatrist Richard C. Pillard (Boston University) and psychologist Michael Bailey (Northwestern University) in 1991, included not only identical and fraternal twins, but a third group, homosexual subjects with adoptive same-sex siblings, genetically unrelated but raised in the same family environment. In the male study, identical twins had a 52% chance of both being gay, compared to a 22% rate for their fraternal twins and only 11% for their adopted brothers. In the study of females, identical twins had a 48% chance of both being lesbian, compared to a 16% rate for sororal twins and only a 6% rate for adopted sisters. Such a result, Pillard and Bailey concluded, shows that genes have a significant influence over sexual orientation, while growing up with a homosexual sibling does not. Moreover, different genes are involved in men than in women; gay men do not have a greater incidence of lesbian sisters; thus, it is hypothesized, two separate and independent genetic influences seem to be operating (Pillard and Bailey, "Innateness"; Pattatucci et al.). In 1993, Bailey et al. conducted a similar study on female twins and found a comparable concordance rate that declined as the degree of genetic relatedness declined (Allen 252).

Such studies encouraged Dean Hamer, a molecular geneticist at the National Institutes of Health, to look for a genetic marker for homosexuality. Recruiting volunteers through advertisements in gay publications, Hamer et al. studied DNA from 40 pairs of gay brothers and found that 33 shared five different patches of genetic material grouped around a particular area on the X chromosome, specifically the 28th region on the X's long arm. This is unusual because the genes on a son's X chromosome are a highly variable combination of the genes on the mother's two X's, and so the sequence of genes varies greatly from one brother to another. As Richard Pillard explains:

Each son gets one of the mother's X chromosomes at random, so the chance of both brothers getting the same chromosome (or the piece of it containing the relevant gene) is 50 percent. The chance of a second pair of gay brothers sharing a marker at the same locus is one in four (one half times one half), the probability generated by flipping pairs of coins. To build a statistically convincing case, the pairs of coins (markers) need to be the same (both heads or both tails) more often than chance predicts. . . . (236)

Out of 40 pairs of brothers, Hamer found 33 twins with similar DNA markers in the Xq28 region. Subsequent studies of heterosexual brothers revealed that most of them did not share these markers, and no linkage was found for pairs of lesbian sisters. So much overlap between brothers who also share a sexual orientation is unlikely to be just coincidence (Henry 37). Hamer concluded that the odds that his results are only random are less than 200 to 1. Homosexuality was the only trait that all 33 pairs shared; the brothers did not all share the same eye color or shoe size or any other obvious characteristic. Nor were they all identifiably effeminate or hypermasculine. They were diverse except for sexual orientation (Hamer et al.; Henry 37; Angier, "Report"). Hamer recently completed two more studies of the Xq28 gene, both of which confirm his original findings (Burr 197), but he has failed to show a similar genetic linkage for lesbianism (Hu et al.).

If homosexuality is hereditary, why does the trait not gradually disappear, as gay males and lesbians are less likely than heterosexuals to have children? Hamer hypothesizes that the genes specific for male homosexuality can be carried and passed on to children by heterosexual women because these "male" genes do not cause the women who inherit them to be homosexual. Simon LeVay (a neuroanatomist at the Salk Institute of Biological Studies) adds that it is possible "gay genes" confer other traits insuring survival, as is the case for the gene for sickle-cell anemia which confers a resistance to malaria ("Sexual" 69). The overwhelming majority of homosexual children are produced by heterosexual parents, parents who may carry the same genes but do not express them, or they may express them in non-homosexual ways: genes that produce same-sex desires or identifications in one individual may produce heterosexual desires or identifications in others (Henry 37). Moreover, the seven subjects who were gay but did not share DNA patterns in Xq28 suggest that other genes may work to enhance or even substitute for Xq28's actions. It may be impossible to determine which genes produce "gay" traits, under what circumstances, and in what stages of an individual's development. Geneticist Jeremy Nathans at Johns Hopkins is currently collecting a large bank of DNA samples from subjects with identifiable sexual histories, but it will be years before the results are known.

Brain Studies

One way genes might affect sexual orientation is by producing enzymes and proteins that determine the structure and function of the brain. Although preliminary and highly controversial, a recent anatomical study suggests that some homosexual brains may be different from heterosexual brains in one of the areas that mediate sexual desire. In autopsies of 41 people, 19 of whom were retrospectively categorized as gay men, 16 straight men, and 6 straight women, LeVay measured the size of a group of cells in the hypothalamus. It was already known that two of the cell-groups were larger in men than in women, and LeVay found the same difference in size when he compared heterosexual men to homosexual men. This area in the hypothalamus of gay men was as small as it was in heterosexual women ("Difference").

It is important to note that the differences in size were statistical rather than absolute; some gay men and heterosexual women had cell-groups as large as those in most heterosexual men. Perhaps they were bisexual, or perhaps the hypothalamus is not the only part of the brain involved in sexual orientation. It is also possible that brain structure changes in response to behavior, rather than preceding and causing it (Rosario 6). Brain cells can rearrange their neuronal connections in response to environmental demands, although how much is unknown. In general, younger brains are more plastic, and while some adjustments continue throughout the life cycle, other neural pathways are optimized before adolescence ends. Same-sex desires are most often reported by gays and lesbians to occur in adolescence, but whether this reflects a developing brain influencing behavior or behavior influencing brain development is unclear (Burr 69; Satinover 101; Pillard and Bailey, "Genetic"; Eric Marcus 10–11; Kandel and Hawkins).

Similar structural differences may occur in the brains of transgendered men who report feeling like "women trapped in men's bodies." Researchers in the Netherlands discovered that a small region (the central subdivision of the bed nucleus of the *stria terminalis*) of the hypothalamus is about 50% larger in non-TG men than in women, but it is almost 60% larger in non-TG men than in MTF transsexuals. Animal studies indicate that this part of the hypothalamus may help coordinate sexual behavior and the release of essential reproductive hormones. In heterosexual and homosexual men, the bed nucleus measures about 2.6 cubic millimeters; in women it averages 1.73; but in MTF transsexuals it averages only 1.3. This is a substantial difference, suggesting that the smaller the bed nucleus, the more "female" the individual feels (Angier, "Study"). This may not be the only etiology for transsexuality. Some forms (such as the XXY syndrome) are clearly genetic, while others may be associated with an area of the brain called the "Sexually Dimorphic Nucleus" (Bill Stuart, "faq2TS"). It is known that human embryos develop recognizably male or female genitalia in the 12th week of pregnancy, but it is not until the 16th week that the SDN is differentiated. Some researchers believe that, depending on the hormonal mix during this four week gap, gender identity may not develop along the same lines as the genitalia (Brown and Rounsley 22).

Some neuroendocrinologists believe that sexual orientation may also be influenced by the early (even prenatal) effects of androgens on the brain cells that control sexual desire. The theory is that if the infant's brain is exposed to high levels of androgens, then the child will become masculinized and feel attracted to women in adulthood. If the brain is not exposed to high levels of androgens, or if hormonal effects are blunted by some other condition, the brain does not masculinize and attraction to men will result. Studies of rodents have shown that some sex-typical sexual behavior can be affected by altering early androgen levels. Female rhesus monkeys exposed prenatally to high levels of androgen subsequently show elevated rates of male-typical (rough-and-tumble) play behavior (Pillard and Bailey, "Innateness"; Berenbaum and Snyder; Meyer-Bahlburg et al.). Whether or not these mechanisms work the same way in human beings is not known.

Similarly suggestive findings have come from studies of girls and women with congenital adrenal hyperplasia (CAH). CAH is a genetically induced disorder that causes a fetus to secrete large amounts of androgens from the adrenal glands, resulting in a newborn girl with virilized genitalia and high rates of masculine behavior. Berenbaum and Snyder have replicated the influence of early androgen exposure on a child's preference for either stereotypical masculine play (e.g., choosing toys consistently more popular with boys than with girls, such as toy cars, Lincoln logs, or a transformer) or stereotypical feminine play (dolls, doll clothing, and kitchen supplies); neutral toys, such as books and jigsaw puzzles, were used as controls. 24 CAH girls, 19 CAH boys, 16 non-CAH girls, and 25 non-CAH boys were told they could play with whatever toys they wanted, and such play was secretly videotaped and shown to two observers, one who knew the children and their CAH status and the other who did not. Two sessions, six months apart, were conducted at the children's homes. Non-CAH boys and girls were also tested to see how well the toys appealed to each sex: scores showed that non-CAH children and CAH-boys were more likely to play with toys our culture assumes should appeal to their sex. CAH girls, however, showed significantly greater preference for boys' activities than did their female non-CAH relatives. While these tests suggested a strong influence of high androgen levels on masculinity in girls, they showed only a weak influence on preference for a particular sex in the playmate. Other researchers have found elevated rates of same-sex attraction among adult women with CAH compared to control women. Women who were prenatally exposed to DES, a chemical that causes masculinization of sexual behavior in some animals, also experienced an elevated rate of homosexual feelings (Pillard and Bailey, "Innateness"; Burr 100–101; Meyer-Bahlburg et al.).

Other parts of the brain may be involved as well but to lesser degrees. Laura Allen and Roger Gorski (biologists at the UCLA School of Medicine) found the commissure of the corpus callosum (a thick bundle of nerves that connects and coordinates the left and right hemispheres of the brain) to be relatively larger in heterosexual women and homosexual men compared with heterosexual men. Some researchers suspect this explains why homosexual men are much more likely to be left-handed, dyslexic, and stutterers—all factors related to left and right hemisphere integration (Gotestam et al.). At the very least, the studies suggest that neuroendocrine influences may have more general effects (Pillard and Bailey, "Innateness"):

In summary the evidence from prenatal endocrine disorders and from the offspring of hormone-treated pregnancies suggests that hormones may contribute to but do not actually determine, the course of sexual orientation in individuals with an abnormal sex-steroid history during prenatal life. (Gooren 1990)

If androgens do play a part in the biology of sexual orientation, they are apparently only one piece of a complex system.

OBJECTIONS TO THE BIOLOGICAL APPROACH

All of the previously mentioned studies have been criticized for their methodology and their assumptions, by other scientists, by anti-gay rights groups, and by pro-gay rights advocates. Theodore Lidz questions Pillard and Bailey's twin studies because they could not establish which of the 100,000 human genes they were tracking. Since they used twins who had been raised together, Lidz maintains it is impossible to separate shared environmental effects from shared genetic effects (Allen 249). Moreover, the study may show only that *something* was shared; it does not prove that what was shared genetically was sexual orientation. Testing subscribers of gay magazines may only reveal that what they have in common is a gene for an extroverted personality, assertiveness, or social activism (being "out" as opposed to being closeted) (257). In addition, bisexual men were counted as homosexual; subjects with diverse behaviors and desires were lumped into the same category regardless of whether the evidence considered was conduct, self-description, or fantasy, some of which may have different etiologies. Some of the brothers refused to answer questions about their sexual orientation, and so Pillard and Bailey relied on the subject's twin to "guess" what his orientation might be (Halley, "Sexual," 540, 543). Stanton L. Jones (Provost of Wheaton College) and Mark A. Yarhouse (Assistant Professor of Psychology at Regent University) see a further complication in how subjects were recruited:

Given the political sophistication of the gay community, it is conceivable that some degree of volunteer bias could have affected the results of the study. If monozygotic twins who had homosexual twin brothers and sisters were more likely to volunteer than discordant twin pairs because they believed the study would produce benefits for the gay community, substantial bias could have swayed the findings. (92)

Several critics of Pillard and Bailey's study argue that genes cannot be considered determinative of sexual orientation if only 52% of identical twin siblings are gay: why are the other 48% heterosexual? Jeffrey Satinover, a retired psychiatrist from Yale University, reasons that

if "homosexuality is genetic," as activists and their media supporters repeatedly claim, the *concordance rate* between identical twins—that is, the incidence of the two twins either both being homosexual or both being heterosexual—will be 100 percent. There would *never* be a *discordant* pair—a pair with one homosexual twin and one heterosexual twin. When we say that "eye color is genetically determined," this is what we mean. That's why identical twins *always* have the same eye color. (83)

However, such an objection may oversimplify how these genes work. Some genes do have complete penetrance: they produce effects in whomever inherits them. But most genes have incomplete penetrance; whether an inherited gene takes effect can depend upon other factors: environment, the influence of other more dominant genes, hormonal events during prenatal and postnatal development of the brain, infections during pregnancy, and mutations in the molecular structure of the gene itself that manifest themselves "downstream," that is, later on in an individual's development. As William J. Turner argues,

in a number of well-defined, genetically determined anatomical and biochemical disorders, MZ [identical] twins exhibit much less than 100%—even as little as 50%—concordance [identical genetic traits]. . . . Indeed, this phenomenon actually calls to attention *the high probability that an unaffected sib or other relative may carry the gene, but in inactive form, as that carried by the affected individual in an active form.* (125–126)

For instance, the Type 1 Diabetes gene has only a 30% chance of being expressed. In a like manner, identical twins could both inherit a "gay" gene, but it would be expressed in only one of them because each individual develops separately.

To illustrate just how complicated it might be to track genetic influences on homosexuality, Chandler Burr reports:

Ten years ago there was a disease of the lungs called, simply, cystic fibrosis. Some kids had it severely, some mildly, but it was a disease. Now that we've found the CF gene and identified 350 completely different mutations inside it, we've discovered there are people with cystic fibrosis mutations who have no perceptible lung disease at all in this "disease of the lungs." We've found people with CF mutations where their only manifestation of the disease is congenital absence of the vas deferens so that they're sterile. . . . We've found that the genes that are used to construct a fly eye and the genes used for a human eye are actually the same genes, but they are called on in completely different ways to do the same job. (217)

Thus, heterosexuals may carry and pass on to their children a full or partial genetic predisposition to homosexuality without experiencing homosexual feelings themselves, and the gene's potential might not be realized for several generations, depending upon what other facilitating or inhibiting genes enter the family pool through marriage. It is not yet known if cultural values, lived experience, biological stressors, or psychological factors can affect the triggering of these genes or their expression in desire and behavior.

Hamer's discovery of a maternal Xq28 gene is more specific, but to prove that this is a "gay gene," it must be precisely located and cloned so that researchers can observe how it expresses the trait. Hamer admits that his work does not establish a genetic basis for homosexuality; he has found only the neighborhood of a gene that is shared by homosexual brothers; it is still not known which gene in that area is involved or how it is related to sexual orientation (Pillard 236–237). Moreover, Hamer selected gay men with gay brothers, no lesbian relatives, and no gay fathers or sons; thus, the selection process itself may have set up a pattern of maternal inheritance (Halley, "Sexual," 533). Garland Allen notes that 92% of Hamer's sample were Caucasian non-Hispanic, 4% African American, 3% Hispanic, and 1% Asian subjects, which suggests that Hamer assumed homosexuality could be categorized as a single behavior wherever it is found—an assumption cross-cultural anthropological studies question, as we will see later in this chapter (255). Hamer also assumed that homosexuality is a constant throughout the life cycle, whereas psychological and sociological studies show that in many individuals it can be fluid (for a more detailed discussion, see Chapter 8).

LeVay's hypothalamus studies have drawn considerable criticism for methodological errors, even from gay rights supporters. As Keen and Goldberg note, LeVay changed methods during his research, measuring both right and left sides of the hypothalamus in 15 brains, only the right side in

14 brains, and only the left side in 12 (54). Twenty-six of the 41 cadavers he autopsied had died of AIDS, but it is not known how AIDS affects brain structure. Byne and Lasco argued that "virtually all men with AIDS have decreased testosterone levels as the result of AIDS itself or of the side effects of particular treatments" and that the size of equivalent brain structures in some animals can be affected by the amount of testosterone in the blood (116). LeVay responded that the six brains of the presumed heterosexual men with AIDS were different in the same way from the brains of the presumed homosexual men with AIDS. Moreover, he found no "dying cells, inflammatory reactions, or other signs of a pathological process at work," but it is also unknown if hormonal damage to brain cells would be visible ("Sexual" 66). Byne and Parsons also noted that studies have shown that the brain can change in response to environment in order to adapt, though it is not known if same-sex experiences would cause different changes than opposite-sex experiences. Thus, Byne and Parsons cannot prove that there is no biological cause, while LeVay cannot prove that there is. Could LeVay have been measuring the *effect* of homosexual experiences rather than the *cause*—a reversal LeVay himself admits is possible (Herman 70; LeVay 66–67)?

Some pro-gay advocates find LeVay's work suspect. Janet Halley questions whether LeVay had accurately determined the sexual orientation of the deceased. Without access to their own assessments or their sexual histories, LeVay relied on medical records and various doctors' unverified evaluations of the patients' prior lives. Halley describes LeVay's binary categories as "startlingly crude" because he sorted his subjects into either the heterosexual category or the homosexual, and if the records did not mention homosexuality, he assumed the deceased was heterosexual ("Sexual" 533–536). Darrell Yates Rist, cofounder of GLAAD (Gay and Lesbian Alliance Against Defamation), argues that LeVay's conclusion—that gay men's brains resemble women's brains—returns us to the outmoded notion that homosexuals are merely gender dysphoric, "hermaphrodites of sorts, sporting feminine brains in masculine bodies—that old German idea of homosexual men, *Warmbruder,* as the third sex" (74).

Opposition to biological theories also comes from a long-standing debate about determinism and free will. Genetic research is seen as an encroachment upon the individual's personal responsibility. In their essay, "The Use, Misuse, and Abuse of Science," Jones and Yarhouse argue that, while it is reasonable to conclude "that genetic, brain structure, prenatal hormonal, and psychological/familial factors may each be a facilitating or contributing cause of homosexual orientation in some individuals," it is unknown if one, some, or all of these influences operate in all homosexuals, and no one has yet proved if these influences render human choice irrelevant and therefore morally neutral:

We again concur with Byne and Parsons, who argue that human choice can be construed to be one of the factors influencing the development of sexual orientation, but that this "is not meant to imply that one consciously decides one's sexual orientation. Instead, sexual orientation is assumed to be shaped and reshaped by a cascade of choices made in the context of changing circumstances in one's life and enormous social and cultural pressures," and, we would add, in the context of considerable predispositions toward certain types of preferences. (105)

It may be simplistic to think in terms of a determinist/choice binary when the mind/brain nexus is so intimately involved in our emotional lives and our conscious choices (Burr 82). How, for instance, would we explain bisexuals who can experience complex and variable combinations of same-sex and opposite-sex attractions, or how desire can be further diversified in transgenderism and transsexualism? This question has already appeared in court rulings. In 1993's *Steffan v. Aspin,* lawyers for a midshipman who was forced to resign from the Naval Academy argued that a biological cause for homosexual orientation suggested it was an immutable trait and therefore should be protected. But the D.C. Circuit Court ruled that biology could not account for the "great 'in between' inhabited by bisexuals," which suggested to the court that "*some* people have *some* choice in their own sexual orientation" (Halley, "Sexual" 514–515). Until we can better understand how body and mind work together in sexuality, Halley warns gay advocates relying on strictly biological arguments that they risk losing in the courts.

Perspectives on how much impact science should have on moral theology follows party lines. Some orthodox Christians reject out of hand the relevance of biology even if influence is proven. Davies and Rentzel argue:

Even if homosexual tendencies were an inherited trait, we would not interpret that as an endorsement of gay or lesbian involvement. Many studies have indicated that tendencies toward alcoholism or depression are inherited. But we do not embrace alcoholism or depression as "acceptable alternative lifestyles." Rather, we try to help people who suffer from these tendencies find healing and recovery.

Science provides facts, not political or religious values. Both hair color and alcoholism may be genetically based, but whether we consider one benign and the other harmful depends on many other questions we must examine first. Is the comparison between alcoholism, depression, and homosexuality useful or inappropriate? What criteria establish the value of traits? How valid are objections to a biological condition when they come from people who do not have it? How valid are the counter-objections by those who have the trait?

Centrist and progressive Christians typically argue for a greater give-and-take between science and religion. While admitting that facts and values are different orders of knowledge that cannot operate freely in each other's field, Jones and Yarhouse maintain that science and ethics are neither independent of one another, nor are they slavishly dependent:

Good science should inform ethical analysis. Ethical and theological analysis should proceed in the context of the best understandings of the subject matter under consideration, and science can provide us with valuable insights and understandings. While science can and should inform our ethical analysis, it will not determine the outcome of that analysis. (118)

Christine E. Gudorf, Professor of Ethics at Florida International University, is more progressive in arguing that the Christian view of "natural law" is itself an attempt to construct ethics out of Scripture and science:

One of the profound historical ironies in modern Christianity is that Catholicism, which had so many clashes with modern science within its resistance to the Enlightenment, nevertheless carried over from its medieval theology a concept of natural law which has allowed it in the contemporary period to integrate the findings of science into theology as further revelation of the Creator embedded in the creation. Thus contemporary Catholicism teaches that in addition to Scripture and postscriptural revelation embedded in the tradition of the church, Christians can discern the will of God in the structures and working of nature, both human and nonhuman. Thus discoveries of science, once verified, contribute to understandings of God's original intention and ongoing will. (134–135)

Clearly, biological research into sexual orientation is a long way from being verified, still farther from revealing God's intentions. But an ongoing exchange between science and religion may be necessary for future progress. Gudorf predicts that progress will require

some developments within the sciences themselves, including a greater openness to religion and theology, and even more fundamentally, a shifting of some emphasis from scientific method and practical applications of science in technology to the philosophy of science and the meanings of scientific discoveries. (136)

Some anti-gay groups reject out of hand scientific research, not for theological reasons but for political suspicions that either the researchers themselves are biased by pro-gay politics or that their reasoning, methodology, and assumptions have been affected unconsciously. Science, like religion or political philosophy, is an attempt to make meaning out of perceived patterns, but how one selects evidence, screens out discordant data, or hypothesizes cause-and-effect relations can be subtly influenced by non-scientific attitudes embedded in his/her historical and cultural moment. The "objectivity" of science when it studies human behavior has undergone tremendous reassessment in the twentieth century. The danger, sociologist Steven Seidman argues, is that "science confers legitimacy and authority on a discourse, its producers, and the social values and ideals of the discourse. In a word, *science is power*" (29). Krafft-Ebing's descriptions of homosexual behavior, considered "objective" a century ago, now reveal the gendered lens through which he observed sexuality (i.e., that homosexuals were men who wanted to be women or women who wanted to be men). Did Hamer rely too much on his own experience as a homosexual to detect self-evident homosexuality in his subjects? LeVay candidly admitted that his shift from neuroanatomical studies of vision to a neuroanatomical study of sexual orientation formed part of the grieving process for his lover who had died of AIDS (quoted in Rosario 12). Did his objectivity suffer as a result? Moreover, to orthodox Christians, science is already a suspect institution, producing secular explanations for human behavior that repudiate religious explanations.

Of course, the door of political influence swings both ways. Anti-gay critics also perceive the world through the lens of a meaning-system and may not be aware of how antipathy for a particular result may blind them to legitimate discoveries. Fliers distributed in Louisville by Freedom's Heritage Forum featured an article entitled, "Don't Believe the Lies from the Laboratory," which opens with

Are gays born or made? It's a question on a lot of people's minds. And *militant gays*, in order to strengthen their *demand* for *special class status*, are *desperate to manufacture evidence* that homosexuality is a genetic condition. Their *strategy: flood the media* with reports of *so-called "discoveries," knowing full-well the average person isn't trained* in telling true scientific evidence from false. (David Williams 55)

How can this debate proceed if people can not even agree on what is good evidence and what is not? Some gay rights opponents refuse to engage seriously the scientific evidence available because they see it as irrelevant in matters of faith, but others fear being deceived. Scientific data is not intrinsically the enemy of belief; it may even help demarcate the line between the physical and the spiritual. But if one believes that physical reality is "fallen" (as a result of Adam and Eve's original sin) and therefore ridden with sin, distortion, and deceptions, then such appeals will be resisted.

Although it is popularly thought that gay rights advocates welcome any and all support from science, at present an intense debate among them centers on the implications of biological evidence for their cause. Jennifer Terry believes that lesbians

in particular, feel a great deal of ambivalence about grounding identity . . . in biological difference since biological explanations have historically been deployed to keep women in a subordinate position to men. (281)

Lindsy van Gelder, a contributing editor to *Ms.* magazine, rejects what she sees as the implication of helplessness and inferiority in the "born gay" defense:

[W]e've essentially thrown up our hands and said, "But we can't *help* being this way."

Inherent in that response is the implication that if we *could* help it, we would. Even when that isn't what we mean, it's what a fair number of straight people hear, including some of our allies. It's easier for some of them to pity us as bearers of a genetic flaw than to respect us as sexual equals. (81)

Moreover, it is feared that once the specific mechanisms for sexual orientation are discovered, anti-gay groups will finance the development of medical techniques to reprogram genetic codes and produce only heterosexuals, or use genetic fingerprinting to "out" LGBTs even before they are born so that deprogramming or persecution can begin in infancy (81). This may not be feasible, however: individual genes can be involved in producing several or numerous effects, so it may not be possible to eliminate a "gay gene" from the human genome without jeopardizing other traits heterosexuals may want to keep. Other LGBTs fear that biological descriptions of difference often lapse into using "deficit metaphors," such as hormonal "imbalances," genetic "mutations," or developmental "accidents," which become part of popular discourse as well, loading the language we use to discuss homosexuality with a negative valence. Schuklenk and Ristow report that the biological argument is already being employed by judges and government agencies against the ultimate goals of the homophile movement because it is used as an "apology" for the existence of gays, who are depicted as an unfortunate blot on nature's good record (22).

CULTURAL INFLUENCES

Biological determinism is also challenged by cultural studies. Formal debates about nature versus nurture have been ongoing since the eighteenth century when English travelers discovered that social and sexual customs varied enormously across cultures. Within the last thirty years it has evolved into a debate between "essentialist" and "constructionist" theories, though these too are mired in a metaphysical quagmire (Stein 101; Seidman 130).

Essentialism views a gay identity as independent of culture, a recognizable difference (whether biologically-based or not) that is noticeable outside of any particular culture or historical period because it is a universal category; same-sex desires do not vary across time, geography, and culture even if local culture stylizes behavior differently or fails to recognize it as a different category at all; homosexuals and heterosexuals are regarded as having a unified sexual identity, internally coherent and behaviorally consistent. Constructionism, on the other hand, regards sexual identity as a specific social creation resulting from the interaction between an individual who seeks to understand him/herself and the explanatory terms provided by his/her culture. A constructed sexuality may be meaningful only within a specific culture and time (Seidman 89). It has been argued that the modern homosexual identity did not take shape until late in the nineteenth century when western doctors and sexologists provided the "explanatory terms" describing and categorizing sexuality. A "homosexual" identity began to take shape with long lists of typical behaviors, perverted desires, faulty patterns of thinking, disordered emotional makeup, and biological anomalies. Although the ancient Greeks observed same-sex behavior, they did not have such "master categories" available; sex acts did not define who or what they were (Halperin, "Sex," 207–208). The nineteenth and twentieth centuries offered a theoretical model by which to name desires, behaviors, fantasies, and identities as either heterosexual or homosexual, and these titles affected every aspect of the person so named. With the recent work of queer theorists, constructionism has taken a "postmodern" turn, questioning the simplistic categories of sexual and self identity (heterosexual/homosexual, man/woman) and allowing for all sorts of variations (butch/femme eroticism, sadomasochism, bisexuality, transgendered practices, transvestism, multiple partner sex, lesbians who have sex with gay men, interracial attractions, casual intimacies, etc.) because it does not posit a stable, unified, and identifiable sexual identity for anyone. Nor does it limit sexual identity merely to sex. An African American, middle-class lesbian's experience may differ profoundly from a white, lower-class, European lesbian: culture, region, religion, age, education, may play simultaneous parts. Individuals experience sexual attraction in a particular class-, race-, or gender-mediated way. There is no core gay identity around which race, class, or age, etc., adds mere nuance or variance; each identification shapes and is shaped by the others. Constructionism is primarily about meaning, the personal and cultural significance of a multiplication of identities (Seidman 92, 122–123, 138, 195; Rosario 6; Corvino xxii).

Vernon A. Rosario offers a useful analogy for understanding how each approach differs and overlaps in the study of sexuality:

As an analogy, the American Revolution created the new possibility for people to identify themselves and *feel* like "American citizens". . . . Those people who were born and raised in the United States and are "natural" American citizens tend to sense this national identity as congenital and integral to their personal identity, and not as a lifestyle choice. This is quite different from the foreigner who, in order to be "naturalized," usually has to undergo numerous, often trying, changes in lifestyle and, ultimately, must make a citizenship choice. Who, then, would you include in a history of "Americans" or a medical study of some aspect of "American" lifestyle:

"Native" Americans, descendants of the Pilgrims, descendants of those forcibly brought over on slave ships, yesterday's "naturalized" citizens, second generation "illegal aliens," all the inhabitants of the "Americas," expatriate U.S. citizens? Both the historical and synchronic identifications of a population involve difficult and arbitrary criteria based on subjects' self-perceptions, and historians' or scientists' "objective" distinctions. (*Science* 7)

What would happen if biological science attempted to assay the essential properties of these disparate groups by tying observed behavior or self-definition to genetic markers? Various associations could have the appearance of "linkage": the Native American gene pool could be tied to political disaffection, the African American gene pool to economic disenfranchisement, and the Pilgrims' descendants to privilege and old money. But these associations are not caused by genes. This is why Hamer's genetic study of self-acknowledged homosexual volunteers may actually be revealing a linkage for the personal qualities required to live publicly as a despised minority (openness, extroversion, assertiveness, courage, liberalism), not necessarily the gene for determining sexual orientation. If orientation is the product of a much larger psychic structure, how much genetic material would a closeted, shy, or orthodox Christian gay man share with a liberal, extroverted, "out and proud" gay man? How many different kinds of personalities can also be gay? How many different kinds of gayness are there? Even seemingly "objective" biological studies will founder if they ignore or oversimplify the diverse sexualities labeled "gay."

It is certainly true that same-sex sexual relations occur worldwide, in every country, in every ethnic group, and in every religion (though not in every tribe), which suggests to biologists that sexual orientation is an essential, transhistorical feature of human nature. But social structures exist everywhere too, and there is a diversity within sexual diversity that current conceptions of genetic and neural mechanisms cannot account for. Ritualized same-sex behaviors and relationships differ significantly between cultures. The same-sex unions celebrated in ancient Greece did not involve two unmarried adults in an egalitarian relationship such as we find today but a married man and a male youth, often a slave (Dynes and Donaldson ix; Kaplan 1885). In Greek thinking, the family served as a model for all sexual relationships: just as a wife was subservient to her husband, so the same-sex youth served as the passive, receptive partner for the husband (Greenberg 149). Yet the boys themselves did not become "feminized" as a result of their sexual role. The Greeks believed that sodomy prepared them not only for battle, but for marriage and, eventually, boys of their own; that belief produced young men who defined themselves as masculine and lived up to manly ideals even though they were penetrated by other males (Dynes and Donaldson x).

Sexual diversity among many African tribes also involves transgenerational relations that do not exclude either party from marriage or social acceptance. Among the Nyakyusa in Tanzania, adolescent males are expected to engage in reciprocal same-sex sexual relations to masculinize them until their early to mid-twenties. As David Greenberg describes it:

At this point, the now-mature young man becomes the older partner of another pre-pubescent boy, ordinarily his wife's or fiancee's younger brother. This relationship continues for roughly fifteen years, until the older partner is about forty. His involvement then ends, except for initiation ceremonies, which include collective homosexual intercourse between the initiates and all the older men or, if he takes a second wife, with her younger brother. Because taboos on heterosexual intercourse are extensive, while there are none on homosexual relations, male sexual outlets are predominantly homosexual between the ages of ten and forty. (28)

Here homosexuality is not "anti-family," as westerners conceive it, but actually binds families together with affection and obligation.

Culture seems to determine what sexual practices are acceptable and meaningful, and in highly specific ways. Although many New Guinea tribes employ rituals that involve semen transfer between men, different tribes see distinct differences between methods of insemination: those tribes that favor fellatio (such as the Kuks, Tchetchai, Sambia, Etoro, and Baruya) regard anal sex as disgusting, while those who favor anal sex (such as the Kaluli and the men of the Auya and East Bay regions) regard oral sex as repulsive (Dynes and Donaldson 132; Greenberg 28). Among the African Bagala, a man who sodomizes a woman can be executed, but sodomy between men is very common and experienced without shame (Greenberg 70). While some pre-Christian Pacific cultures saw no shame for boys who were sodomized, others did, mocking them as "girls" until they matured into men (Dynes and Donaldson 132). Attitudes towards individuals who cross gender lines also follow a cultural logic. Because Sambian men traditionally considered women to be inferior, male transgenderism and transvestism was condemned, but in Native American tribes, where women enjoyed comparable rights and privileges with men, transgenderism and transvestism were often acceptable (Greenberg 46–47).

Does social constructionism account for all same-sex relationships? Ritualized homosexuality among the Nyakyusa in eastern Africa occurs in the context of kinship structures and marriage, and so the men and boys who are lovers are not thought of as abnormal or different (Adam 21–25). But does this mean there were no innate homosexuals in these groups? Some clandestine same-sex relationships do remain in the Nyakyusan tribe after the young men turn 25, even though they are socially discouraged. Can these sexual minorities—the Nyakyusan who desires same-sex sexual relations long after he is married, the adult Greek man who desired to be penetrated—be considered innately gay, as the essentialists would argue? Do permanent same-sex couples in cultures lacking a "homosexual" label still think of themselves (and experience themselves) as "different," as non-heterosexual? The problem here is that one culture is trying to approximate meaning in another culture when all cultures create meaning from their own unique experiences, and all cultures define what constitutes evidence to support that meaning.

Like medieval Christianity, non-western societies constructed genital romances, reading the body as a text to define the person inside the body, but these readings interpreted the metaphor of anatomy differently. Anthropologist Gilbert Herdt's study in Melanesia found that a tribe he called the Sambians (to protect their privacy) "perceive no imminent, naturally driven fit between one's birthright sex and one's gender identity or role" ("Fetish" 54). They believe that while a female child is born with all she needs to grow into a woman, a boy lacks semen and will not develop masculinity naturally, for the mother's milk, menstrual blood, and caregiving only reinforce femininity. To prevent this, boys over the age of seven are housed in forest lodges with the men of the tribe, where they pass through a series of rites: tanning of the skin, nose-bleeding, dressing in warrior decorations, but most important, the frequent swallowing of semen from as many adult males as possible. The Sambians believe that semen masculinizes boys, making them strong warriors and marriageable partners who will father children and defend the tribe (*Same* 112–123). Since only semen can beget semen (Herdt, "Fetish," 54–55), the men restrict intercourse with women to prevent them from growing too strong and challenging the men's authority: "The entire cluster of homosexual beliefs and practices is kept secret from women, lest they learn that their subordination is a precarious accomplishment, rather than part of the order of nature" (Greenberg 29).

Ritualized same-sex relationships are by no means unique to the Sambians; they were, at one time before the arrival of Christian missionaries, shared by 60 other societies in New Guinea, the New Hebrides, and Australia (Herdt, *Same,* 82). But is ritualized insemination to instill masculinity a homosexual practice, a hypermasculine practice, a misogynist (hostile to women) practice, all three, or none of the above (Adam 27; Herdt, *Same,* 13, 65)? Herdt argues that

for the Sambia, sexuality is a ritual process, involving the body as a kind of temple and template of society, in which sex can never be isolated or separated from the larger social context of family, kinship, religion and community. . . . Their society did not have a concept for homosexual or gay, and these notions, when I translated them in the appropriate way, were alien and unmanageable. (*Same* xiv)

In this tribe, same-sex intimacy between young men is not seen as a private choice, an orientation, or a preference: socially, they are expected to have occasional sex with each other, and sometimes this leads to a permanent "best friends" relationship (Sorenson). In East Bay, Melanesia, young single men who are good friends or even brothers may take turns accommodating each other sexually, but they are not considered—and do not consider themselves—lovers (Greenberg 66). 90% of the Sambian males terminate their sexual relations with older men once they marry; if they continue to participate in the semen rituals, it is always as contributors of semen to a boy, not as recipients (Herdt, *Same*, 114). Are they "gay"? Can we say that Sambian men reserve "gay" desires for specific situations even though these encounters are not considered "gay," extramarital or separated from family life? And what of the 10% who continue to have sex with other men in their adult years? Are they the "real" gays, or do they expect continued masculinizing benefits from the ritual to fulfill their husbandly and fatherly duties? Or are they merely heterosexuals unhappy with their wives and their roles as husbands and fathers? It is difficult to translate Sambian ideology into western terms. Among seventeenth century Japanese samurai, male-male sexual relations were fully consonant with the ideals of masculinity; but in Mexico it is believed that effeminacy and male homosexuality are inextricably linked (Carrier). In each culture, individuals behave and self-report in different ways. Social factors determine how we think about the erotic, how we define it and its boundaries, which we then experience as natural (Seidman 148).

Sexuality may have important biological components that are universal, but identities seem to involve important cultural constructions. Demographics and community dynamics are just as much a part of diverse sexualities as they are a part of heterosexuality. Ritualized homosexuality in New Guinea occurs almost entirely in tribes that dwell in the lowlands, which are ecologically, culturally and sexually different from tribes on the highlands or adjacent islands (Herdt, *Ritualized*, 48–51). The number of women available in a particular group apparently has little to do with ritual homosexuality. The Bena Bena people in the highlands have more men than women but no institutionalized homosexuality, as do the Akwe-Shavante tribe of Brazil (Greenberg 31). Ritualized homosexuality is always practiced *within* a kinship structure so that it *does not challenge* gender role prescriptions in the family or in the community. Nyakyusan women do not define themselves as lesbians, women-centered-women, or bisexual; nor do they leave their husbands or form independent couples, because their culture has not constructed such a role for them to consider. In twentieth-century America, gays and lesbians establish their own social structures and institutions (bars, clubs, self-help groups, bookstores, newspapers, etc.), self-consciously theorizing and labeling what they feel and do both as individuals and as a group (Lockard 83–84). This does not mean that a San Francisco gay man or lesbian is the "real" homosexual and the Nyakyusa husband or wife is not. Herdt advises that such binaries be avoided: the identity categories "homosexual/heterosexual" in the nineteenth century and "gay/straight" in the twentieth century should be understood not as universal but as suggestions of common themes around the world (*Same* xvi).

The new LGB, who self-identifies openly, forms romantic relationships, performs a religious ceremony celebrating a committed union, or constructs a gay politics, gay sensibilities, or a gay theology, is a creation of modern times—even if same-sex sexual relations are as old as humankind. As David Halperin speculates:

Does the "paederast," the classical Greek adult, married male who periodically enjoys sexually penetrating a male adolescent share *the same sexuality* with the "berdache," the Native-American (Indian) adult male who from childhood has taken on many aspects of a woman and is regularly penetrated by the adult male to whom he has been married in a public and socially sanctioned ceremony? Does the latter share *the same sexuality* with the New Guinea tribesman and warrior who from the ages of eight to fifteen has been orally inseminated on a daily basis by older youths and who, after years of orally inseminating his juniors, will be married to an adult woman and have children of his own? Does any of these persons share *the same sexuality* with the modern homosexual? ("History?" 46)

Reasoning that all sexualities are culturally constructed, William Simon argues that while pre-modern societies enforced sexual conformity through a patriarchal system, modern societies create sexual pluralism through a system that fosters individuation (13). The meaning of any sexual episode is subject to multiple uses and revisions; as the meaning of experience and the experience of meaning change, we will continue to see the development of not only a plurality of homosexualities but a plurality of heterosexualities because our concepts of the sexual may not be limited to the seeming stability of organs and orifices (27, 30).

If the modern LGBT is a product of the times, on what basis can sexual minorities lobby for protected status? Many LGBTs (usually male) use essentialist arguments to maintain that their condition is immutable, like race or ethnicity, not a choice, and so legal guarantees should be made of their equality with heterosexuals. Others (usually female) prefer to use a constructionist argument, which may or may not argue immutability, but which applies to both homosexuality and heterosexuality and so implies equality. In contrast, Stanford Law Professor Janet Halley argues that neither essentialism nor constructionism is necessarily gay-affirmative because anti-gay rights groups freely use both to justify discrimination ("Sexual" 566). Didi Herman notes:

For conservative Christians anti-immutability is perfectly consistent with their theological knowledge. A "gay identity" did not exist in the Bible; the sins of Sodom were behavioral, not ontological. Homosexuality identity is thus a modern and, in their view, a human invention. Interestingly, this understanding of sexuality resembles that of radical feminist and gay theory, rather than the mainstream gay rights movement. In contrast, however, the CR is quick to dismiss with derision any suggestion that *gender* is socially constructed. Masculinity and femininity are neither behaviors nor identities; rather, they are God-given, biological essences. (73)

Moreover, even constructionism implies reductionism because individual agency can be elided by social pressures (Smith and Windes 149). Halley believes that pro-gay litigators who base their "suspect status" arguments on immutability not only risk misrepresenting and dividing the LGBT community, but they risk losing their cases as well:

In recent military cases [such as *Dahl v. Secretary of the United States Navy*], the government has sought to justify its anti-gay policy by an unstable amalgam of essentialist and constructivist models: the military, it is said, should defer to the strong feeling among heterosexual male soldiers that homosexual men are essentially unlike them, *and* to the same soldiers' terrible anxiety that their proximity to gay men erodes their own *heterosexuality*. ("Sexual" 566)

Halley contends that LGBTs should avoid questions of immutability and instead look for common ground in order to articulate the personal, social and political meanings of being LGBT. This is also common ground for heterosexuals too, who are amalgams of the fixed and the fluid, the cultural and the biological, the sexual and the political. The sameness and the difference that the soldiers in *Dahl* feared and desired simultaneously are dynamic tensions that appear within LGBT populations, individuals, and society.

If sexuality is socially constructed, will giving social approval to sexual diversity encourage higher rates of LGBTs, luring otherwise "straight" children into shifting their sexual orientation or becoming confused about their gender? This prospect has been an effective weapon in anti-gay crusades, warning that the LGBT population could swell to 20%–30% if young people thought it was socially acceptable (Porteous, "Eyrie"). Cultural studies offer a qualified answer. On the one hand, all adolescent boys participate in Sambian fellatio. On the other hand, it is not at all certain these Sambian males can be defined as gay since some of them openly object to ritualized fellatio, some do it only because their culture requires it, all go on to marry, and only 10% continue to form same-sex sexual relationships (Herdt, *Same*, 114, 120–121). The gay male populations in Paris and London were comparable in size in the nineteenth and twentieth centuries, despite the fact that since the late-eighteenth century France had decriminalized homosexuality while England retained severe penalties (including capital punishment) until 1967 (Whitam and Mathy 4–5). Today, in Denmark, the Netherlands, Iceland, Hungary, Norway, Luxembourg, and France, LGBs have been accorded full equal rights as citizens, including military service (Bawer 50), with no ballooning numbers of LGBTs. Or perhaps "legal equality" is not the same thing as "social approval" and does not affect the construction of a sexual identity. No one knows how biological, familial, psychological, and cultural factors combine or operate separately to influence sexual orientation. Perhaps, we may come to see that sex is not simply a natural force threatening social order (and thus requiring marriage—and only marriage—to contain it), but that it is already a part of social order.

8

Diversity within Diversity: Postmodern Sexual Identities

I label myself as a human being. I don't like labels, though. I'm afraid too
of placing myself into a category I can't maintain.
—*Quoted in Martin S. Weinberg et al.,*
Dual Attraction: Understanding Bisexuality

It is commonly asserted by pro-gay activists that 10% of the American population is homosexual, while anti-gay groups insist it is only 1–2%. Each
side uses figures to calculate how much political influence LGBTs should
enjoy. Science has been unable to settle the dispute because of the conceptual problem of fitting methodology to an intrinsically diverse population.
Over the last fifty years surveys have reported incidence ranging from
1.2% to 22%, and so 10%, while convenient, is oversimplified (Keen and
Goldberg 51). Variations can be attributed to sampling bias, ideological
bias, or the impact of AIDS, but a more thorny problem is theoretical: how
do we decide *who* is *what* orientation? Are sexual orientations stable or
fluid? Can they be determined by sexual behavior, fantasy, desire, ideology,
personal aims, or some combination? Do different individuals stress each
component differently? What kinds of survey questions can distinguish
multiple, varying, localized components? Do sexual categories disserve
LGBTs because defining who is considered a "real" gay or lesbian marginalizes (and therefore polices) individuals who do not behave, feel, or identify in the same way?

Although it is popularly believed that Alfred Kinsey's pioneering study in
the 1940s proved that 10% of the American population was homosexual,
he argued against such an easy categorization (Cabaj and Stein 46). Kinsey

and his colleagues at Indiana University conducted the first large scale sex survey in history, involving 11,240 men, and found that 37% of them had at least some same-sex experience to the point of orgasm at some point in their lives. 25% had more than incidental experience. 18% had as much same-sex as opposite-sex experience for a period of at least three years. 10% were largely homosexual, with some heterosexual experience. Four percent were exclusively homosexual throughout their lives (*Sexual Behavior in the Human Male* 650). In a subsequent study, Kinsey reported the numbers for women were lower by half (*Sexual Behavior in the Human Female* 474–475). In 1991 Rogers and Turner found that only 5–7% of American men reported some same-sex contact in their adult years. A year later Laumann et al. found that only 2.8% of men and 1.4% of women self-identify as being homosexual or bisexual, and only 2.7% of men and 1.3% of women report homosexual activity in the preceding year. Overall, 3.8% of women and 7.1% of men reported at least one same-sex encounter since puberty (Laumann et al. 293–294).

Several factors may account for these varying numbers. Kinsey worked in pre-AIDS times. A question like "have you ever had anal intercourse?" is more likely to be answered with a "No" today because, in the age of AIDS, many gay men have switched from that high risk behavior to low or no risk behaviors (oral sex, mutual caressing, or celibacy); even a non-specific question, like "Have you had sex with a man?" may be narrowly interpreted by the respondent as a question about anal sex and their HIV status (Keen and Goldberg 50). Consequently, many closeted gays make it a blanket policy never to tell anyone of their orientation. The Chicago study reported that only 7.1% of male respondents admitted to any same-gender sex since puberty, but one of the study's own authors, Stuart Michaels, in *Time* magazine's cover story, confessed that this figure was too low: "This is a stigmatized group. There is probably a lot more homosexual activity going on than we could get people to talk about" (Tremblay). Even before AIDS, anal sex was not a reliable gauge of homosexuality since various studies reported that 5% to 41% of gay males never engaged in it and 16% to 50% engaged in it regularly; the percentages vary considerably from one gay subculture to another, and differ among racial and ethnic groups (Schwanberg; Reinisch et al. 137; Voeller 260). There is no universal marker for sexual identity.

Surveys of marginalized groups are very difficult to conduct. Stigmatization can begin even before LGBT youth become aware of who they are. Hershberger and D'Augelli found that less than 30% of teenagers who engaged in same-sex sexual relations thought of themselves as homosexual. Because courts readily deny LGBTs child custody, parents usually conceal their homosexuality from family members (Patterson 34). Although it can be important for a doctor to know of a patient's sexual orientation, the Gay and Lesbian Medical Association found that 64% of medical personnel believed that "out" LGBT patients risk receiving substandard care; 52% had actually seen their colleagues either deny care or give substandard care to known gay and lesbian patients; and 84% of the lesbians feared reprisals if they returned to their physicians for new ailments (O'Hanlan). If people are willing to risk their health, why would they confess all to a stranger conducting a sex survey? This may be especially true of bisexuals, who feel unsupported by both gay and straight communities (Levine and Evans 17; Golden 29).

Surveyors face a variety of problems gathering their information. Kinsey interviewed almost anyone he could find, including men in prisons and reform schools as well as students and volunteers from gay social networks, which may have inflated the number of same-sex reports; on the other hand, Kinsey used face-to-face interviews, which may have intimidated some of his subjects to underreport. He also asked about adolescent experiences, which other surveyors usually ignore (Cabaj and Stein 47). So it is difficult to pin down how much the Kinsey figures are biased or in which direction, if not in both directions. Nearly every other survey conducted since Kinsey has differed in some significant way, either in its execution or interpretation (Keen and Goldberg 49). Some surveyors interview on the telephone, which may increase the respondent's fears that his/her private life has become public property. Choosing numbers from a telephone book omits anyone who has not lived in one place long enough to get listed: how, for instance, can a phone survey reach teenagers who are homeless because they are LGBT? Studies have reported that 16%–38% of runaway teens are LGBT (Human Rights Watch 74). Geography also skews results. Surveys conducted in rural areas typically report a 2% incidence of gay men, while urban areas yield 15% (Herdt, *Same,* 173). Even within a single city there are variations since LGBTs may be concentrated in certain areas and not others (Tremblay).

Political bias can also affect results. Brian Clowes argues that Kinsey's own sexual orientation biased him towards finding pro-gay evidence, choosing four techniques that inflated the numbers: interviewing sex offenders (who, Clowes suspects, would more likely be homosexuals), not revealing his sources (something all surveyors do to protect privacy—but it does prevent a detailed review of how well Kinsey selected his sources), fudging statistics, and hiring biased researchers (116). Tim LaHaye thinks Kinsey's figures are inflated because he included over 10,000 college students among his interviewees: "college young people are notoriously more sexually permissive and curious than any other group in our society" (19). How well do college students represent the general population? Are same-sex sexual relations more common in prison because there are more homosexuals there or because incarcerated heterosexuals seek sexual release? There is no physical evidence that Kinsey fudged his figures, but was he unconsciously biased? Opinions vary. While Kinsey's biographer, Cornelia

Christensen, claims that "Kinsey came to the study of human sexual behavior as a biologist, not a social reformer" (95), Regina Morantz believes that he was driven to normalize homosexuality: "cloaked in the unbiased empiricism of the dispassionate scientist lay the emotional preferences of a moral crusader" (566).

Political influence, of course, can cut both ways. Laumann et al. argue that sex surveys (such as those conducted by *Playboy* and *Redbook* magazines) attract respondents who are already biased for or against sexual diversity (22). Conservatives Judith Reisman and Edward Eichel accuse Kinsey of bias in their book, *Kinsey, Sex, and Fraud: The Indoctrination of a People,* but then present their own "unbiased" conclusions that only 1% of the population is gay or lesbian, the lowest estimate of any survey ever conducted. Congress tried to approve funds for two large national surveys to settle the controversy, but the measure was killed for fear that even a study would confer unwarranted legitimacy on sexual diversity. How pure can science be when caught in the middle of an intense political battle? Stephanie H. Kenen asks three good questions: "Who counts when you're counting homosexuals? Who doesn't? And, finally: Who does the counting?" (211)

A more perplexing problem with sex surveys is theoretical: at what percentile do we decide *who* is *what* orientation? Is a homosexual someone who has never had intercourse with the opposite sex, or has same-sex relations 75% of the time and opposite-sex relations 25% of the time? Or 50%–50%? Or 10%–90%? Heterosexuals do experiment (the use of gay men by heterosexual men is quite common as long as it is only the gay man who is penetrated), but typically they do not feel that such behavior defines their orientation (Whitam and Mathy 3–4). As one interviewee said:

I am also not really gay. Gay sex is something that I do 2–3 times a week. It amounts to so little of my time. If you were to add up the time I spend looking for and having sex with men it would total 1–2 hours weekly. The rest of the time I am heterosexual, married, a family man. (Jagose 7–8)

Angela Pattatucci et al. have found a variation of this logic in women; as one respondent said: "I'm not a lesbian. I just fell in love with this one woman" (Burr 173). The personal and the sexual do not always correlate to produce a categorizable identity. Indeed, as Eliason and Morgan report, there is actually little agreement as to what a lesbian is in the lesbian community itself. Is a woman a lesbian if she merely has sex with women? Or if she finds personal fulfillment in a non-sexual love relationship with another woman? Must a woman label herself "lesbian" in order to be one? Is self-labeling enough? Some women report choosing to be lesbians at some time in their lives, others feel that they were "born lesbian." Is one "less lesbian" than the other? Contrary to popular belief, lesbians who endorse choice do not place more emphasis on a feminist definition of lesbianism than lesbians who endorse biology, and lesbians who endorse "born" do not emphasize the physical aspects of lesbian desire more than lesbians who endorse choice (50—51).

Most people who identify as homosexuals have had past heterosexual experiences, usually in adolescence, and often they tried to change their orientation by dating the opposite sex. Researchers typically find that 25%–35% of their lesbian subjects had been married, and 58%–84% reported heterosexual experience (Kitzinger and Wilkinson 96). Many gay men and lesbians like the opposite sex, form close friendships with them, may date them, and sometimes even have sex with them: in one survey, 46% of self-identified lesbians also engaged in heterosexual sex—a third of these with gay or bisexual men (96), perhaps because these men were less prejudiced about lesbians. But does this make women less lesbian? Pat Califia argues that such questions reveal the problem with current sexual categories. She finds it

very odd that sexual orientation is defined solely in terms of the sex of one's partners. . . . I have sex with faggots. And I'm a lesbian. . . . Sex with men outside the context of the gay community doesn't interest me at all. In a funny way, when two gay people of opposite sexes make it, it's still gay sex. ("Gay Men" 29)

Anatomy does not, by itself, define what constitutes her sexual encounter.

Sexual behavior is not the defining factor of orientation. Kinsey found that 62%–79% of the men who self-identified (declaring "I am gay" to the interviewer) also reported having sex with women at some time in their lives. Nearly 50% of college-educated women reported some same-sex contact past puberty, while only 2%–3% were exclusively lesbian their entire lives. Of those who *always* referred to themselves as lesbian, 43% had had sex at least once with a man (Reinisch et al., 141, 144). Kinsey found that when people were asked to self-identify, only those who were exclusively homosexual even mentioned the word. Others did not feel defined by their same-sex experiences, even if these were considerable. When a man says, "I am not gay. If I was gay I would kiss the men I have sex with. I never kiss men," he is recognizing that different acts carry different meanings in different contexts.

So is sexual orientation what you *do* or how you *feel*? Is it whom you fall in love with, or whom you feel sexually attracted to? Identity and behavior are independent variables: a man who sleeps with both sexes may still define himself as heterosexual: the desire for other men is regarded as only "horniness," an eroticized friendship ("fuckbuddies"), an affiliation. As Herdt concludes:

In a variety of cultures around the world, and even within many communities within the United States, certain individuals of both genders and of distinct ethnic groups engage in homoerotic encounters, but they do not identify themselves as "homosexual" or "gay" or "lesbian" or even "bisexual." Quite the contrary, they may even be appalled by the idea of homosexuality when it is explained to them, and they cannot think of what being "that way" would feel like even when it is pointed out that they typically have sexual relations with the same gender. They may regard themselves as "heterosexuals," "straights," or just "human beings" who on occasion participate in homoerotic encounters for various reasons, including pleasure, money, social expectations, and the absence of other sexual opportunities. (*Same* 4)

In surveys conducted in the United States, the United Kingdom, and France, Sell, Wells, and Wypij found that when respondents were asked about specific same-sex behavior, the percentage who acknowledged it ran 6.2% (U.S.), 4.5% (U.K.), and 10.7% (Fr.) for males, and 3.5% (U.S.), 2.1% (U.K.), and 3.3% (Fr.) for females. But when asked to report not only sexual experience but also "sexual attraction" to the same sex, the numbers tripled: 20.8% (U.S.), 16.3% (U.K.), and 18.5% (Fr.) for males, 17.8% (U.S.), 18.6% (U.K.), and 18.5% (Fr.) for females. How many more respondents would be added if the study had asked questions about love, fantasy, or friendship as opposed to behavior (for instance, satisfying same-sex fantasies during intercourse with the opposite sex)?

At the very least, a person's sexuality is comprised of three independent variables—behavior, desire, and identity—which may correlate, overlap, or operate independently in different individuals. Some can satisfy heterosexual desires in a same-gender encounter, while others can satisfy homosexual desires in an opposite-sex encounter, which could explain how some LGBs remain married and sexually faithful for many years. William Simon theorizes that heterosexuals can derive pleasure not from but through the feelings attributed to their partner, fantasizing what the partner is experiencing, and thus sympathetically putting oneself in the position of the other sex. This "drive to be both sexes" means that "the more explicitly heterosexual the fantasy, the more inevitable is the bisexual nature of the experience" (90). At the very least, we can say that what one fantasizes or feels exceeds categories. Laumann et al. found that 59% of the women and 44% of the men felt desire for the same sex but did not think of themselves as lesbian or gay and did not act on the desire. Only 24% of men and 15% of women identified themselves, their desires, or their behavior as lesbian or gay. One percent of the men and women identified as gay or lesbian, felt desire for the same sex, but never acted upon the desire and so had no history of same-gender sexual behavior to report, which can affect the final figures of the survey (298–301). Some sex-surveyors define homosexuality very narrowly: respondents have to be actively and exclusively or predominantly gay, and they have to be "out" to family members and to an outside investigator. But, as Simon argues, "not all who desire behave congruently with that desire, just as behavior is not necessarily immediately congruent with desire" (121).

As long as human sexuality is so complex, surveys with unexamined, simplistic assumptions will ask naive questions that elicit problematic answers:

It should be obvious . . . that the mere continuing of accumulation of more information, of more data, will not move us forward substantially. We are not dealing with an issue of information—at least, not of information alone; it is not so much a matter of *what* we think about the sexual as it is a matter of *how* we think about the sexual, not a matter of explanation, but one of understanding. . . . Rarely has the gap between theory and ongoing research been so wide. . . . (26)

BISEXUALITY

Surveys are particularly unsuited for estimating the numbers of bisexuals, who are virtually invisible: they have no separate community in which to develop a culture, a discourse, or a theorized identity. Despised by heterosexuals, distrusted by homosexuals, they have only recently begun to coordinate civil rights efforts with gay and lesbian groups. In past sex surveys, bisexuals were often lumped into either the homosexual category or the heterosexual. Many surveyors would not categorize respondents as bisexual unless their sexual activity occurred simultaneously with partners of both sexes over a period of a year or more, which severely underrepresents their numbers (MacDonald). Focusing on sex acts rather than erotic or romantic feelings, affiliation, attraction, emotional preference, or fantasy betrays the popular prejudice that bisexuality is merely sex and lots of it. What can reductive criteria make of a 65-year-old man a Kinsey researcher interviewed: who had been happily married for 45 years, but after his wife's death, he fell in love with a man and maintained a long-term monogamous relationship with him (Reinisch et al. 143)? In a group of 100 elderly women, Monika Kehoe found nine who self-identified as "bisexual," but not *simultaneously* bisexual:

[I] have always thought of myself as bisexual. Did not marry (heterosexual) until age 42. Have always been monogamous, whether in lesbian or heterosexual relationships. At age 50 I chose to spend the rest of my life as a lesbian.

Another woman, a 75-year-old widow, had been married for 37 years but considered herself bisexual because she had had a same-sex relationship for two years half a century earlier (47–48). Diversity is typically overlooked by surveyors whose conceptions of what they are looking for profoundly affect what they find. Sociologist Paula C. Rust believes that bisexual behavior may be as prevalent as homosexual behavior, especially when lifetime cumulative sexual behavior is considered (see Milton Diamond, "Homosexuality"; Rogers and Turner; Rust, *Bisexuality*, 31). To find out if bisexuals are more sexually active than homosexuals or heterosexuals, she questioned 577 subjects, ages 15 to 82, with most in their 20s and 30s. The rates of involvement were nearly identical: 33.7% of bisexuals, 40.7% of lesbians and gay men, and 33.3% of heterosexuals were sexually inactive ("Monogamy and Polyamory" 135–36).

Popular attitudes towards bisexuals are shaped by lurid magazine articles on swingers, sensationalistic TV talk shows on adulterous spouses, and movies (Roberts 69). In his review of more than 200 films over the last 80 years, Wayne M. Bryant found that, until very recently, bisexuals were typically depicted as oversexed thrill seekers, hustlers, sadistic killers and psychopaths. Biphobic stereotypes mimic those commonly heard about gay men—that they are hypersexual, sexually addicted, promiscuous, and duplicitous, that they are not just immoral but amoral and will have sex with "anything that moves." Ironically, such comments can come from both heterosexuals and homosexuals. Homosexuals often view bisexuals as sexually "confused," "traitors to the cause of lesbian/gay liberation," or homosexuals who are too cowardly to come out of the closet and lose their heterosexual privileges. Heterosexuals describe bisexuals as sexually "confused," "fence-sitters," or heterosexuals who are just "playing around" or "trying to be cool." Both groups have accused bisexuals of being self-absorbed, shallow, narcissistic, untrustworthy, and morally bankrupt (Weinberg et al. 205–206; Udis-Kessler 45–46).

But psychological studies show that bisexuality is not associated with psychopathology or maladjustment in either men or women to any degree exceeding that found in heterosexuals. Nor are most bisexuals "confused" or "in denial" about their sexual identity (Cabaj and Stein 154–156; Fox 33). Few engage in swinging (most swingers are married heterosexuals with children), and roughly 10% of bisexuals prefer long-term monogamous threesomes, sometimes called a "group marriage" (Rust, "Monogamy and Polyamory," 139). Some may be bisexual for only part of their lives and then become exclusively heterosexual or exclusively homosexual. On average, bisexual men and women become sexually active several years later than monosexuals: for men, in their middle to late teens, for women not until their early 20s (Fox 25). Some gays and lesbians regard bisexuals as "lesbians-who-sleep-with-men" or "gays-who-sleep-with-women" (Hutchins 254), but bisexuals themselves often report that they fall in love with "persons," not with a particular gender (Leland et al. 50). Some bisexuals do respond to each gender equally, but others show a preference for one gender over another. They may describe themselves as 75% inclined toward the opposite sex and 25% toward the same sex. For some, these figures change over time. Pattatucci et al. found that "it is not unusual for a small portion of women to report feeling themselves to be straight at age sixteen, perhaps lesbian at age twenty-four, maybe bisexual at age thirty-eight, and straight again at age fifty-five" (Burr 169; Evans and Wall 17).

Consequently, the determination of a bisexual identity is extremely diffi-cult and politically charged. Deciding who is "really" gay or "really" les-bian or "really" bisexual depends on how well human beings fit into rigid categories. In a study of self-identified lesbians with at least ten years of prior heterosexual experience, Kitzinger and Wilkinson found that "essen-tialist" theories of sexual orientation failed to account for the dynamic nature of sexuality in some people, whether they identify as bisexual or not. One woman reported:

The first time I fell in love with a woman I was 25 and pregnant with my second child. I thought, "What's this? Are you bisexual or what?" And then I pushed it to the back of my mind. There was no way I could deal with it because I had these chil-dren, and a husband, and no way of supporting myself. So I just didn't think about it. (98)

In fact, she did not finally identify herself as lesbian until she was in her 40s. Another woman said:

After I came out as lesbian at the age of 42, I remembered the passionate affair I'd had for 2 years with another girl at school. We told ourselves that it didn't mean anything; we were just practicing for the real thing. (99)

Such a scenario occurs more often for women who don't "come out" until later in life. They may go through a period of questioning whether they are lesbian or bisexual, and they may be criticized by other women who have felt same-sex attraction all their lives. Katherine Raymond found herself in the position of the outsider in both heterosexual and homosexual communities:

Since my sexuality has evolved to include attraction to both women and men, I've experienced a similar sense of awkward disjuncture in the presence of straight acquaintances who use "queer" as a pejorative term, as well as with lesbian friends who refer to straight women with barely-veiled contempt. In each of these situations I find myself wondering: Who do I side with? Who do I speak for? Who is it my place to defend? Who is it my place to criticize? If I voice my objections, will I actu-ally succeed in changing anyone's opinions, or only in alienating myself? (60)

These questions may strike exclusive homosexuals not as honest dissent but as dangerous disloyalty. The gay and lesbian communities are political enti-ties as much as affectional ones, providing a geographical and cultural area of safety, unity, and validation for their members who face harassment and bigotry. By developing rules for belonging, such as dress codes, politically correct vocabulary, tastes in food and music, and formulas for relation-ships, gay and lesbian communities create a social world in their own image, but it is a constructed and sometimes simplified image (Schus-ter 67). Identity-based politics—arguing for rights based on the shared and immutable characteristics of a group—relies on the assumption that people who share a sexual identity will also share attitudes, experiences, behaviors, desires, values, and politics. The reality is that individuals—bisexual and monosexual—are more diverse than the shared sexual categories suggest (Steakley *im passim*).

One bisexual woman named Joanne found that the group dynamics of her lesbian community pulled her apart emotionally. She had lived as a heterosexual for

15 yrs of my adult life; then came out as lesbian at the same time as discovering the feminist community; spent 7 years doing that and really learning a lot. I felt very at home among the lesbian community but it was mostly separatist [women only] and I have a son. I also like a lot of men; I have always needed to integrate into many communities because I am creative and intuitive, and dogmatic society is difficult for me. I finally got frustrated with the narrowness of the community I was in; and started hanging out with gay men because it was more fun. [T]hen I got involved with one, which of course, made us both "bi." . . . I'm finding that there are a lot of women who, when they become bi, leave "women's community". I found it kind of boring to have to explain to all the gay people I knew that I had changed my definition; it was too much like apologizing and begging for approval, which is of course, a humiliating and unnecessary stance to adopt. ("Lez Opinions")

Group identities tend to marginalize desires that do not fit the approved image. Lesbians who identify themselves as "butch" or "femme," who enjoy sado-masochism, pornography, or anonymous sex without love are often denounced as "male identified." One such lesbian is Margaret Nichols, who describes herself in this way:

I am a Sexually Incorrect lesbian. . . . I've always harbored a secret love of makeup and dressing up. . . . On the other hand, I am aghast at the thought of calling myself a femme. . . . I repudiate politically correct lesbian lovemaking . . . [which] consists of the following: Two women lie side by side (tops or bottoms are strictly forbidden—lesbians must be non-hierarchical); they touch each other gently and sweetly all over their bodies for several hours (lesbians are not genitally/orgasm oriented, a patriarchal mode). If the women have orgasms at all— and orgasms are only marginally acceptable because, after all, we must be process, rather than goal, oriented—both orgasms must occur at exactly the same time in order to foster true equality and egalitarianism. (I'm not kidding about the orgasm stuff: A "feminist" critique of a paper I published in the journal *Women and Therapy* included the charge that my thinking was "male-identified" because I talked about treating anorgasmic lesbians. The critic charged that orgasms shouldn't be important to lesbians, only to men. I've given up a lot for the lesbian-feminist movement, but this is where I draw the line.)

Nichols feels that by formulating a lesbian feminist sexuality as the opposite of male heterosexuality, her community repudiated any desire that resembled male desire and so desexualized lesbianism and pathologized other lesbians as sexually perverse—the very charge heterosexism levels at LGBTs. D. Travers Scott adds that hegemonic gay communities which police the affectional and behavioral "purity" of their members are, in fact, internalizing orthodox ideology about gender roles and thus undermine the gay rights movement (67).

Category dissidents are the queers of the gay community whose marginalization keeps other LGBTs in line. Carla Golden reports that identity policing begins early on when young women may still be trying to discover who and what they are:

The assumption was often made about lesbians who were unwilling to state that they were (forever) uninterested sexually in men, that they must be having difficulty coming out, or were unwilling to accept a stigmatized identity. Sometimes they were assumed to be going through a bisexual phase, or worse yet, to be male-identified and operating under a false consciousness. (29)

In her book, *Bisexuality and the Challenge to Lesbian Politics: Sex, Loyalty and Revolution,* Paula C. Rust interviewed hundreds of lesbian and bisexual women to find out how "biphobic" stereotypes were conceptualized and supported. Nearly one-fourth of the lesbian respondents said that they believe bisexuality does not even exist as a legitimate identity. One said:

To be bisexual would mean that a person were simultaneously involved in an intimate sexual relationship with a man and a woman. It is possible but would be better described as schizophrenic. (48)

Other lesbians reasoned that bisexuality was simply impossible because

one has to have stronger feelings one way or the other. . . . It is very hard for me to conceive of a woman who is emotionally and physically attracted to women being also similarly attracted to men. I do not feel the two can co-exist. (48–49)

The word "conceive" pinpoints the issue. Some lesbians recognized that other women behaved bisexually, but they were unable to construct a theory for it: how could the subjective life of a person survive such radical disjunctions? Are bisexual desires/feelings/aims radically different from monosexual ones, or are they same regardless of gender? Heterosexuals may find it difficult to concede that homosexuals have their own version of the "genital romance," but that conception of transcendent unity falls to pieces when shifted between genders in bisexuality. Is a conceptualized sexual identity even necessary to bisexuals, or do they enjoy two separate but equal identities? If so, how are they related? What determines which is in ascendance? Significantly, Rust found that those lesbians who reported feeling "some" sexual attraction toward men were more likely to believe that bisexuality exists as a legitimate sexual identity, more likely to perceive greater similarity between bisexual women and lesbians, and more willing to associate with bisexual women, than lesbians who were exclusively attracted to other women (*Bisexuality* 113). Experience provides some measure of empathy, but even these respondents were unable to conceive of bisexuality in non-binary terms. They looked upon it as merely an overlapping of lesbianism and heterosexuality, not a third, legitimate sexuality. Like heterosexuals, most exclusive lesbians tend to see bisexuals as biased toward either true heterosexuality or true lesbianism.

Will bisexuality deconstruct restrictive binary conceptualizations, as bisexual activists hope? Little is known about how bisexuals even arrive at their conclusion that they do not fit either the heterosexual or homosexual paradigm (Schuster 61). Bisexuals tend to assume that an intellectual understanding of their difference is unnecessary, as long as self-realization is emotionally fulfilling. In Kitzinger and Wilkinson's study of bisexual women:

A sense of self-discovery came through vividly in some women's accounts: they talked exuberantly of being reborn, of becoming alive or awake for the first time, of seeing the world anew. That moment of first naming was described as "an explosion of aliveness," "like waking up having been half asleep all my life," "like a conversion experience," and "like emerging from a chrysalis." (100)

But is bisexuality the delimiting term they are looking for? What have they "converted" to if not another category, and one in which the word "sexual" is still central? A chrysalis does become something else, but its newness is intimately related to the old.

Bisexuals tend not to address this issue, relying on their experience as if it were an internally consistent essence that lay beyond questioning. Indeed, they have used it as a weapon: in Rust's survey, 32% of bisexuals claimed that everyone is bisexual, and that homosexuals and heterosexuals are merely repressing their innate capacity for multiple attractions. Such a view replaces one kind of repression with another; one's relationship requires the denial of part of one's essence. It is true that some bisexuals assume they have two essences, but they admit they can be only one essence at a time. Others believe that they can be deeply involved emotionally and sexually with both men and women simultaneously. So what is the nature of the desires involved? Does a bisexual have *different* desires, needs, pleasures elicited by or fulfilled with different genders? Or are the *same* desires, needs, and pleasures fulfilled by both genders, perhaps in different ways? Can a bisexual experience a relationship without gender as a determining component? Or is a bisexual someone who can appreciate the different benefits two genders offer in a relationship? As Naomi Tucker has pointed out, "some of us are bisexual because we do not pay much attention to the gender of our attractions" while other people are bisexual because "we do see tremendous gender differences and want to experience them all" (Rust, *Bisexuality*, 240). Are there still only two genders in bisexuality, or is gender difference a fiction that can be played with, created, destroyed, and recreated again and again, because it is as much an artificial construction as a sexual orientation? If so, is bisexuality merely another production of culture's binary thinking and therefore not inherently liberating at all?

Perhaps because there has been little progress in theorizing bisexuality and its relationship to homosexuality and heterosexuality, very few bisexual respondents in Rust's survey wrote about bisexuality in political terms, but this did not necessarily evidence political apathy. Unlike lesbians, no bisexual women talked about their "heterosexual privileges"; on the other hand, no bisexual woman accused other bisexual women of lacking political commitment to gay rights. They did not apparently think of the bisexual identity as ideologically significant in and of itself, but only as it was connected to gay and lesbian ideology (*Bisexuality* 215). They were thinking of themselves as "half-gay" or "half-lesbian." Without a theoretical construct of what bisexuality is, they identified with the nearest available model of difference but without reconciling it conceptually with their heterosexual attractions. The frequent citation of Freud's speculation that we are all born bisexual allowed them to avoid constructing an explanation for what appears to be a contradictory identity.

TRANSGENDERISM AND TRANSSEXUALISM

Gender ideology has also confused popular understanding of transgenderism and transsexuals. Firm figures exist only for transsexualism, which is much rarer than homosexuality, occurring at a rate of roughly 1 in every 10,000 births. About 45% of all transsexuals are FTM but are generally invisible because MTF transsexuals receive the largest amount of media exposure owing to the higher value culture places on the male sex and the "dishonor" he brings upon himself when he gives up his ordained gender. Although it is popularly assumed that transsexualism is a form of homosexuality, surveys show that it has little directly to do with sexual preference. Gays and transvestites do not generally experience the body-identity gender conflicts experienced by transsexuals. FTM transsexuals, for instance, have fantasies they are males while having sexual relations with other women, while lesbians are very much aware of themselves as women (Scanzoni and Mollenkott 214n.27). Transvestites, who outnumber transsexuals by 60 to 1, are largely heterosexual (often married with children). Transsexuals, both before and following surgery, may be heterosexual, bisexual, lesbian, or celibate (Chambers; Bill Stuart, "Transvestites").

Homosexuality and transgenderism are often, erroneously, conflated in both popular and professional discourse. Psychoanalyst Charles Socarides claims that transsexuals are only delusional homosexuals who want to have same-sex sexual relations but think they will suffer no guilt if they convince themselves they are literally the opposite sex. Robert Stoller blames dominating mothers of transgendered patients for alienating their daughters or feminizing their sons. But, in studies, the childhoods of transsexuals show a great deal of variety (Milton Diamond, "Self Testing," 119):

As important as environmental factors may be, to date they have not given us any more conclusive answers for causation than hereditary influences have. While some transsexuals report coming from seriously dysfunctional families, many do not. With regard to child rearing, transsexuals report a wide range of experiences, from hideously abusive to extremely loving and supportive. (Brown and Rounsley 25)

Even supportive specialists may adhere to an explanatory model for transsexuality that oversimplifies some transsexuals' experiences:

In other words, transsexuals are persons born with a perfectly normal and healthy brain of one gender, but in a body with a perfectly healthy and normal anatomy of the opposite gender. The affected person lives with a struggle to reconcile their natural personality, gender identity, and body image with their physical body and social status until a time in their life when the conflict becomes too great to bear and they seek medical help to change their anatomy and social role. No effective psychotherapeutic treatment for transsexualism exists, since the only defect is the mismatch of body and brain, and a healthy gender identity (even a mismatched one) cannot be changed; therefore the only effective treatment is to surgically change the gender of the body to align with the person's natural gender identity, a "sex change." (Chambers)

Because gender dysphoria is conceived solely on the male/female duality, a candidate for sex-reassignment surgery who has feelings considered "normal" for his/her bodily gender is usually rejected for treatment. That is, a transsexual man who lives as a woman can not confess to his doctor that he ever experiences penile pleasure (Sandy Stone). Not surprisingly, in the 1980s there was not a single preoperative MTF transsexual for whom data is available who reported penile sexual pleasure while living in the "gender of choice." This prohibition on diversity continued postoperatively. Full membership in the assigned gender was conferred by reported orgasm, real or faked, accomplished only through heterosexual penetration. To acknowledge any gender-incongruent desire would be to risk "role inappropriateness," leading to disqualification. Stone argues that transsexuals are pressured into enforcing a kind of gender conformity because the field of sex-reassignment surgery is dominated by doctors who are not transgendered themselves. The Harry Benjamin International Gender Dysphoria Association's standards of care decree that a candidate for hormone therapy and sexual-reassignment surgery must have the written approval of a certified therapist after no less than three months of care; he or she must live full-time in the new gender for at least a year before being accepted for surgery; and a partner in a heterosexual marriage might not be eligible for the operation. Transsexuals feel strongly that this reluctance to create gay or lesbian couples is homophobic (Stone 291–292).

According to Stone, neither the doctors nor the transsexuals have taken the step of questioning the "trapped in the wrong body" model as an adequate descriptive category, which oversimplifies the multiple experiences people do in fact have. Doctors and therapists frequently ask this question of a prospective transsexual: "Suppose that you could be a man [or woman] in every way except for your genitals; would you be content?" Only one answer is presumed to be clinically correct and will lead to reassignment surgery. Small wonder, then, that so much of transsexual discourses revolves around the phrase "wrong body." But for many transsexuals, gender identity is different from and even irrelevant to physical genitalia. Stone worries that, by creating totalized, monolithic identities ("I am really a woman," "I am really a man"), transsexuals have foreclosed the possibility of authentic relationships as more complex beings, blends of masculinity and femininity. Dallas Denny warns that sex reassignment could just be an "assimilation" into another kind of closet, conforming to society's gender categories rather than defining oneself. If the dysfunction lies in the culture, not the individual, the transsexual would then be exchanging one set of rules for another and living in essentially the same state: having some of one's feelings suffocated by a narrow paradigm (40).

Judith Butler, Professor of Humanities at Johns Hopkins University, agrees that gender is another kind of closet just as restrictive as the homosexual closet. Although writing here about stylized behaviors among butch and femme lesbians, Butler reasons that gender is more performative than essential:

If gender is drag, and if it is an imitation that regularly produces the ideal it attempts to approximate, then gender is a performance that *produces* the illusion of an inner sex or essence or psychic gender core; it *produces* on the skin, through the gesture, the move, the gait (that array of corporeal theatrics understood as gender presentation), the illusion of an inner depth. In effect, one way that genders get naturalized [experienced as natural] is through being constructed as an inner psychic or physical *necessity*. And yet, it is always a surface sign, a signification on and with the public body that produces this illusion of an inner depth, necessity, or essence that is somehow magically, causally expressed. ("Imitation" 317)

The genital romance of heterosexuality represents itself as both a biological necessity and a spiritual ideal to be sought, an endless, convoluted, self-perpetuating system in which we perform a gender in order to think of ourselves as that gender.

Orthodox views of sexuality state that sex (male/female) produces gender (masculine/feminine) which causes desire towards the opposite sex. According to Freud, certain identifications (for example, with parents) are early

and therefore primary in forming a gendered self, while others (for example, with siblings) come later and are secondary. The Freudian explanation
for how gender identities develop is linear; all influences happen in a set historical order (pre-oedipal identification with mother, oedipal rivalry with
father, post-oedipal identification/conflict with mother or father) producing
an inviolable self-other relation: you identify with one sex and you desire
the other. Freud reasoned that if a woman desired another woman, deep
down she must identify with men. Butler argues that gender is not a core
aspect of identity but rather a performance because human beings behave
differently at different times. She suggests that gender should be thought of
as free-floating and fluid rather than fixed:

When the constructed status of gender is theorized as radically independent of sex,
gender itself becomes a free-floating artifice, with the consequence that man and
masculine might just as easily signify a female body as a male one, and woman and
feminine a male body as easily as a female one. (*Gender Trouble* 6)

Butler advocates "gender trouble" as a way of challenging orthodox
notions of gender identities. By dressing up as a member of the opposite sex,
drag artists subvert ideas of gender norms: "in imitating gender, drag
implicitly reveals the imitative structure of gender itself—as well as its con-
tingency" (*Gender Trouble* 137). Although Butler does not offer any other
concrete examples of how people might go about subverting gender roles,
the pop singer Madonna is often cited as an example of someone who does
not restrict herself to traditional gender roles. In the video of her song, "Justify My Love," for example, there are several characters who are dressed
and behave in ways which make their sex and gender indeterminable. Kate
Bornstein reports that she lives out this situation on a daily basis:

I know that I am not a man and most of the time I feel like I am not a woman. I
keep one foot in the place called woman because otherwise sometimes you can blow
away into madness. There is no other place to touch down in this culture, except
among people who are laughing about gender: the drag-queens, the cool butches,
and other transgenderists who are laughing and not trying to be one or the other.
(Shannon Bell 110)

In rejecting a binary view of gender relations, Butler argues that people
can form and choose components from their own individual identities.
Indeed, according to Anne Fausto-Sterling, Professor of Biochemistry at
Brown University, a new group of TGs has arisen who call themselves
"transgenderists" (or "gender benders") because they define themselves
rather than giving doctors, society or group pressure the privilege to dictate
who they are and how they should feel. Traditionally, transgendered individuals choose surgery or cross-dressing to move from being unambiguous
men to unambiguous women as if there were no territory in between.

Transgenderists do neither; they do not want to *pass* as the opposite sex, for they regard either gender as an arbitrary set of constructed behaviors ("Five"), as attested to in this letter posted on the transsexual newsgroup (alt.transgendered, 20 May 1994) and reprinted by Karen Nakamura:

My name is Deborah. I'm 24 (male-to-female), 5'6", 110 lb., married, hetero from Maine (US). I've been dressing femininely since I was about 8 or so. . . . My feminine characteristics have always been stronger and more visible than masculine ones.

The line that some people have used in the past, *"I'm a woman trapped in a man's body" doesn't feel right*—I believe we all have feminine and masculine characteristics at our disposal, and thankfully science has given us more of the ability to show or hide as much of each as we desire. (For a price, of course.)

I haven't figured out just how I should label myself (I hate labels anyway). I see mixed definitions of "ts" and "tv," and don't understand really what each one is. Attempts by science to classify these feelings aren't working very well. Popeye said it best—"I am what I am!" (82–83)

Just as Sambian men in New Guinea challenge western notions of what constitutes "homosexual" behavior and what constitutes "heterosexual" behavior, transgenderists undermine gender norms by crossing the borders in multiple, divergent ways. Preliminary research suggests that transsexuality is also responsive to cultural constructions: a joint study by Flinders University in South Australia and St. Jorgen's Hospital in Sweden suggests that MTF transsexuality is far more prevalent in macho societies: Australia, with its polarized conception of sex-roles, has four times the rate of MTF transsexuality than Sweden where sexual diversity is tolerated (Peters). Personal choice is influenced by the way a culture constructs the choices to be made.

INCONCEIVABLE VARIATIONS

Because the terms "homosexual" and "bisexual" enforce a restricting duality, Carol Queen and Lawrence Schimel use the term "pomosexual" to refer to anyone whose affectional, sexual, or gender characteristics surpass a fixed identity (20). Derived from the word "postmodernism," signifying a break from modernist, essentialist notions of identity (as natural categories), a pomosexual deconstructs gender and sexual binaries by crisscrossing the definitional boundaries they set up to illustrate how one identity category shades into—and is contaminated by—the other. Judging others by these binaries may oversimplify the subjective experience of sexuality by tying it too closely to specific acts and specific pieces of anatomy from which sexual categories are drawn, as Kathy Rudy argues:

The homo/hetero system presumes as well that everyone has either an obvious penis or vagina, that every person has an uncomplicated, positive relationship to that organ, and that owning that piece of equipment necessarily correlates to "who we really are." (99)

And "who we really are" serves two opposed purposes simultaneously: while discovering one's identity and sharing it publically (as in "coming out") empowers an individual, it can also be used to oppress that individual and the group similarly labeled (Rudy 100). Since both heterosexuals and homosexuals share a variety of sexual acts, there may be no "really queer" acts that constitute a queer identity. A particular sex act need not produce a gay identity or promote a gay-positive consciousness. The genital romance—whether straight or gay—may only be an illusion created by categorical thinking.

Judith Halberstam, a columnist for the radical lesbian magazine, *On Our Backs*, calls for entirely new sexual vocabularies to acknowledge the growing trend of hybridized sexual and gender styles. New queer identities are appearing with a dizzying multiplicity: gay men with surgically produced vaginas, lesbians with surgically produced penises, aggressive femmes, women who are butch in the streets but femme in the sheets, lesbians who like men, drag queens (men who dress like women), drag kings (women who dress like straight men), fag drag (women who dress like gay men), women who fuck only gay men and women who fuck like gay men, dyke mommies, transsexual lesbians, and male lesbians. Halberstam reasons that so many border crossings have occurred, anyone who tries to dress or behave according to the requirements of a gender and sexual identity is "in drag." If identity, gender, orientation, are artificial constructions, the telling point may lie in desire. It does not matter what identity theory or community standards dictate gays and lesbians should be like; what really counts is desire, which

has a terrifying precision. Pleasure might be sex with a woman who looks like a boy; pleasure might be a woman going in disguise as a man to a gay bar in order to pick up a gay man. Pleasure might be two naked women; pleasure might be masturbation watched by a stranger; pleasure might be a man and a woman; but pleasure seems to be precise. ("F2M" 212)

Halberstam cites an interview with a pre-operative FTM transsexual called Danny as an example of just how precise desire is regardless of identity categories. Danny describes her desire to have sex with men *but only as a man*. Danny stresses that, as a woman, she had restricted herself to having only oral sex with men, denying them access to her vagina (because, she felt, oral sex does not imply a particular gender). But now that Danny is preparing to be surgically reassigned to become a male, he demands that his partners recognize him as a man before he has "gay sex" with them. In other words, they must recognize his male desire in order for him to feel a proper part of lovemaking. He refuses to let them penetrate him vaginally, even though it is still available for use, because he feels his desire is now male. Moreover, he has found willing partners, gay men who desire gay men with vaginas.

How can such shifts in sexual aim, exceeding conventional descriptive categories, be explained by the gender-based Freudian model?

The female-to-gay-male (FTGM) transsexual and the male-to-lesbian transsexual (MTLF) pose an enormous conceptual challenge for the gender paradigm by which sexuality is traditionally judged. If a woman is attracted to men (whether heterosexual or homosexual), she can fall in love and have vaginal or anal intercourse with them as a female. But it is inconceivable that she would want to be surgically reassigned to become a man in order to be a gay lover with only gay males. It is inconceivable because it violates the imaginary balance of sexual psychopathologies (by which homosexuality is judged only a mirror image of heterosexuality). If lesbians are "women who really want to be men," it is traditionally theorized, then their pursuit of women is an attempt (however futile) to restore gender balance. But the FTGM is neither a lesbian (though she desires queer sex) nor a heterosexual (though she desires men); she identifies as a gay male who has no interest in vaginal intercourse. Although having sex with a man as a woman would restore opposite-sex pairing, *only anatomy would be aligned.* Does sexual reassignment surgery work for FTGMs? A recent Dutch study of nine FTGMs in varying stages of treatment showed they were just as satisfied sexually and psychologically as self-identified gay men. Moreover, the FTGMs' gay male sexual partners were equally satisfied with their preoperative lovers who still had a vagina (Coleman et al.). What this suggests is that there is no necessary association between gender identity, gender role, sexual orientation, anatomy, or sexual aim. No theory has been proposed to explain why transsexuals can occupy contradictory positions, even though Magnus Hirchfeld recognized this confusion as early as 1910.

According to Halberstam, the number of women who want to be surgically altered to become men is increasing, and this includes lesbians who belong to lesbian communities, which has sparked considerable debate. Is the lesbian who desires to become a man still a lesbian? Will she cease to be a lesbian after surgical reassignment? Will she exercise privileges as a man that denigrate lesbian sexuality? Will desire change? And what happens to the lesbian who is the partner of the FTM lesbian transsexual? Would having sex with a FTM transsexual constitute heterosexuality because a penis is involved? Will the lesbian partner be incorporated into a heterosexual relationship, perspective, or desire (for if she desires the male body which belongs to her lesbian lover, has she lost touch with lesbian erotics)? To which is lesbian desire directed—the gender of the body or the gender of the person in the body—and do persons have a gender (*Female Masculinity* 141–173)?

Halberstam insists that a FTM transsexual should not be considered "butch" because maleness is not the same thing as being butch: "butch does not require penile proof, a fleshly monument to 'real' masculinity. Butch is a belief, a performance, a swagger in the walk; butch is an attitude, a tough line, a fiction, a way of dressing" that is specifically geared to work in a lesbian relationship ("F2M" 223). Butches see no contradiction between their butchness and their identity as women, nor do their lovers, and so the overwhelming majority (but not all) of butches do not desire to be surgically altered to become males. The butch-as-man stereotype fails to explain butch experiences and desires, particularly if she does not find any value in men. Nor do all butches find themselves attracted only to femmes (as the binary would insist). A survey of butches by Loulan revealed that 50% were primarily attracted to femmes, while 25% were attracted mainly to other butches.

Because masculinity and femininity are, at least in part, culturally produced, butch and femme lesbians occupy multiple positions. Some butches claim that their demeanor and dress are absolutely essential to their identities. Others take a more pluralistic view: "Some of us [butch dykes] are faggots, some are boys, some are bitches with dicks, some are boys who love to get fucked or fuck their femme tops just the way she says." The butch-femme dynamic is complex, with old borders remembered and yet subverted by femme tops, butch bottoms, femmes butched-out (cross-dressing) in male drag, butches femmed-out in drag, and even the butch fag in drag (the butch lesbian who, when she dresses in femme clothing, feels like a gay man dressing for a woman). Some butches look like female sex goddesses. JoAnn Loulan's research shows that 95% of lesbians are familiar with butch/femme codes and can rate themselves or others in terms of those codes, and yet the same percentage feels that butch/femme was "unimportant in their lives." Even more important, Loulan found that there were no significant differences between the sexual activities of her respondents. Indeed, they were often the opposite of what the labels would suggest: butches were more likely to never vaginally penetrate their lovers, while femmes penetrated their lovers more frequently than anyone else. Thus, some lesbians routinely joke about being a "butchy femme" or a "femmy butch" or feeling "kiki" (going both ways) because categories fail to enclose experience.

Inness and Lloyd question the essentialist notion that butch lesbians must be attracted to femme lesbians, mimicking heterosexual relationships. They cite Trish Thomas's declaration, in her essay, "Straight People Call Me Sir," that

To the femmes I'm immediately suspect. They figure if I'm butch and I don't go for femmes, it's because I secretly hate femmes, because I secretly hate women, because I secretly hate myself. Either that or I'm simply a closet femme who's trying to weasel in on the already slim supply of eligible butches. Femmes, on the other hand, are allowed to go for butches—that's normal.

To the butches, I'm the ultimate threat. If you're butch, you gotta have a femme under your arm at all times, that's how you know you're butch. So, when I hit on another butch, it naturally throws her off balance. (9)

Thomas' critics explain contradictions in desire as emanating from a hidden, and pathological, desire which, when understood properly, resolves the contradictions. No "real" butch pursues other butches, so she must be something else. But Thomas sees the term "butch" as socially constructed and riven with internal contradictions. This raises a number of intriguing questions. Can anyone be a butch just by saying so, or are there certain criteria a woman must meet before she can be called butch? Does a woman need to self-identify as butch in order to be butch? Is a lesbian butch because of how she looks, to whom she is attracted, who is attracted to her, or because of what she does in bed? All of these questions have been answered in conflicting ways. Cherrie Moraga, for instance, claims that "to be butch, to me, is not to be a woman." Because butches seem to imitate men, Moraga assumes that they despise femininity, which disqualifies them as lesbians. Lesbian feminists in the 1970s condemned butches and urged other lesbians to assume an "androgynous" ideal. Ironically, as Inness and Lloyd point out, many aspects of androgyny were indistinguishable from butchness: wearing non-constrictive clothing, such as flannel shirts, jeans, and hiking books; short, boyish haircuts; becoming carpenters or auto repairwomen. The 1980s saw a reaction against androgyny to more pronounced sexual styles; butch/femme was seen as an iconoclastic taboo-smashing strategy. What was once considered innate had become fluid.

9

Define "Illness": Rival Theories of Pathology and "Ex-Gay" Ministries

Anti-gay rights groups, citing several psychoanalysts, argue that homosexuality is a pathological lifestyle, a neurotic or addictive condition resulting from poor parenting, which cripples self-other interaction, self-insight, and self control. Pro-gay rights groups, citing behavioral psychologists, argue that homosexuals resemble heterosexuals in social functioning, emotional well being, and personality characteristics. Two fundamentally different approaches to understanding human behavior—psychoanalytic and behavioral—have created a long paper trail of published articles and books that flatly contradict each other. Some psychoanalysts claim that homosexuality can be cured but provide no consistent, replicable documentation that it is a developmental disorder or that patients have changed sexual orientation; psychiatrists and psychologists commonly claim that homosexuality is an immutable condition which cannot be "cured" without harm to the individual's emotional makeup, but they have not discovered a physiological mechanism or a psychological origin. Sifting through these competing views requires understanding the relative merits of Freudian and behavioral approaches to human psychology.

Psychoanalysts and psychologists became interested in sexual orientation because it seems to follow a developmental course. Many gays and lesbians become aware of their attraction to the same sex fairly early in life, even if they do not label it until much later, as this 19-year-old lesbian relates:

I always knew that I was a dyke. My mother was always trying to get me to dress more like a girl, you know, dresses and all. Once in a while I would just do it to make her happy, but I always felt so uncomfortable. Before I came out, I was in denial, I used to also say that I liked boys, I even went out with a few of them on dates, but, they never did anything for me. I'd try to get into kissing them and all that, but, I knew that inside it was girls that really did something for me. (Mallon 83)

In one study, three-fourths of gay men remembered having strong and persistent homosexual attachments to other boys prior to adolescence; 66% of lesbians first experienced same-sex fantasies and dreams prior to age 14 (Saghir and Robins 208). D'Augelli and Hershberger interviewed 194 LGB youth and found that first awareness of same-sex desires typically occurred at age 10, although disclosure to another person was generally delayed until about age 16. A few (13%) claimed they could remember same-sex interests at age 5 or less. It is impossible to assess how much adult bias contaminates early memory, but 91% of respondents reported awareness by age 15. Self-labeling ("I am gay") tends to follow about 4 years later (430). Much the same story is heard from TG/TS individuals. Mildred L. Brown reports that 85% of her patients recognized their difference by the time they began grade school. One patient, Greg, claimed:

My mother knew that I was transgendered from age four on. . . . Even at such an early age, I was very conscious of how different I was and how much more feminine I looked and acted than the other boys. I was always being told by my mother to do things differently. "Don't hold your books like that; girls hold their books like that. Don't walk like that; girls walk like that. Don't cross your legs; only girls cross their legs like that." Eventually I began to feel like I was a total failure. (30–31)

In a series of interviews with a transgender support group, sociologist Douglas Mason-Schrock found that transsexuals commonly told stories of discovering their "true self" early in childhood, as one MTF transsexual said:

I guess that it would be whatever the medical term or psychological term is. I'm not exactly sure. But it always has been there since I can remember; probably at four years old I felt more female than . . . male.

Mason-Schrock concludes:

During support group meetings and interviews, and on computer networks, transgenderists often said, "I've felt different *as long as I can remember*." Early memories of feeling ambivalent about gender, or memories of doing gender unconventionally, were regarded as key pieces of evidence for transsexuality. Transsexuals viewed childhood as a time when their authentic impulses had not yet been stifled by restrictive gender boundaries. At that time, the "true self" reigned. (179)

But what is this "true self"? Some LGBTs see it as an unalloyed, immutable core defining who they have always been and always will be. Others see their sexual or gender identities as a complex integration of recognitions and reinterpretations that evolve over time as feelings and circumstances change. Carla Golden interviewed college-age lesbians and found that some claimed to be "born lesbian," feeling "different" from other girls even in childhood; others did not have as conscious a sense of being different, nor did they necessarily view their same-sex attractions as fundamentally different from opposite-sex attractions (25–26).

Psychotherapists who consider homosexuality a developmental disorder stemming from bad parenting reject the authenticity of LGBT claims that they have discovered a true, innate, and immutable self. Typically, they regard the sometimes complex process of self-identification as evidence of confusion or self-deception. In his book *The Gay Invasion: A Christian Look at the Spreading Homosexual Myth*, William D. Rodgers believes that gays can convince themselves that what they feel is normal, self-evident, and unchangeable:

Homosexuals learn to practice public deceit so often that, after a time, they cannot distinguish between truth and falsehood in their own private thoughts. And "coming out of the closet" is merely an extension of that self-delusion.

Gays con themselves, believing that if they accept their sexual abnormality as normal for them, then other people will have to accept it too. They tell themselves that once they "are declared," the terrible secret burden which they carry will be lifted. They tell themselves that they will be happy, really happy for the first time in their lives.

But, "The heart," Jeremiah lamented, "is deceitful above all things, and desperately wicked: who can know it?" (17:9). (45–46)

Jeremiah pinpoints the problem here. Who *is* in an authoritative position to know another person's innermost thoughts, or even one's own thoughts? Rodgers assumes he is, as do Golden's respondents. Golden's subjects privilege their judgement over Rodgers because they experience their desires directly, which the lesbian community validates with an explanatory ideology in which same-sex desire is experienced as subjectively fulfilling. Rodgers privileges his judgement because he presumes he is qualified to see the "truth" his patients cannot see, and he also works within a community that offers a supporting ideology in which homosexuality is considered objectively disordered. But self-deception can cut either way, whether one is a therapist or a patient. LGBTs and reparative therapists each rely on discourses and theoretical models developed to find coherence in experience, but what kind of coherence one finds depends on the model one applies. Those patterns that do not fit the model can either be reinterpreted to fit or ignored. Often this process is neither conscious nor deliberate, nor is insight impossible or introspection valueless, but it is not unproblematic. The central issue in the rocky history of psychology in the twentieth century has been just this point: how much access does the mind have to its own processes? The Freudian unconscious, religious cult indoctrination, "brain washing," inadequate integration of left and right lobes of the brain, and the contentious debates about False Memory Syndrome (recovering previously repressed memories of sexual abuse decades later) serve as warnings that introspection is far from infallible. Not only can one's desire to believe produce a fraudulent sense of conviction, but one's feelings, sensations and conclusions can be profoundly influenced by the political ideology and religious principles to which an individual subscribes.

Both patients and psychotherapists tend to evaluate their own mental and emotional states using theory-based interpretations endorsed by the prevailing belief system they work with, which can compromise therapeutic insights. As Adolph Grunbaum has argued:

More often than not, a patient who seeks treatment from a Freudian doctor already brings some psychoanalytic beliefs into the therapy, or is at least receptive to etiologic interpretations of his conduct based on the analyst's theoretical stance. No wonder that analytic patients then find the rationale offered to them credible. But this credulity is hardly tantamount to privileged cognitive access. (30)

Freud himself, the founder of psychoanalysis, realized that there are many ways by which an analyst may overtly or covertly persuade patients to accept an incorrect hypothesis (Grunbaum 31). Fisher and Greenberg discovered that even normal "individuals will enthusiastically accept bogus interpretations as accurate descriptions of their own personalities" (364). If, for instance, they adopt the psychoanalytic explanation that aggressiveness is really a defense against shyness, or that the absence of guilt proves some unbearable guilt has been repressed, patients are more likely to recover memories that accord with these conceptual models. The same rule holds for the psychoanalyst directing the treatment. Freudian analysts tend to find oedipal conflicts in their patients' memories, Adlerians find masculine strivings and inferiority, Horneyites idealized images, Sullivanians disturbed interpersonal relationships, and so on, confirming the theories and interpretations of their analytical training. Phillip McCaffrey extends such contextual responsiveness to dreamwork: since the "analysands of Freudians show a remarkable preference for Freudian-style dreams while Jungian patients adopt a more appropriate Jungian style," McCaffrey concludes that "it is sometimes difficult to sort out the dream from its telling and its interpretation" (133). The National Association for Research and Therapy of Homosexuality (NARTH) admits that 99% of its patients enter therapy believing that treatment "can be effective and valuable" and that 95% of the therapists believe that orientation can be changed (Mills). With such high motivation on each side, a truly critical self-examination is crucial.

But even with a willingness to question oneself, self-deceit can be hard to detect because the psychoanalytic relationship encourages both the patient and the analyst to establish a transference relationship. Freud realized that every patient develops a transference, attributing feelings to the analyst that belong elsewhere. Women whose neuroses centered around their fathers typically formed a transference relationship with a male analyst, experiencing it as intense interest, love, anger, fear of rejection, or bitterness, which replicated their unconscious feelings. By making the patient aware of these inappropriate feelings, the analyst can then begin analyzing them in order to discover to whom they really belong and how they might be resolved on a conscious level. But it is also possible for the analyst to develop a countertransference and fail to identify his/her own desires and how these might be interfering with analytical insight. Who we are, what we desire, and how we think about our desires can affect what we see in others, especially if our operating theory assures us we cannot be wrong.

Psychotherapists especially run the risk of countertransference with homosexual or transgendered patients because sexual diversity elicits strong emotional reactions that can lead them to pathologize their patients. In his review of psychoanalyst Edmund Bergler's work with homosexual patients in the 1950s and 1960s, Kenneth Lewes found evidence of a strong countertransference that Bergler apparently did not recognize:

What is so extraordinary about Bergler's work on homosexuality is the intemperate and abusive tone he adopted when describing his patients. He was frequently annoyed and exasperated by their behavior, by their "unique . . . megalomaniacal superciliousness" and their "amazing degree of unreliability. . . ." "There are no happy homosexuals," he claimed, denying his patients' assertions to the contrary. "The amount of conflicts, of jealousy, for instance, between homosexuals surpasses everything known even in bad heterosexual relationships." . . . And Bergler never ceased to be amazed at what he saw as "the great percentage of homosexuals among swindlers, pseudologues [confabulators who mix fact and fantasy], forgers, law-breakers of all sorts, drug purveyors, gamblers, pimps, spies, brothel-owners, etc." (113–114)

Bergler's emotional investment in pathologizing homosexuals led him to accuse other analysts who disagreed with him of "resistance." He warned American parents that teenage children could be recruited into homosexuality–contradicting his own operating theory that homosexuality starts in infancy. He swept away homosexuals' claims that they did not feel guilty for their orientation as evidence of their sociopathology or sadistic perversion. Moreover, Bergler seemed entirely unaware of the social forces at work in his patients' lives, for instance, that an individual condemned as deviant by his/her culture, family, and religion, would suffer any psychological consequences requiring treatment (Lewes 153–155). It is impossible now to tell if Bergler's vitriol was the result of his own prejudice or a logical extension of the homoprejudice already built into psychoanalytic theory, or both. Historically, psychoanalysis has been theorized and practiced exclusively by heterosexuals. No major analytic institute will admit a homosexual to candidacy (a policy Freud himself objected to), and until 1980 no analyst has ever written an article on homosexuality and countertransference, even though much has been published on countertransference in regards to a variety of other issues. The result is a school of thought that does not systematically acknowledge the findings of other scholarly disciplines that show homosexuality is not pathological (Lewes 229, 238–240). Christian psychotherapists must be especially wary and open to searching self-scrutiny because they operate within two communities and philosophies that interpret human experience in a hegemonic way that discounts contradictory evidence.

THE PSYCHOANALYTIC THEORY OF HOMOSEXUALITY

Psychoanalysis set the terms by which western culture examined homosexuality for much of the twentieth century, but, as we will see, Freud borrowed from gender ideology that goes back to the ancient Greeks. Freud reasoned that a meaning, wish, or memory which the patient could not bear to think about (and so was repressed into an unconscious form) could be acted out in a symbolic way, as behavior, a symptom, or a dream. If a patient suffered from hysterical blindness (blindness with no physical damage to the eye or brain), Freud reasoned that there was something that he/she unconsciously did not wish to see. Interrogating a patient's ideas allowed the psychoanalyst to see how various events in this patient's past fit together to form a coherent narrative, a story line that could make people sick or well. Much of psychoanalytic technique resembles literary interpretation, connecting symbols, metaphors, gestures, word choices, the rhetorical and compositional features of storytelling until a thematically coherent narrative is produced that explains why the patient is ill.

Psychoanalysis is founded upon the premise that all children pass through two fundamental stages of erotic organization: the pre-oedipal and the oedipal (based on Sophocles' play of the ancient Greek King Oedipus who is fated to murder his father and marry his mother). The infant begins life in the pre-oedipal stage when its mother is its whole world and it is hers. This attachment is intimate and defining; the mother's touch, attention, and nursing surround and stimulate the child. The child enters the oedipal stage when it perceives the father as a rival for the mother's attentions. Not wanting to share her, it may wish doing away with the father. But because the oedipal stage has introduced the child to a social world, it also becomes aware of the incest taboo, and so its desire for her is repressed into the unconscious. The child fears that the father will retaliate by castrating it. In order to make peace, the male child identifies with the father, imitating him, raising him to the level of an ideal. If the child is female, she already feels castrated, Freud reasoned (reading anatomy as psychically definitive), and so as an adult she tries to regain the lost penis through intercourse with a husband, or by becoming pregnant, especially with a son. The phallus represents power, and girls hope to grow up and become mothers of sons in order to exercise power over them.

Freud theorized that homosexual orientations resulted from an inadequate resolution of the oedipal phase, a neurotic (unconscious) compromise between warring needs. A boy who identifies with his mother instead of his father may take the role of a woman with another man in adulthood; a girl who identifies with the father risks becoming a "mannish" lesbian. But because Freud assumed that sexual orientation was a product of the oedipal crisis, and therefore a gender issue, he arrived at several, inconsistent conclusions depending on who identified as which gender and how that gender was symbolically positioned in unconscious fantasy. In some statements, he regarded homosexuality as a natural component of libidinal drives, that everyone is born bisexual and that heterosexuality or homosexuality resulted from repression of the other orientation. Homosexuality, then, could not be a sickness. But in other writings he described it as an "inversion" (turning away from what is normal), a "turning inward" of the desire instead of outward, a fixation in childhood, or an inhibition of instincts. Depending on which passage is cited, Freud claimed that homosexuality was normal or an illness, a variation of sexual function or an "arrest of sexual development" (Lewes 29–31).

Freud's first explanation for the origin of homosexuality was also his clearest: in his monograph on Leonardo da Vinci, the mother is excessively attentive to her son, which overstimulates him. He assumes that she is like him, has a penis too, but when he discovers his mistake, castration anxiety causes him to despise her as sexually mutilated, and so he seeks out a "woman with a penis," another effeminate boy (Lewes 36–38). In Freud's second theory, the son identifies with his mother, selecting love objects who resemble his mother's truest love—himself—and so homosexuality is a pathological narcissism (Lewes 38). In his case study of the "Wolf Man," Freud theorized that his patient had identified with his father, but this identification was undone when he was seduced by an older sister. He then shifted from an active masculine character to a passive feminine one and desired to be penetrated by the father. Rather than try to be *like* the father, he chose to be loved *by* the father, or by substitutes for the father, other men. But here things get complicated, because Freud assumed that innate instincts are already homosexual in some children, and so they pass through the oedipus phase differently than heterosexual children do (Lewes 39–41). Finally, in his fourth theory, Freud reasoned that the oedipal child represses murderous jealousy towards rivals for his mother's affections and replaces it with the opposite, feelings of love, converting his male rivals into love objects. Nevertheless, the child unconsciously believes that his father hates him, which creates paranoia. Consequently, many American psychoanalysts in the 1950s and 1960s believed that all paranoid individuals were homosexuals in denial, and that homosexuals themselves were inevitably paranoid in some fashion (Lewes 42).

Freud died in 1939 before he could reconcile these conflicting explanations, and subsequent theorizing by his followers only multiplied the number of ways homosexuality could be conceived. One of the most influential reparative psychoanalysts, Irving Bieber, proposed that a gay man was produced by a seductive mother who undermines her son's masculinity by dominating him and minimizing her husband's role in the family: the son becomes a romantic substitute for a distant husband/father and becomes fixated on her, growing up fearing women yet identifying with them, desiring to take the place of a woman sexually (Lewes 208). Other psychoanalysts theorized that the trauma causing it must occur earlier than Freud had thought, in the pre-oedipal stage, when narcissistic oral drives were paramount. Edmund Bergler reasoned that the shock of weaning made some infants feel overwhelming rage against the mother; the subsequent guilt caused it to fantasize masochistically that it must be beaten by the father, substituting its buttocks as the object for rage in place of the mother's breasts. Thus, Bergler argued, the homosexual seeks to heal himself by incorporating the penis orally as well as anally, unconsciously equating the penis with the breast, the vagina with the mouth, and sperm with milk. Metaphorically, it all made sense (Lewes 112–113).

American analysts created four alternative explanations for lesbianism. The first theory reasons that a daughter who identifies too strongly with her seductive father yet fears men will adapt by taking the man's place sexually in a lesbian relationship with a safer maternal figure, another woman. The second claims that lesbianism is rooted in unfulfilled maternal needs during the early mother-daughter period (this can include mothers who seek their own sexual satisfaction through playing with their daughter's genitalia). Third, a girl who does not identify with her mother because she is "weak, pathetic, vulnerable or in some way inadequate," will then identify with the father and experience "gender identity problems, finding herself incapable of living as an authentic woman." Fourth, a woman who is sexually abused by a man will come to fear male sexuality (Herman 95).

Psychoanalytic theory has appeal because it explains sexual diversity in terms that heterosexuals can already understand: the exchange of gender roles. Rather than being intractably *different* and perhaps incomprehensible, LGBT desires are viewed as perversions of the *same* desires heterosexuals feel. The formula for producing a homosexual is to make a young heterosexual feel inadequate: "I am a failure = I am castrated = I am not a man = I am a woman = I am a homosexual" (Lewes 168). Like ancient Roman doctors, psychoanalysts regarded homosexuals as flawed because they shared certain symbolic characteristics with the opposite sex. But by trying to frame sexual orientation in terms of gender, psychoanalysts found that the result was not just another duality but a permutation of sexual/gender positions. In his survey of published theories, Kenneth Lewes found that psychoanalysts eventually theorized twelve possible outcomes for the oedipal conflict—six of which produce homosexuals, six of which produce heterosexuals. All twelve are the result of oedipal trauma, and so all twelve fulfill Freud's definition of a neurosis. As the oedipus crisis is conceived, it simply is not possible for anyone to pass through it without repressing an erotic attachment for one or the other parent, and both heterosexuality and homosexuality are compromise formations, neuroses built out of conflict (82–86).

Neither has oral trauma served well as an etiology for homosexuality because it confuses narcissism (which is pathological) with narcissistic object choice (which is not). As Lewes argues, choosing an external object automatically means that the individual enjoys good object-relations to some extent, and heterosexuals often find similarities in their lovers that satisfy narcissistic desires. Moreover, psychoanalytic theory cannot conceive of a boy growing up heterosexual unless he identifies with the father, but there is no clear reason why it should be only the father he identifies with: one identification does not preclude another, and simultaneous identifications with both parents are not only possible but common (85, 180–182, 217–218). In his essay, "The Psychogenesis of a Case of Homosexuality in a Woman," Freud seems to have anticipated Lewes' point:

A man with predominantly male characteristics and also masculine in his erotic life may still be inverted in respect to his object, loving only men instead of women. A man in whose character feminine attributes obviously predominate, who may, indeed, behave in love like a woman, might be expected, from this feminine attitude, to choose a man for his love object; but he may nevertheless be heterosexual, and show no more inversion in respect to his object [than] an average normal man. . . . [Mental] sexual character and object choice do not necessarily coincide. (*Standard Edition* 18: 155–172)

Even masculine males have important feminine characteristics, and it can be argued that a partial feminine identification is necessary to keep a young boy from so completely identifying with his father that other men become love objects. Although American psychoanalysts regarded the child's relation to the mother as purely affectionate and to the father as one of rivalry, in fact the child's relationship with the mother can be just as ambivalent and competitive as with the father (Lewes 85). Love and hatred, identification and rejection, attraction and fear are not so easily divided between the parents as was once assumed.

Behavioral psychologists today argue that the gender explanation for homosexuality is outmoded and confusing, that the gay population is far too diverse—in both behavior and self-image—to be reduced to postured femininity or postured masculinity (Schor and Weed *im passim*). Masculine and feminine styles of behavior occur in both gay and straight populations. Although LGB audiences generally applaud movies like *Victor/Victoria, La Cage aux Folles, The Crying Game,* and *The Birdcage* for their sympathetic treatment of sexual diversity, many also worry that straight audiences will mistakenly think that cross-dressing or cross-gender expression is somehow an essential ingredient to homosexuality. Bieber himself admitted that some of his patients and their parents did not fit into any of his gender paradigms; indeed some were the opposite of what psychoanalytic theory anticipated, but he discounted such exceptions to maintain the rule (Bieber 318).

By the end of the 1960s, it was becoming well recognized that cure rates for the psychoanalytic treatment of homosexuality were discouragingly low (Lewes 233). Patients who did not change their sexual orientation were dismissed as morally recalcitrant. Analysts resisted attributing these case failures to deficiencies in theory or technique. Why one child's sexual nature was affected by a particular set of family events while another's was not could not be explained consistently using psychoanalytic theory, except by the vague concept that somehow an innate constitution or predisposition was operating. Although Freud accepted the idea that everyone was bisexual at birth, American psychoanalysts did not, which put them in a theoretical dilemma: if there is no bisexuality in infantile sexuality, how can homosexuality be a perversion, which, by definition, is the survival of infantile sexuality into adult life?

Nor were harsher therapies any more likely to effect a real change in orientation. From the 1930s to 1960s, American doctors tried various medical interventions: surgically removing the uterus of lesbians and the testicles of gay men, injecting lesbians with estrogen, or performing lobotomies. Aversion therapy came in four forms: jolts of electricity when the male patient responded sexually to a picture of another male; images of vomit associated with same-sex eroticism; injections of apomorphine to induce nausea or Metrazol, a cardiac stimulant that provoked grand mal seizures; castration (Carlston 188). In 1972, R. G. Heath implanted electrodes into the brain of a gay man to stimulate his pleasure centers while a female prostitute attempted to seduce him. None of these therapies produced a cure. While some gays changed their behavior, dating and even marrying women, it is uncertain that they changed their orientation since they continued to feel sexually and romantically attracted to other men (Burr 124; Cabaj and Stein 4, 530–533).

BEHAVIORAL PSYCHOLOGY

In the early 1950s Evelyn Hooker, a young psychologist at UCLA, investigated the assumption that homosexuals suffered from psychopathology.

She was puzzled that her gay students seemed normal when her own academic training taught her to regard them as sick. Hooker gave three psychological tests to 60 males (30 homosexuals and 30 heterosexuals), scored the tests, and then sent them to two other professional psychologists, one of whom was the renown Bruno Klopfer who believed that homosexuals were pathological and that such tests would reveal this. Neither expert was able to distinguish from the test results who was homosexual and who was not. Hooker concluded that there was no correlation between homosexuality and psychopathology (Burr 85–86), a generalization that has since been qualified by Jones and Yarhouse, who point out that her subjects were not selected to be a "representative sample of homosexual persons," and her recruitment strategy eliminated participants who were undergoing psychotherapy or psychiatric treatment (109). At best, say Jones and Yarhouse, "the Hooker study proved that Hooker's group of homosexuals were no more distressed than" her heterosexual subjects (109).

Still, Hooker's results contradicted conventional wisdom and spurred other studies which found no consistent or pervasive psychopathology or social maladjustment in homosexuals beyond the levels found among heterosexuals. These studies persuaded both the American Psychiatric Association (APA) and the American Psychological Association to rule officially that homosexuality is not a sickness:

Psychologists, psychiatrists and other mental health professionals agree that homosexuality is not an illness, mental disorder or an emotional problem. Over 35 years of objective, well-designed scientific research has shown that homosexuality, in and of itself, is not associated with mental disorders or emotional or social problems. Homosexuality was once thought to be a mental illness because mental health professionals and society had biased information. In the past the studies of gay, lesbian and bisexual people involved only those in therapy, thus biasing the resulting conclusions. When researchers examined data about these people who were not in therapy, the idea that homosexuality was a mental illness was quickly found to be untrue. (American Psychological Association)

Nor do behavioral studies show any consistent evidence that transgendered/transsexual persons are psychopathic simply because they identify with another gender (Denny and Green 97). This doesn't mean that individual LGBTs are immune to psychiatric or psychodynamic illness, only that homosexuals as a group exhibit the same variety of psychological profiles as heterosexuals.

American psychoanalysts condemned the APA's ruling. Charles Socarides, in an essay entitled, "The Erosion of Heterosexuality: Psychiatry falters, America sleeps," argued:

This psychiatric nonsense and social recklessness bring with it many individual tragedies, as men and women who no longer appreciate their own appropriate sexual roles create confusion in the very young for generations to come. Gender identity disturbance is bound to increase, and more true homosexual deviations result as parents distort the maleness or femaleness of their infants and children.

Brian Clowes voices a commonly held belief among anti-gay groups that the APA's ruling was politically expedient:

What the homosexuals do not mention, of course, is that this sudden change in attitude was not based on any new scientific evidence. . . . It was a purely political move, induced by a relentless saturation campaign of deception, intimidation, and unethical collusion between the APA committee and activist sodomite groups. (116)

Although the vote in the APA had been called for by those who opposed declassifying it as an illness, Clowes maintains that gay activists "intimidated psychiatrists all over the nation" to sway the vote, even though it was conducted anonymously, by mail, and involved well over ten thousand members (Keen and Goldberg 66). Pro-gay groups admit applying political pressure but respond by asking: if there is abundant evidence that homosexuals are inherently psychologically sick, why have psychotherapists not been able to conduct methodologically-sound surveys of their own to support their position? If both sides offered comparable studies, some resolution of the issue might be had. But psychotherapists have been unable to provide empirical evidence that would help behavioral psychologists replicate their claims, either because such claims are unfounded or because it is presently impossible to correlate measurable behavior with psychodynamic meaning (see below).

Behavioral studies have challenged nearly every psychoanalytic hypothesis about homosexuality. Various surveys report that childhood sexual abuse has no impact on whether a child grows up to be heterosexual and homosexual; that gay men do not consistently have domineering mothers or weak fathers; that bad experiences with men do not make women into lesbians, nor do bad experiences with women make men into homosexuals. Surveys of the childhoods of LGBTs have found the same variety of happiness and sadness, successes and failures, fulfillment and frustration, as in the childhoods of heterosexuals (Bailey et al.; Patterson; Eric Marcus 60; McCary and McCary 257; Tasker and Golombok; Milton Diamond, "Self-Testing," 119). Ritch C. Savin-Williams, of Cornell University, concludes from this research:

In many important ways, however, lesbian, bisexual, and gay male youths are similar to other adolescents. They experience puberty, friendships, family conflict, peer pressure, and concerns about their future. Undeniably, some encounter developmental issues not faced, at least to the same degree, by heterosexual peers, such as violence, abuse, and rejection from family and peers because of their sexuality. Growing up with forbidden and unacceptable sexual attractions, fantasies, and identity may well alter a youth's developmental trajectory. At the most fundamental level, however, bisexual, lesbian, and gay male youths are, first and foremost, adolescents, sharing with others of their age group basic developmental concerns and processes. (56)

Gays and lesbians are more likely to have higher rates of alcoholism or drug use than heterosexuals, and they are more likely to seek therapy, but do these statistics mean that they are intrinsically unhappy being homosexuals (as anti-gay groups reason) or unhappy because they are socially condemned (as LGBT advocates reason)? Christine E. Gudorf warns us:

While it is possible to interpret higher rates of alcoholism and psychological therapy for homosexual persons as evidence of the sinfulness of homosexual behavior, such an argument is inherently dangerous: statistics for other minority populations, including racial minorities, migrant workers, and the most severely impoverished in general, demonstrate similar patterns, yet few would want to morally stigmatize poor, dark-skinned, or migrant populations. A link more likely than depravity between these populations and the homosexual population is discrimination and low social status. Strong cultural homophobia, which makes the lives of homosexual persons much more difficult, is generally understood as one important factor in elevated use of alcohol, drugs, and therapy among homosexual persons. (130)

Since neither the psychoanalytic nor the behavioral approach offers a convincing explanation for the origin of sexual diversity, it is presently impossible to prove or disprove the question of intrinsic pathology, especially since each approach offers its own definition of what constitutes pathology. But behavioral studies do tell us that homosexuals function socially and intellectually as well as heterosexuals, and that the significant difference between them centers on orientation: homosexuals do not feel as emotionally or sexually satisfied with heterosexual relationships as they do with same-sex relationships. Saghir and Robins' St. Louis survey found that while all of the heterosexuals interviewed reported adequate and positive satisfaction gained from relationships with the opposite sex, 57% of the homosexuals felt "complete indifference" sexually and emotionally for members of the opposite sex. For 43% of gay men interviewed, heterosexual experience was rated as "partially pleasurable but not adequately so." As one subject said:

I felt that while the sense of [sexual] release was enjoyable, it was not satisfactory because there was no real emotional involvement or intellectual agreement and common interests and language. I feel a greater sense of companionship with guys than girls. With men, sex is more satisfying to me emotionally, intellectually and sexually. (Saghir and Robins 93)

Surveys of lesbians report similar results. Although 100% of the heterosexual women interviewed said they attained a "satisfactory emotional and sexual involvement" in relationships with men, none of the lesbians interviewed found any emotional or sexual satisfaction with men (252). None of the heterosexual women felt emotionally or sexually indifferent to men, but 61% of the lesbians did. Contrary to the popular stereotype, only 4% of the lesbians interviewed felt a "strong hostility to men" (252). From a psychoanalytic perspective, these reports are considered "denials" or "deficits" because heterosexuality is the assumed norm. The model of unresolved oedipal conflicts would discount the respondent's conscious experience and reduce them to symptoms of denial.

SEXUAL PRACTICE

In the rhetorical war over sexual diversity, anti-gay groups tend to look upon orientation primarily as a sexual issue, rather than a complex psychosocial identity. Once LGBT persons are reduced to sex, they are assumed to be pathologically obsessed with it, and because they cannot marry, their single status defines them as incapable of true intimacy (Rudy 60). LGBTs feel caught in a catch-22: as gay Episcopalian Louie Crew argues, "on the one hand, the church condemns us for allegedly not forming stable relationships. . . . On the other, the church strictly forbids us to form such relationships" (Scanzoni and Mollenkott 139). Anti-gay groups do not see stability as an environmental issue but as an intrinsic, pathological feature of homosexuality. Brian Clowes, following conclusions from Bergler, Bieber and Socarides, claims that "committed and loving" same-gender couples are "extremely rare," about 2%, and that the average homosexual "marriage" lasts less than two years, with half of the partners cheating "incessantly" during that time span (118):

The homosexual addict is compulsive. He is completely out of control in many instances. He may make occasional half-hearted attempts at limiting or controlling his behavior, but such attempts generally fail. . . . The homosexual addict is an escapist. He avoids responsibility for his actions and blames everyone else for anything in his life that is not to his liking. (116)

"Without exception," reparative therapist Rodgers adds, "practicing homosexuals are sex obsessed. They place their sexuality before everything else in life; before family, before friends, before God" (42).

Rodgers' own patient list may, indeed, be largely comprised of homosexual sex addicts, but it is a mistake to assume that any therapist's clientele represents accurately the general population, since LGBTs without psychological problems do not seek out therapy and so are underrepresented. As behavioral surveys show, heterosexual and homosexual populations largely resemble each other—some prefer recreational or anonymous sex; some prefer love in committed relationships; and some prefer both—only the number of sexual encounters and partners varies between the two groups. Some studies report low numbers. Researchers Saghir and Robins found in their St. Louis survey that most gay men were less sexually active than most heterosexual men—with one exception:

Lesbians	Heterosexual females	Frequency of intercourse
76%	32%	less than once a week
17	56	1–3 times a week
7	12	4 or more times a week

Gay males	Heterosexual males	Frequency of intercourse
58%	65%	less than once a week
32	35	1–3 times a week
10	0	4 or more times a week

The heterosexual women were more sexually active than the lesbians, and straight men and gay men were roughly equal except for 10% of the gay men who were more active than any of the heterosexual men. How active varies according to location and timing. Surveys in the 1970s found that three quarters of urban male homosexuals reported having more than 30 partners in a lifetime, a third had between 100 and 500 partners, and one-quarter had 500 or more partners (Bell and Weinberg 85). After the outbreak of AIDS, a study of 655 San Francisco gay men found that the average number of partners per month decreased to 2.5 in 1985 (Weinberg et al. 204–205). By 1992 Laumann et al. reported an average of 42.8 lifetime sexual partners for gay men as compared to 16.5 for heterosexual men (315).

But is promiscuity intrinsic to homosexuality or a response to environment? Clearly, promiscuous gay men in large cities can be more active than promiscuous heterosexual men. In San Francisco's Castro district or New York's Greenwich Village, gays form communities, businesses, newspapers, clubs, churches, political action committees, and extensive circles of friends among whom they readily find partners. In smaller towns and rural areas, LGBTs tend to be more isolated. Second, women are more severely censured than men for sex outside of marriage, and they face the additional problem of unwanted pregnancy, so promiscuous heterosexual men find fewer willing partners than promiscuous gay men do. Laumann et al. found that while 5.1% of adult males have had 5 or more sex partners in the previous twelve months, only 1.7% of adult females have had 5 or more (177). Third, outside of marriage men tend to focus more on sex than on relationships whether they are straight or gay (Burr 176–177); the all-male urban cultures of bathhouses and bars cultivate the sexual more than the romantic or domestic (Macedo, "Sexuality," 98–99). Fourth, since anti-gay landlords, employers, neighbors, and random bashers can more easily identify and target gays and lesbians if they are living together as long-term couples, it is physically safer for them to be single (Cabaj and Stein 108).

Without the substantial social support of marriage and religious institutions that heterosexuals receive, gay couples vary considerably in their commitments and success. In a 1988–89 study, 1,266 couples—comprised of 706 lesbian couples (56%) and 560 male couples (44%) with an average age of 35 years—were surveyed by Bryant and Demian, who found that the average life span of a relationship for women was 4.9 years and for men 6.9 years. More than 100 of these couples had passed their 15th anniversary. One lesbian relationship had lasted 43 years, and three male couples had stayed together for more than 40 years. 19% of lesbian couples and 13% of male couples had been together one year or less. Significantly, when church approval is added to relationship dynamics, longevity increases: the Episcopalian diocese of Rochester, New York, has been blessing same-sex relationships for the past twenty years, producing a higher success rate for homosexual couples staying together than for heterosexual marriages (Elizabeth Stuart 102).

Without the risk of pregnancy or the structures of marriage, gay and lesbian couples do tend to be less monogamous than straight couples. Bryant and Demian surveyed gay and lesbian couples who were as successful at monogamy as heterosexuals: 91% of the women and 63% of the men had agreed on monogamy; 7% of the women and 26% of the men agreed on monogamy with certain, mutually-acceptable exceptions; 3% of the women and 11% of the men reported no demands on exclusivity. 90% of the women and 63% of the men reported "never" having broken their sexual agreement; 8% of the women and 28% of the men "rarely" broke them; 8% of the women and 28% of the men "sometimes" broke agreements; and 1% of the women and 8% of the men reported breaking sexual agreements "often." Even in the 1970s, before AIDS, three studies showed that 65% of lesbians had maintained an intimate, stable relationship for 1 to 9 years, and 17% had maintained an intimate, stable relationship for more than 10 years (McCary and McCary 253). McWhirter and Mattison studied 156 male couples who had been together from 1 to 37 years and concluded that "gay men can and do establish long-term, committed relationships, which are characterized by stability, mutual caring, generosity, creativity, intimacy, love, support, and nurturing" (Cabaj and Stein 324). Other studies have found much less success. Jones and Yarhouse cite a survey by Blumstein and Schwartz of 1,000 gay and 800 lesbian couples who reported a non-monogamy occurrence rate across the life of the relationship as 79% and 19% respectively; only 36% of gay men and 71% of lesbians valued sexual monogamy (111). This shift suggests that what gays and lesbians want out of a relationship may change as they age, as community ideologies evolve, as they theorize and redefine what happiness is, and as they respond to religious and familial support.

THE EX-GAY MOVEMENT

Rebuffed by the APA, Christian therapists created a new approach in the 1970s and 1980s called "ex-gay ministries," such as Homosexuals Anonymous, Metanoia Ministries, Love in Action, EXIT of Melodyland, and Exodus, which proposed to cure homosexuals by returning them to their original heterosexual state. Exodus International is today an umbrella organization for 75 to 110 ex-gay groups (Mills). Its Doctrinal and Policy Statement shows how theological principles and psychoanalytic principles were combined:

EXODUS cites homosexual tendencies as one of many disorders that beset fallen humanity. Choosing to resolve these tendencies through homosexual behavior, taking on a homosexual identity, and involvement in the homosexual lifestyle is considered destructive, as it distorts God's intent for the individual and is thus sinful. Instead, Christ offers a healing alternative to those with homosexual tendencies. EXODUS upholds redemption for the homosexual person as the process whereby sin's power is broken, and the individual is freed to know and experience true identity as discovered in Christ and His Church. That process entails the freedom to grow into heterosexuality. (Bob Davies)

Framed in the natural law theology of Aquinas, sexual diversity is shifted from a demonic *other* to a misapplied *same,* a misguided attempt to find meaning in humankind's fallen nature where no saving meaning exists. Original Sin functions like Freud's oedipal trauma, repressing humankind's ability to use right reason, blinding the homosexual to God's plan. LGBTs are viewed as victims—of sin, of a fallen world, and of themselves. Consequently, ex-gay counselors have often made appeals to orthodox hardliners to be more sympathetic to the "plight of the homosexual," to overcome their fears and "un-Christlike" attitudes, and reject hateful stereotypes (Herman 49–50). Janet Folger of the Florida-based Coral Ridge Ministries' Center for Reclaiming America states that her group's effort

is really not at all about hate, it is about hope. And really what we are trying to say to people is, "We love you, and that there are options" [to change]. . . . What we are saying is that if you are open to the information, and you are tolerant of another viewpoint, for example, then maybe these folks, these tens of thousands who walked away from homosexuality, maybe they have something to say. Maybe their message should be heard in a national debate." (Davis)

And some pro-gay Christians, such as Christopher Camp, praise anti-gay Christians as true believers:

The majority of the people involved in the [ex-gay] movement are very sincere and they're good people who mean well. . . . They would give you the shirts off their backs. They'd give you all their money, and even put you up in their houses for free. They'd feed you and take care of you as one of their own. (Davis)

However, the Christian ministries' claim to produce cures remains unproven by scientific standards. Because reparative therapists are not trained in the theoretical and methodological rigors of the "hard" sciences (relying instead on interpretation and the symbolic/semantic play of memory and self-expression), they can not provide reliable surveys to chart their success rate statistically or through long-term follow up interviews. Bob Goetze has compiled a list of small anecdotal studies of some patients but admits that they include "too few subjects to be 'statistically significant.'" But, he adds judiciously, "it does not matter whether one is able to apply the results of one study to all homosexual people. What we are looking for is evidence that some people have experienced change." Goetze's qualification does not necessarily undermine his effectiveness as a therapist. No psychoanalyst can promise change for everyone, or even the same kind of change, since patients' histories, needs, personalities, and insights are diverse. But the issue of sexual diversity is so inflammatory that claims are made on each side that tend to gloss over individual differences. First, not all "ex-gay" therapists are as cautious about making generalizations as Goetze is. Anthony Falzarano, who founded Transformation Ex-Gay Ministries, publically stated that not only did he become a homosexual because he was molested by his older brother, but that "80 percent of homosexuals have been molested or raped as children," a statistic without any corroborating evidence from scientific surveys, police records, or from Falzarano himself (Mills). It may be that 80% of Falzarano's clients *were* molested, but since therapists tend to attract a more troubled clientele than is typical of the general population, making generalizations for a whole group is risky. Moreover, some reparative therapists may make the mistake of attributing their patients' present unhappiness to their homosexuality, when the two may really be separate issues. Christopher Camp, who spent ten years in reparative therapy, believes that many homosexuals go to these ministries for emotional problems (with parents, social condemnation, substance abuse, or self-esteem) that have nothing to do with homosexuality itself (Davis). If treatment makes the patient happier, the therapist may misinterpret happiness as a successful amelioration of the homosexual neurosis.

Nor is the fact that some patients cease homosexual activity by becoming celibate or even married proof that orientation or identity has been changed. While sexual behavior can be cataloged and tabulated, sexual identity is a subjective and cultural construct; no test can reliably tell that what an ex-gay feels is or is not heterosexuality. It has been argued that the patients who successfully give up same-sex relationships and become "heterosexual" may really be bisexuals who now act upon a readily available orientation (Sample 126). Goetze discounts this possibility, but his definition of a bisexual is narrow—someone who is "as sexually oriented toward members of both sexes, to essentially the same degree and with the same intensity"—which excludes a large number of bisexuals. Underestimating the bisexual population might explain Schmidt's notation, in his report on reparative therapies, that

client motivation is of course a major factor in all success reports. Other positive variables include youth (under thirty), anxiety over the homosexual condition, recent onset of homosexual activity, some heterosexual experience, lower level of effeminacy in men or masculinity in women, higher education level, loneliness and desire for marriage and children. (154)

Several of Schmidt's variables imply that suitable candidates for becoming "ex-gay" are not those who would be ranked as "exclusive homosexuals" in a Kinsey rating. Prior heterosexual experience suggests that these individuals can function in heterosexual relationships, either because they *do* have desires for the opposite sex, or they are able to draw upon same-sex desire to perform sexually with the opposite sex. But even this argument may be circular because it oversimplifies how individuals experience and cultures construct sexualities. How do we separate the same-sex urges "ex-gays" experience from those which heterosexuals experience? If desire can escape the categories we impose, how do we judge anyone's identity? It may be reductionistic to assume that desire alone determines sexual identity.

Although NARTH claims that 30–50% of patients report long-term "significant" change in behavior or sexual orientation, individual Christian therapists have much less success. Hal Scholl's Spring Forth Ministry loses 19 out of every 20 participants (Schmidt 153, 155). Tim LaHaye admits candidly that conversions from homosexuality to heterosexuality are "extremely rare": "Everyone who knows anything about homosexuality has to admit that it is usually very difficult to extricate a person from this life style" (112). Dr. Ralph Blair reports that all of the early movement's leaders who claimed to have been cured of their homosexuality have now dropped out: Guy Charles of Liberation in Jesus Christ, Roger Grindstaff of Disciples Only, John Evans of Love in Action, Jim Kasper and Mike Bussee of EXIT at Melodyland, Greg Reid of Eagle Ministries, Rick Notch of Open Door, and many others. John Evans remembers

the heart-breaking struggle in my life and the lives of other gay Christians as we prayed and pleaded with God for deliverance from our homosexual nature. I allowed Kent [Philpott] to attempt to cast out of me what he described as "the demon of homosexuality." Although I was completely open and honest before God, my homosexual feelings remained. . . . We all battled with our own homosexual feelings but claimed to be "ex-gay" by faith and waited for the day it would become a reality. There are some gay Christians still claiming to be "ex-gay" but these statements are being made by faith as they continue to suppress their homosexual feelings. (Blair 7–8)

Anthony Falzarano disagrees with Evans, explaining that patients have to have "a Christian conviction or a Judeo-Christian conviction that [homosexual behavior] is wrong" in order to be cured (Davis).

Part of the problem is the use of the word "cure." Each side disputes what it means. Over the years the initial claims of total conversions from homosexuality to full heterosexuality have been gradually qualified. Exodus now offers not "full reorientation" but "partial" recovery: a significant number of these patients, while identifying themselves as "ex-gay," do not usually function as heterosexuals sexually. Goetze sees partiality, not as a failure in the operating theory or technique, but as a qualified success:

Change can be an increase of something. A woman who was only occasionally attracted to other women, might find the frequency of those attractions increasing. Or, it can be a decrease. A man who was very sexually active, may decrease his sexual activity. Change can also mean acquiring something one has not had before. A lesbian woman may find herself acquiring a sexual attraction to men. And it can mean eliminating, or no longer having, something which one used to have. (Goetze)

Because an orthodox moral theology, not psychological principles, sets the terms for what qualifies as success, the bottom line is behavioral, avoiding sinful acts. Thus, chastity becomes a mark of psychotherapeutic progress. John White avoids claims of complete cures by advocating total abstinence for his patients, admitting that heterosexual sex would produce "pain" and even "profound depression" for ex-gays; Kent Philpott of Love in Action goes further when he asks "the homosexual to give up all for Christ—give up sex, a secure lifestyle, friends, maybe even his job"; and David Field argues that, since homosexuality is a permanent condition, celibacy must be permanent as well, even though he admits that such a demand is "harsh":

Eve was created to relieve Adam's loneliness. But how can a modern Adam's loneliness be relieved if no Eve satisfies him and if he is denied the intimate relationship with another Adam that his heart craves? (Blair 45)

From an orthodox perspective, no human relationship can compare with one's relationship to God; a life of chaste loneliness is preferable to offending the Almighty. As White puts it, "Would you despise intimacy with the Almighty in insisting on more of human intimacy?" (Blair 44).

An illustrative case of the incompatibility of terms "redemption" and "cure" was published in 1980 by the Inter-Varsity Christian Fellowship as an example of a successful cure. The text is the confession of a woman writing under the pseudonym Nancy, who describes how she struggled with lesbianism. Nancy was unable to reconcile the conflict between what she felt and what Scriptures asserted was proper and true. She asked a Christian friend for advice, who said:

When you're involved with a woman in a gay relationship, you may feel there is no greater joy in the world. You will love her and be loved in return, you'll share at a deeper level than you've ever known before and she will return your sharing with tenderness and compassion. You'll think that there was never a better love than this and never will be. You're wrong. You'll think that your love is different and unique and goes beyond the mores [moral attitudes] found in the Bible. You're wrong. You may even feel that your love for each other is equal to if not better than the love between a husband and a wife—or you may even feel married to each other. But you're wrong again. You could never give each other the greatest love possible. You may love each other, yes, but you are not giving each other the love that Jesus gave us. (19)

Everything Nancy felt for women was "wrong" even though it felt right because, in accordance with Orthodox theology, sin corrupts perception and judgment. Thus, she must abandon the feelings she has in order to free herself. Suppressing feelings constitutes redemption, but is it a cure? Pro-gay groups would argue that Nancy has simply retreated back into the closet, denying her true identity, which will eventually damage her sense of self-worth. Syndicated gay-press columnist, Richard Mohr, has said:

Each time a gay person finds the closet morally acceptable for himself or others, he degrades himself as gay and sinks to the level of abjection dictated for gays by the dominant culture. No gay person with sufficient self-respect and dignity can be required to view himself or other gays in this way. (Wockner 75)

In 1998 the APA board of trustees passed a resolution condemning reparative therapy, and there are some members who are now calling for an official ban on the practice (Haldeman).

Politics, science, and religion all meet on the question of what Nancy thinks she is doing. Should reparative therapy be banned because people like Nancy use it to renounce their sexuality? Psychologically, repression is not a cure; it does not resolve unconscious conflict or erase unwanted desires. Theologically, it is a common solution, because all sinners are required to do is say "No." Analyzing or exploring evil makes no sense because, by orthodox definition, it lacks a divine purpose, sense, and benefit. If Nancy believes she has made an acceptable trade-off, a redemption rather than a cure, on which side should freedom stand? If renunciation of her actual desires restores her to a religious community she wants to be a part of, who is in an authoritative position to judge what is best for her? Admittedly, Nancy is in tough spot: if she chooses to value her feelings over her beliefs, her church would accuse her of moral degradation, and if she is a true believer, she may feel condemned to Hell; if she chooses to value salvation over earthly and personal happiness, gays and lesbians would accuse her of political surrender. Each side defines Nancy's decision in their own terms, asking her to give up something she values for what they value.

Scientifically, Nancy's improved feelings about herself cannot be used as evidence that a psychological cure has been effected or that her homosexuality was an illness to start with, but can we condemn her decision to value the consolations and benefits of faith over sexuality if that choice is consonant with her beliefs? What makes religion and gay pride valuable—developing a discourse that brings meaning and value to one's personal life—also undermines their authority to test themselves or offer definitive proof that can be generalized for everyone. Redefining sin as an illness to be cured, or self-denial as expediency, confuses religious discourse with scientific discourse for political reasons. Each side in the debate claims the other is deceiving itself, tempting each to make dogmatic and universal what may be personal, subtle, and indefensible, connected to more interesting questions about meaning and fulfillment than "which category do you belong to"?

Part Three

Politics and Sexual Diversity

The great enemy of the truth is very often not the lie—deliberate, contrived and dishonest—but the myth—persistent, persuasive and unrealistic.
—*John F. Kennedy*

10

Demonizing the Enemy

It is easier to nauseate than educate.
—*Tony Marcos*

If the complexities of biblical scholarship and psychological research do not marshal public opinion, there are always tried and true tactics for fighting the political battle of gay rights. Most LGBTs and orthodox Christians dislike using inflammatory rhetoric, but because the issues are so complex and so vital to each, public announcements seeking converts or votes for state ballot initiatives are often fought with oversimplified manifestos, fearful predictions, or dehumanizing stereotypes. In a 1987 fund raising letter, the Reverend Jerry Falwell claimed that gays were going out of their way to donate blood three times more often than other citizens because "they know they are going to die—and they are going to take as many people with them as they can" (Sara Diamond 101). The Reverend Fred Phelps describes homosexuality even more bluntly:

JEFFREY DAHMER—*A TYPICAL FAG! YES! JEFFREY DAHMER IS MERELY A TYPICAL FAG IN FULL FLOWER!* All fags have the same nature and character as DAHMER who molested & killed 17 boys, & then ate their flesh after having sex with their dead bodies. *YES!* All fags, "as natural BRUTE BEASTS, made to be taken and destroyed, are murderers, liars, filthy and lawless." (2 Pet. 2:7,8,12; Jn. 8:44) Most are thwarted by societal constraints from reaching full flower, but *ALL* are *JEFFREY DAHMERS.* ("Week 181")

In response, some gay activists call orthodox Christians "hate mongers" and "extremists," with Pat Robertson earning the title of "Ayatollah Robertson." In a 1993 Cincinnati election, opponents of gay rights legislation were labeled "bigots and homophobes who belong in a post-office lineup with the KKK" (Button et al. 173). When the anti-gay rights Measure 9 was fought in 1992 in Oregon, proposed censorship of gay books in public schools was compared to Serbia's ethnic cleansing, and the gay news magazine, *The Advocate,* illustrated its cover story with a swastika and the headline, "The Rise of Fascism in America" (Gallagher and Bull 59). Liberal ally Isaac Asimov showed little tolerance when he ridiculed the Christian Right in an article in *Macleans* magazine:

And it is these ignorant people, the most uneducated, the most unimaginative, the most unthinking among us, who would make of themselves the guides and leaders of us all; who would force their feeble and childish beliefs on us; who would invade our schools and libraries and homes. (Liebman and Wuthnow 157)

Former head of the Christian Coalition, Ralph Reed, no stranger to propaganda himself, complains: "Religion has become equated with fanaticism, orthodox faith with fascism, and politically involved people of faith are painted as zealots. As a society, we have become biased against bigotry itself except when that bias is directed at religion" (6). Ironically, Reed's sense of persecution echoes the victimization of LGBTs. Both sides have found themselves trapped in an escalating war of mutual demonization.

Hyperbole is the weapon of choice in the sex wars, but it is a dangerous one, for it oversimplifies not only the group it targets but the group that uses it. Often it is picked up by opponents, recontextualized, and used effectively in counter propaganda to represent the enemy as dangerously radical. One classic example occurred on February 15, 1987, when a "gay poet and a gay revolutionary from Connecticut" named Michael Swift published this piece in the *Gay Community News:*

We shall sodomize your sons, emblems of your feeble masculinity, of your shallow dreams and vulgar lies. We shall seduce them in your schools, in your dormitories, in your gymnasiums, in your locker rooms, in your sports arenas, in your seminaries, in your youth groups, in your movie theater bathrooms. . . . If you dare to cry faggot, fairy, queer at us, we will stab you in your cowardly hearts and defile your dead, puny bodies. . . . The family unit—spawning ground of lies, betrayals, mediocrity, hypocrisy and violence will be abolished. . . . All churches who condemn us will be closed. Our only gods are handsome young men. All males who insist on remaining stupidly heterosexual will be tried in homosexual courts of justice and will become invisible men. . . . Tremble, hetero swine, when we appear before you without our masks. (Rueda and Schwartz 26)

Although the editor described it as a work of satire poking fun at the hyperbole it uses, it was immediately included in that week's *Congressional Record,* and has been frequently reprinted in anti-gay rights tracts as a serious manifesto. Clowes advises his Catholic readers:

Perhaps no single work has summarized the actual, unobscured objectives of the homosexuals as well as [this] essay. It quite adequately sums up the entire homosexual agenda. . . . Although homosexual strategists loudly insist that this essay is a joke or a dream, their actions demonstrate differently. Swift's short essay gives the lie to the already-strained myth of homosexual "tolerance." (117)

Anti-gay propaganda feeds upon radical images. The Christian Coalition's video coverage of Gay Pride parades ignores the more conventional LGBTs with their business suits and children, focusing instead on the half naked revelers in leather, chanting slogans, and advocating confrontation, not dialogue. As Candace Gingrich said in an interview to the *Baltimore Alternative:*

Most times, the only gay or lesbian face people know of is who they see in the pride parade. To judge us on that would be like judging heterosexuals after watching the Mardi Gras. (Wockner 80)

The Lambda Report publishes salacious extracts and personal ads from gay publications with nude photographs, requests for sado-masochistic partners, and references to pedophilia to suggest that all LGBTs are sexually radical (Herman 79). Thus, when Tim LaHaye warns his readers of the future he thinks most gay people want, he sees an apocalypse of biblical proportions:

In other words, as we approach the end of the age and the return of Christ, we can expect that homosexuality, among other degenerating sin practices, will increase. In fact, Daniel 11:37 contains an interesting prediction about the anti-Christ, who is destined to rule the world just prior to our Lord's return to set up his Kingdom. "Neither shall he regard the God of his fathers, *nor the desire of women.* . . ." This suggests that the anti-Christ *may* be a homosexual. If he is, that would explain the significance of the influential group of international homosexuals who are rumored to be gaining worldwide political influence. (204)

LaHaye is making symbolic connections between the lavishly profane outfits gay partiers wear in Pride parades and the horrific depictions of Satan in medieval Christian art. Pat Robertson also saw metaphorical similarities between his Satanic enemies when he complained a year after his unsuccessful presidential campaign in 1992:

Just like what Nazi Germany did to the Jews, so liberal America is now doing to the evangelical Christians. It's no different. It is the same thing. It is happening all over again. It is the Democratic Congress, the liberal-biased news media, and the homo-sexuals who want to destroy all Christians. Wholesale abuse and discrimination and the worst bigotry directed toward any group in America today. More terrible than anything suffered by any minority in our history. (Boston, *Dangerous,* 161)

These remarks brought a hailstorm of protest from Jewish Holocaust groups who did not see a fair comparison, but Robertson believes that his enemies are demonically possessed, and so, when he quotes pro-gay texts, he focuses on the most radical, the most subversive, the angriest passages, convinced that they are only the tip of the iceberg and that centrist LGBTs secretly agree with the radical margins.

Although most gay groups prefer legal challenges and education over confrontation and demonization (Button et al. 73), there are some who regard their opponents as genuinely evil, and they are tempted to try dirty tricks for a good cause. On the Queer Resources Directory, one such writer, Stuart Norman, reasons that

because the RW [right wing] has declared war on us, and in war all morality is lost, can't we use some of their tactics and strategies against them? They do not fight fairly; we can't afford to, either. Yes, we may be accused of lowering ourselves to their level, but think what will happen if they win. Not only will our community suffer, but others as well. Their kind of discrimination knows no bounds.

Norman advises stronger measures than appeals to reason or tolerance, and offers to his readers possible counterattack strategies, among which are:

• Liken the right wing and fundies to Nazis, KKK, etc. . . . If we have to use fear tactics, then exploit the possibility of a right wing, religious dictatorship.

• We may be able to get more media attention by using sensationalistic rhetoric against the fundamentalists.

• We need to expose the raw hatred beneath the rhetoric of apparent concern and theological justifications. Therefore we must be able to argue against their belief system to expose the reality beneath, and to push the buttons that trigger the irra-tional hatred, then we can demonstrate what the fundies really stand for.

• Attack the credibility of evangelists. It is well-proven than many have been char-latans and criminals, exploiting their followers in pursuit of political power and wealth.

• If fundies wish to discriminate against us, then we can do the same against them. Should we call for discriminatory laws against fundamentalists, limiting their right to employment, housing, etc.? Probably not, but we can privately discrimi-nate against them and make it widely known that we will discriminate against them.

It is tempting for each side to assume that the other cannot possibly believe what it does without pathology, criminality, or diabolical possession. As the "other," they are, by definition, dysfunctional, abducted mentally by forces too weird to be understood.

Centrist pro-gay national organizations now warn their members against using incendiary language. The Gay and Lesbian Alliance against Defamation (GLAAD) issued a bulletin advising caution when members respond to Dr. Laura Schlessinger's anti-gay remarks. Schlessinger, a best-selling author and host of a syndicated talk-show that reaches 20 million listeners daily, pronounced homosexuality to be a mental disorder, labeling gays and lesbians as "biological mistakes." When Joan M. Garry, GLAAD's Executive Director, met with Schlessinger, she received the following challenge:

If your organization doesn't agree with me then they will attempt to shut me down. Which, frankly, you've got to tell your people that when they do public attacks, it makes me more popular. It gets me more sponsors. It's counterproductive."

GLAAD recommends to its members that they send only polite replies:

Obviously, she is expecting (perhaps even hoping for) angry letters with attacks as personal as those she directs—fodder to use against us on the air. So we are requesting that you write to her and register your opinions as clearly and strongly as possible without rising to her "bait." Think about your own experiences and help her see the impact her words have upon real people—how her words fan the fires of prejudice and discrimination.

Will a kinder, gentler approach avoid demonizing stereotypes and advance the debate? And who will enforce it? Who will unravel the accumulated misrepresentations of the past? It could be a daunting task. Consider the case of Dr. Paul Cameron, who founded the Family Research Institute in 1987 to use "science" to convince voters that homosexuality is not only a crime against nature but against humanity. FRI publishes a national sex survey Cameron had conducted in the mid-1980s, even though, by scientific standards, its methods were sloppy and the results invalid. Interviewers simply knocked on doors and handed a 550-item questionnaire to the first adult who answered. Interviews were not conducted face-to-face, some respondents had possession of the questionnaires much longer than others, and some of the questions were confusing. As two of Cameron's former colleagues, Drs. Robert D. Brown and James K. Cole, declared in a published letter to the *Nebraska Medical Journal*:

What we have then is an extremely lengthy questionnaire, dealing with highly personal matters and with no cited reliability or validity data, being distributed door-to-door by strangers. In no respectable community of survey researchers would this be characterized as scientific. (412)

Brown and Cole also noted that Cameron omitted significant information about the sampling process: he referred to a "systematic area cluster sampling" process, yet no information is given on how sampling areas were selected or how many. The numbers themselves suggest there was nothing systematic about it. Omaha (pop. 300,000) yielded 979 responses while Los Angeles (pop. 4,000,000) yielded only 934. More than 56.5% of all those who were provided questionnaires did not even respond. "Experienced and qualified researchers," Brown and Cole state, "would not base any definitive conclusions on such a limited return," particularly since the sampling method was biased toward soliciting homosexuals, and some of the respondents did not respond seriously to the more outlandish questions but tried to provoke the surveyors with outlandish answers (411).

Brown and Cole also noted major discrepancies in the data analysis as well as data interpretation. Of the 550 questions on the survey, Cameron made conclusions pathologizing homosexuals based on less than 30 items. Brown and Cole argue:

Statisticians know that performing statistical tests on over 550 items will result in approximately 20–30 appearing to be statistically significant just by chance alone. Is this only an interesting coincidence? If you drew cards from a poker deck enough times, you are bound to draw a good poker hand sooner or later. . . . Cameron's credibility as a scientist whose data and data analyses can be trusted has been seriously compromised by evidence that he has systematically distorted data to support assertions he has made regarding homosexuality. . . . What we have left is gross overgeneralization and misrepresentation of useless data. (412–414)

When the Nebraska Psychological Association and the Midwest Sociological Society examined Cameron's study, they too found critical methodological problems: the number of homosexuals he interviewed were far too small to represent America's gay population. Cameron concluded that his homosexual respondents were "pathological" because they had admitted to at least one incident of "oral/anal kissing," but he failed to mention that a majority of his heterosexual respondents also reported oral/anal contact. In 1982 and 1984, the Nebraska Psychological Association censured him for his sloppy research. The Midwest Sociological Society censured him in 1985, and the American Psychological Association expelled him from its membership (David Williams 30).

None of this has made Cameron retract, reconsider or revise his work. Instead, he published a study of obituaries, collected randomly from gay magazines, which claimed:

Compared to white women generally, lesbians are 425 times more likely to be murdered, 875 times more likely to commit suicide, and 437 times more likely to die in auto accidents. All told, lesbians are 10 times more likely than all homosexuals to die violently and 549 times more likely to die violently than white women generally. (*Lifespan* 5)

He also published an essay arguing that pedophilia is intrinsic to homosexuality. Cameron based his claim on the work of A. Nicholas Groth, the nationally respected Director of the Sex Offender Program at the Connecticut Department of Correction, but Cameron grossly misrepresented Groth's research. Groth complained to the Nebraska Board of Examiners of Psychologists:

homosexuality and homosexual pedophilia are not synonymous. In fact, it may be that these two orientations are mutually exclusive, the reason being that the homosexual male is sexually attracted to masculine qualities whereas the heterosexual male is sexually attracted to feminine characteristics, and the sexually immature child's qualities are more feminine than masculine. . . . In any case, in over 12 years of clinical experience working with child molesters, we have yet to see any example of a regression from an adult homosexual orientation." (180–181)

Groth charges that Cameron fudged the statistics of Groth's own work in order to prove that homosexuals were dangerous to children. He had done the same thing in 1984 when he testified in Texas at a trial on homosexual rights. The presiding Judge, Jerry Buschmeyer, examined the evidence and concluded that Cameron had lied to the court:

His own statement that "homosexuals are approximately 43 times more apt to commit crimes than is the general population" is a total distortion of the Kinsey data upon which he relies—which, as is obvious to anyone who reads the report, concerns data from a non-representative sample of delinquent homosexuals. . . . His sworn statement that "homosexuals abuse children at a proportionately greater incident than do heterosexuals" is based upon the same distorted data. . . . (David Williams 31)

Nevertheless, over the last sixteen years, Cameron has been invited to speak to many conservative groups around the country who believe him to be scientifically informed, gaining the respect of national conservative leaders like Pat Robertson and writers like Robert Magnuson. Colonel Ronald D. Ray used Cameron's conclusions to argue in his book, *Gays: In or Out? The U.S. Military and Homosexuals,* that all homosexuals be excluded from the military because "almost all homosexuals engage in sexual practices which are inherently degrading or humiliating and are rarely practiced by heterosexuals" (36). When Idaho's anti-gay rights initiative of 1994 was advocated, voters were given Cameron's contention that gay men were 34 times more likely to commit murder, 90 times more likely to molest children, and so addicted to masochism they should enjoy getting beat up by gay bashers. The initiative lost by only 3,098 votes out of 420,000 cast (Witt and McCorkle 60, 63).

Once demonizing myth gets published as fact, it can be recirculated endlessly, until its origins are lost and its validity becomes unquestioned even by people of good will simply because it is so widespread. Echoes of

Cameron's disinformation can be heard from Paul Volle, Chairman of the Christian Coalition of Maine, who claimed that "gays commit over 33% of their sex acts with children. Of the pupil molestations, homosexual teachers commit as many as 80% of those acts" ("Stupid").

In a book lauded on the cover as "the premier interdisciplinary resource for thinking Christians grappling with the perplexing moral status of homosexual behavior," Thomas E. Schmidt relies on Cameron's figures to calculate that 3.2 million American boys have been molested by homosexuals (115). Brian Clowes uses Cameron's claim that homosexual teachers are 90 to 100 times more likely to molest students than heterosexual teachers (121). Yet criminal and sociological inquiries show that a child is 100 times more likely to be molested by a heterosexual family member than by a gay or lesbian non-family member (Jenny et al.). Groth and Birnbaum studied 175 men who had been convicted of sexual assaults against children between 1970 and 1975: none of the offenders showed any preference for adult homosexual relationships; in fact, they frequently expressed a strong sexual aversion to other adult males, reporting that what they found attractive about immature boys were their feminine features and the absence of secondary sexual characteristics such as body hair and muscles (180–181). Children's Hospital in Denver found that only 1 of 387 cases of suspected child molestation involved a gay perpetrator. Jenny et al. found that men who molest young boys are, by a wide margin, heterosexuals who are currently involved in sexual relationships with women, do not feel attracted to other men, and do not engage in same-sex sexual relations with men. And yet 49% of Oregon citizens, persuaded by misinformation, voted for a 1992 ballot proposal that would have required high school teachers to publicly denounce homosexuality by equating it with pedophilia, sadism, and masochism and describing it as "abnormal, wrong, unnatural, and perverse" (Nava and Dawidoff 68).

How will a new civility in the gay rights debate deal with misinformation, and who will judge what should be corrected, invalidated, or censored? Each side tends to embrace evidence favoring its own position. Brian Clowes charges that Kinsey's sex surveys were not only bad science but political propaganda to pressure government policy changes. Gay groups, the press, and politicians readily adopted the 10% figure to justify gay rights without examining critically what the figure meant. Clowes sees a snowball effect in how the opposition uses science: Kinsey's research led to Hooker's gay-friendly studies, which led to the APA's reversal depathologizing homosexuality, which encouraged researchers to conduct gay-friendly brain studies and genetic surveys. Discoveries of "gay brains" or "gay genes" were trumpeted in news media as "proof" that homosexuality was not a choice. But since Clowes considers Kinsey's methods "sloppy" and results "utterly meaningless," merely a form of "pure propaganda . . . ridiculously far from the mathematical or statistical science pretended" (see Chapter 8 for criticisms of Kinsey's work), he judges subsequent research as tainted and politically motivated (116). Clowes' fear is that voters will decide the gay rights question by supplanting moral considerations with the unquestioned authority of secular science, which, from his perspective, is influenced by both liberal politics and anti-Christian prejudice. Part of this fear arises from a suspicion that gay scientists fudge their results, but it is also consonant with orthodox views of how easily human reason and perception can be corrupted by humankind's "Fallen state": sinners tend not to see their sins objectively; true objectivity is seeing God's design in the universe. Pro-gay rights groups believe that science can reveal the truth of their difference; anti-gay rights groups believe that science without a guiding theological-based faith can mistake Error for Truth. How, then, can the two sides agree on what counts as credible scientific evidence and what is not when each side approaches credibility and objectivity from such different philosophical perspectives?

Hate Speech or Righteous Speech?

What qualifies as "hate speech"? Warning that homosexuals are prone to violence and murder, Brian Clowes reasons:

Self-Hate—Other-Hate. It is obvious that a group of people who enjoy—or who are truly addicted to—being sodomized, tortured, and degraded have extremely low self-esteem. . . . Their activities and publications clearly show that they are filled with rage and self-hate. . . . Therefore, it is not at all surprising that homosexuals occasionally erupt in explosions of extreme violence against others. (137)

Is Clowes led to such conclusions by a personal hatred towards LGBTs disguised to look psychologically sound, or by the orthodox model of perversion which connects one perversion to another, multiplying deviance in a way he finds both believable and frightening? Is he sifting through evidence unaware of how his ideology affects his perceptions of LGBTs, or is he aware but dismisses evidence contradicting his belief because he believes it has been concocted by pro-gay forces or by the devil himself? Can his theological orientation protect him against the accusation of prejudice?

Scanzoni and Mollenkott have argued that "what distinguishes prejudice from a simple misconception is emotional resistance to new evidence" (158). Under this rubric, Clowes may be judged prejudiced if he willfully fails to acknowledge evidence that LGBTs are neither pathological nor antisocial. But how accountable are individuals for misconceptions validated by the ideological system they grew up in and which makes sense of conflicting evidence, indeed, shapes the way they experience dissonant evidence? Does the intensity of anti-gay rhetoric suggest that anti-gay groups are caught in a moral bind: committed to preserving self-validating dogma that defines new evidence as false? Scanzoni and Mollenkott urge Christians to avoid prejudicial stereotypes by maintaining "habitual open-mindedness" while reexamining evidence, "making every effort to avoid boxing people into rigid categories" (159). But how successful would such an appeal be when it already invalidates orthodox thinking? If one believes that God himself sorted everyone into two categories (male/female, good/evil), and that satanic forces trick human beings into confusing categories (disguising evil and falsehood with the veneer of goodness and truth), how would he/she regard the invitation to open-mindedness that more readily accepts the homosexual's claim to be good? Take, for example, a recent dispute in print between James Dobson and John D. Woodbridge. Dobson, head of Focus on the Family, declared:

Nothing short of a great Civil War of Values rages today throughout North America. Two sides with vastly differing and incompatible world-views are locked in a bitter conflict that permeates every level of society. . . . We are engaged in a battle—not primarily with our philosophical opponents—but against "Satan, who leads the whole world astray." (Rev. 12:9) (28)

Woodbridge, Professor of Church History at Trinity Evangelical Divinity School, argued that such "cold war rhetoric" is itself the problem, that civility alone can bring the two sides together:

Repeated recourse to the language of war makes it harder to love our enemies—and it is already hard to do so—because it flames angry feelings. Second, culture-war rhetoric leads us to distort others' positions, to see enmity in place of mere disagreement. It leaves no room for nuanced positions, or for middle ground. . . . Sadly, Christian activists have sometimes yielded to culture-war temptations. Unsubstantiated charges, fear-mongering, global denunciations, and the "demonization" of opponents have surfaced in newsletters and public rhetoric. This approach may raise money, but it does not raise the moral tone of the debate. (23, 24)

But is money the only reason Dobson does not lower his moral tone? What if demonizing speech results not from (or merely from) "angry feelings" that motivate opposed world views, but from the world views themselves, which produce and necessitate absolute, adamant opposition to a perceived threat? If only heterosexuals can experience and appreciate the "genital romance" of procreative sex, and if only LGBTs can experience and appreciate the fulfilling meaning of sexual diversity—if thinking is shaped by different experiences and incompatible discourses—can civility be enough to bridge two estranged worlds? Does a middle ground even exist on which either side can find a ideologically sound position? Or is the very idea of a middle ground little more than wishful thinking, a utopian desire to domesticate politics by minimizing what separates disputants? How does one even take the first step: deciding if an opponent's beliefs are a satanic conspiracy or bigotry, or if they are part of an exploration of—and passionate disagreement about—the meaning and value of life?

A tentative gesture toward civility was taken recently by the Reverend Mel White, who appealed to Pat Robertson and Jerry Falwell to stop recirculating Cameron's demonizing claims:

How many frightened, lonely youth have killed themselves because of what they read or their parents have heard on your telecasts or read in your books or mailings? How many American families have been torn apart, how many teenagers have run away or been discarded, how many acts of discrimination or violence have been aimed against gay and lesbian youth because of the homosexual myths and stereotypes that you promote and sustain?

The tragic, trickle-down effects of homophobic rhetoric have been demonstrated over and over again. What you say about homosexuality on the "700 Club" moves with devastating consequences through our homes, our schools, and our churches. The disinformation you distribute appears and reappears in sermons, Sunday school lessons, counseling sessions, and in heartbreaking confrontations between young people, their parents, and their peers. (311)

Robertson did not respond but Falwell did, and a meeting between the two, each accompanied by 200 of their associates, took place at Falwell's Thomas Road Church in Lynchburg, Virginia, on October 23, 1999. Falwell made it clear that he would not change his view that the Bible condemns homosexual activity, nor would he ever support legal recognition of same-sex unions. White left theological negotiations to future discussions but pressed the point that Falwell's repeated condemnations of homosexuals as sinners and social reprobates constitutes hate language that incites violence. Falwell disagreed, arguing that the Bible requires him to call a sin a sin, but he promised to tone down his rhetoric and delete Paul Cameron's pseudo-science from his publications (Brennan). Although Falwell denied that his speeches contributed to violence against homosexuals, he acknowledged White's criticism that his language has been strident:

"We plead guilty to that, and we will try to do better," he said, "and I will use what influence I have across the evangelical landscape" to encourage others to do likewise. "Most Christians believe the gay life style is wrong," Falwell said, but "we've got to, in the next century, make the world believe we love the sinner more than we hate the sin." (Niebuhr)

Falwell and White then apologized for demonizing each other in the past and praised each other for taking the first step toward a higher level of discourse.

Will they succeed? Falwell later acknowledged that his meeting with White had angered some of his followers: "I'm getting a lot of heat, lots of letters, lots of e-mail, from my friends, my supporters who are saying, 'Hold on man. What are you doing?'" Outside of Falwell's church, 40 anti-gay Baptists demonstrated, some shouting, some holding signs, such as "Jerry And A Fairy Equal Sin." Members of Heritage Baptist Church, from Mount

Enterprise, Texas, objected to any meeting between Christians and homosexuals: "We've supported Jerry Falwell over the years . . . and he has
thrown in the towel" (Orth). When Falwell originally told his advisers of
his plans to include a sit-down dinner with White, they persuaded Falwell
to dispense with the food, citing I Corinthians 5:11, where the Apostle Paul
warns against associating "with anyone who calls himself a brother but is
sexually immoral. . . . With such a man do not even eat" (Murphy, "Falwell"). When White et al. arrived, they found only bottles of Poland water
on the tables. If Falwell cannot move on the subject of sharing food, has he
even room to examine larger issues? Richard Cizik, spokesman for the
National Association of Evangelicals, has reported that the reaction among
Christian evangelicals has been at best mixed: "Some are very supportive
and think Falwell has done the right thing. Others are suspicious that these
kinds of efforts aren't productive in the long run."

Evangelicals are not the only ones disappointed in White's policy of reap-
proachment. Of the four groups who protested the meeting, one was Oral
Majority, a radical gay group based in Florida. OM's Bob Kunst denounced
both White and Falwell: "'They're both a disaster,' said Kunst, calling
White a 'self-hating homosexual' and Falwell a war criminal in the war
against AIDS" (Orth). Two Spirit Laughing, the Internet name of a former
editor of a lesbian/gay newsletter, *Update,* asserted:

. . . for those who find a *great deal* of comfort in the CHRISTIAN RELIGIOUS
discussions held recently between the clown prince of televangelists, Jerry Fartwell,
and the well-intentioned but strictly CHRISTIAN RELIGIOUS worker Mel White,
please take a few moments to ponder what real effect this will have on anything,
beyond a bit of short-term fuzzy publicity for Fartwell, and a regrettable increase in
the clamor among the easily persuaded for them there loud-mouthed bad queers to
stop criticizing pseudo-religious hate-mongers (actually IRS-savvy political power
brokers). . . . Don't give up, don't give in, and don't forget.

Will the dialogue of Falwell and White have much effect on their peers,
many whom do not share their religious or political views? What kinds of
policies can come out of a "love the sinner but hate the sin" approach? Is
love possible without justice? In many states, ballots have appeared pro-
posing to fire LGBT teachers, not because the teachers themselves are
hated, but because of the concern that children may model themselves on
adult LGBTs simply by being in their presence. Orthodox Christian theology has traditionally feared the power of deviant sex to create social and
psychological disorder because humankind's fallen nature is seen as vulnerable to perversion despite family studies suggesting that no significant psychological differences are found between children raised by heterosexuals
and children raised by gays or lesbians—much less teachers (Bailey et al.;
Patterson 44; Eric Marcus 60; Mohr 39). Tasker and Golombok found no
deficits in the mental health, self-esteem, or social adjustment; nor did chil-

dren raised by lesbian mothers show any greater incidence of gender identity confusion or cross-gender behavior (205). Children raised by gay
fathers have also been found to be psychologically healthy and overwhelm-
ingly heterosexual (Cabaj and Stein 384–385; Barret and Robinson 85).
Can secular science allay theologically-based fears?

To complicate matters, stereotypes do not need to rely on individual
spokesmen to make them powerful if they are deeply rooted in the institutions that most affect LGBT lives. In many courts of law lesbian mothers are
deemed unsuitable as parents on a number of grounds: that they are emotionally unstable, that they are not maternal, that they or their partner might
sexually abuse their children, that they are not child-oriented, that children
brought up by homosexual parents will become homosexual themselves,
that such children will be less psychologically healthy, more liable to mental
breakdowns, or exhibit behavioral problems, that such children will suffer
in their own social relationships if their friends find out about their parents'
homosexuality (Patterson 39; Tasker and Golombok 203; Falk 941). None
of this is supported by research, but gay men and lesbians are often denied
the adoption of an orphaned child, and they are more apt to lose custody of
their own biological children in divorce cases. In a recent court case, Circuit
Judge Joseph Tarbuck of Pensacola gave custody of an 11 year old girl to her
father, who was a convicted murderer, solely because the mother, Mary, was
a lesbian. John Ward confessed to murdering his first wife, Judy, after an
argument over custody of their children; he served eight years in prison.
Even though the father had never taken care of his daughter for more than
four days in a row, and even though he was behind in child support pay-
ments, the judge declared: "This child should be given the opportunity and
the option to live in a nonlesbian world" ("Lesbian Appeals").

Elizabeth Gibbs argues that there is no scientific evidence to support such
judicial decisions. Studies suggest that lesbian women are at no greater risk
for psychiatric disorder than heterosexual women (Falk 943), that lesbian
mothers are just as child-oriented, warm and responsive to the children, and
nurturing and confident as their heterosexual counterparts (Tasker and
Golombok 205–206). Lesbians' romantic and sexual relationships with
other women have not been found to detract from their ability to care for
their children (Patterson 39). Nor does the absence of a father in single parent households (headed by either a heterosexual woman or a lesbian
woman) have any significant effect on the psychosexual development of the
children involved (Green et al.). Most scientists who study the issue now
believe that "there is no evidence that the development of children with gay
parents is compromised in any significant respect relative to that among
children of heterosexual parents in otherwise comparable circumstances"
(Patterson 33). But little of the evidence has seeped into public discourse on
gay rights, and it is unlikely to because stereotypes have the advantages of
being brief, dramatic, and ideologically congruent.

11

Gay Bashing
and Social Control

THE THEORY OF PERSECUTION

Anti-gay activists deny that their depiction of homosexuals as anti-family sexual predators incites hatred or violence against gays, and most orthodox churches officially condemn gay bashing. Pro-gay advocates believe that demonization itself invites violence. Attorney Kendall Thomas argues that while "homosexual sodomy statutes express the official 'theory' of homophobia, private acts of violence against gay men and lesbians 'translate' that theory into brutal practice" (1485). When individual citizens act on behalf of the state, they erase the boundary between public and private, an erasure *Bowers v. Hardwick* legitimized as constitutional. Legally, Hardwick has no private area in which to be homosexual; his sexuality is always a public concern, an intrusion into and disruption of social order, even when conducted in the privacy of his own home, and so he deserves punishment. The harassment of African American males by the Ku Klux Klan was rationalized on similar grounds: incursions by black men into white public areas endangered "white culture," and the most inflammatory image depicting the mixing of races was, not surprisingly, a sexual one: that of black men molesting white women. Propaganda against gay men substitutes the image of a molested boy for the white woman. Thus, gay rights advocates argue that queer bashing has the same function that lynchings had for African Americans: to keep a whole stigmatized group afraid to assert its rights, to keep it invisible in the closet (Mohr 5). History suggests that whenever a social group is demonized, it automatically becomes a target for harassment and violence. The targeted minority may be defined by race, religion, ideology, or merely geographic location, but the disparaging myths generally follow the same formula: to portray the Other as immoral and degenerate (Rubin). For centuries the Jews in Europe were labeled sexually deviant, sexually addicted, carriers of disease, slaves of Satan, and the enemies of God, virtually the same accusations made of LGBTs today. Does this commonality prove a shared goal? (Boswell 14–15; Blumenthal, "History/Hysteria").

Gay rights advocates point to similarities between fascist ideology and orthodox Christian theology to imply that traditional thinking links despised groups in a chain of binaries that reinforce one another. Gestapo leader, Heinrich Himmler, adapted the "natural law" theology of sexuality to portray homosexuality as "anti-family." State policy encouraged all German women and men to produce children with clearly marked gender roles, boys destined to be future warriors, girls to be future mothers. The Nazis outlawed anything deemed destructive to family values: contraceptives, abortion, prostitution, and homosexuality. The Reich legal director, Hans Frank, proclaimed that homosexual activity meant the "negation of the community"—not only because it did not produce children but because it encouraged social tolerance. On May 14, 1928, the Nazi party issued an official policy towards homosexuality:

Community before Individual:
   It is not necessary that you and I live, but it is necessary that the German people live. And they can live only if they can fight, for life means fighting. And they can fight only if they maintain their masculinity. They can only maintain their masculinity if they exercise discipline, especially in matters of love. . . . Anyone who even thinks of homosexual love is our enemy. We reject anything which emasculates our people and makes them a plaything for our enemies, for we know that life is a fight, and it is madness to think that men will ever embrace fraternally. Natural history teaches us the opposite. Might makes right. And the stronger always win over the weak. (Porter xii)

The gay embrace undermines gender, racial, and national distinctions that properly structure the world and society. Like Eric Fuchs who argues that only heterosexuals experience "in their flesh the order of differentiation which structures the world," the Nazis reasoned that gender differences stand as a structural model for all group dynamics. To maintain their natural superiority, men, nations and races must exploit the subordinated Other, women as breeding stock, nonwhites as slaves, non-Aryans as enemies, or else become exploited themselves, feminized and weakened by tolerance and democracy. The Nazis fought homosexuality with propaganda, repressive laws, prison sentences, and finally death in concentration camps. No one has a final count of the homosexual dead, but estimates vary between 20,000 and 500,000 (Feig 80–84; Porter x).

   Orthodox Christian thinking also ties perversions together, but with
important differences. Pat Robertson declared in 1992 on his televised 700
Club that fascism and homosexuality were compatible:

When lawlessness is abroad in the land, the same thing will happen here that hap-
pened in Nazi Germany. Many of those people involved in Adolf Hitler were
Satanists, many of them were homosexuals—the two things seem to go together.
("Religious Political")

The traditional model for perversion connects the flip side of binaries—
order/disorder, truth/heresy, God/Satan, heterosexuality/homosexuality,
and freedom/fascism. The distaff position signals a usurpation of right reason and a violation of God's plan, which set up all binary structures in the
first place. As America's sodomy laws suggest, social deviance and sexual
deviance are allied in traditional thinking, and so Robertson reasons that
fascists, like homosexuals, must also be sexually disordered. Thus, while
having the appearance of stability and logic, binary thinking contains slip-
pages as each term bleeds into the other, producing variations. Neo-nazi
groups in the United States also use traditional binaries to establish a natural hierarchy of value. Take the Blue Boys, a small group of young gay bashers in Los Angeles who cruise Hollywood with blue aluminum bats looking
for victims. When interviewed, the group's leader, Cap, formulated his own
theory of perversion to justify his actions:

Fags call each other fags, and a fag thinks that everyone is a fag. I tell you, [the] Blue
Boys are male. We're heteros. We have girlfriends and wives. We're out there fucking
chicks every night and we have nothing to do with any fag shit. . . . These queers
fucking deserve [AIDS]. They are going around spreading their disease wherever they
want under the rules of privacy given them by this fraudulent Constitution, with niggers in the Supreme Court saying what we can do and what we cannot do. This
nation was built by white people for white people and is not to be confused with a
bunch of faggots and niggers taking over. (Herek and Berrill 194, 197)

The position of the "enemy" can be filled by any of the three despised groups:
gay men (who are emasculated but threaten to emasculate heterosexuals),
"chicks" (who must be sexually exploited to prove one's manhood), and
African Americans (who compete with whites for political power). Life is a
struggle between the strong and the weak; thus, democracy is fraudulent
because it is altruistic, protecting the weak who then conspire to dominate the
naturally superior, sexually correct Nazi males. While Robertson would consider the Blue Boys to be Satanic, in fact, their beliefs resemble those of Christian Reconstructionism, a fringe group which holds that only white, Anglo-
Saxon/Germanic Christians should exercise dominion over all the earth
through the power of God's Law (Robinson, "Christian"). Binaries do not

line up the same way for everyone. How one positions oneself in a binarized social hierarchy (as an outsider or insider, Christian or Jew, black or white, male or female) changes the way binaries are connected, and, consequently, whom one is allied with or against.

Although African Americans have also been victimized by prejudice and demonized as sexual predators, and consequently commonly assumed to be allies of LGBTs, in fact, as a group they are less liberal about social issues than white Americans, and many oppose homosexuality on religious grounds, as a sinful lifestyle that forfeits any right to legal redress. Some black gays have encountered racist white gays (blacks seldom occupy leadership positions in gay rights groups); others resent any comparison of suffering or disenfranchisement between LGBTs and African Americans as denigrating the latter (Gallagher, "Blacks and Gays," 400; Button et al. 186, 89–90). Like the Blue Boys, some African Americans theorize a hierarchy of value in which ranking becomes the only access to power and self-esteem: devalued by white culture, straight blacks can at least feel superior to gays, especially gay blacks. Indeed, the combined effect of being despised by whites for being black and by blacks for being queer has produced an attempted suicide rate for gay men and lesbians of color that is almost double that of white gay men and lesbians (Tremblay). In a review of statements by black intellectuals and religious leaders, Howard University Professor Ron Simmons found a variety of pathologizing explanations for why some African Americans are gay, all of them tied to racial and gender binary oppositions: that it is an emasculation of black men by white oppression, that it is a sinister plot perpetuated by diabolical white racists who want to destroy the black race, that it is a white man's disease. Nathan and Julia Hare, in their 1984 book, *The Endangered Black Family: Coping with the Unisexualization and Coming Extinction of the Black Race*, argue that black children are feminized by white female schoolteachers as part of a genocidal plot masterminded by the "white liberal-radical-moderate-establishment coalition" (211–212). Minister Louis Farrakhan, leader of the Nation of Islam, argued in 1990 that adulterers, child molesters, rapists and homosexuals should be executed for the benefit of family and national values:

Do you know why [in biblical times] they [stoned you to death] for adultery? Because there is nothing more sacred than marriage and family. Nothing. . . . And every time you stone [an adulterer] you're killing the thought in your own mind. . . . You make an example [by stoning someone] because the individual is not more important than the community [or the] nation. So you sacrifice the individual for the preservation of a nation. (Simmons 222)

Like Himmler and Robertson, Farrakhan bases his condemnation of sexual diversity on the premise that it is detrimental to all structured social relations. He uses anti-gay remarks to rekindle pride in straight black men, to reassert their value and power in a white nation that discounts them, but he reads value as requiring a despised Other. Simmons sees this goading tactic as ultimately self-destructive:

Persecuting gays reinforces a false sense of manhood. Rather than confront the real enemy—those who actually cause and control the oppression—their frustrations caused by powerlessness are soothed by intimidating those who they consider weak. It's easy to prove your manhood by putting down "faggots."

Simmons' argument is that homoprejudice suppresses any emotion that diverges from fixed gender roles: "in the black community, a male is often forced to denounce sexual diversity in order to avoid suspicion [and] too often the homophobia and heterosexism within the African American community forces men to be the 'hardest hard,'" nullifying "unmanly" feelings (214, 217) as well as heterosexual females who may fear that being strong, ambitious, or self-assured may open them to charges of lesbianism.

Farrakhan's prescription to kill a person to kill the thought, silencing yourself by silencing others, suggests that anti-gay violence is an attempt to erase difference, not just in others but in oneself, and this may be why gay bashings are more vicious than other kinds of violent crimes, to erase any hint of likeness or self-doubt. In a review of gay bashings resulting in murder listed in 17 newspapers and two police department files over a five year period, researchers found that most victims were "more apt to be stabbed a dozen times or more, mutilated, *and* strangled, [and] in a number of instances stabbed or mutilated after being fatally shot" (Comstock 47). Melissa Mertz, coordinator of the Victims of Violent Assault Assistant Program of Bellevue Hospital in New York, reports:

Attacks against gay men were the most heinous and brutal I encountered. . . . They frequently involved torture, cutting, mutilation, and beating, and showed the absolute intent to rub out the human being because of his [sexual] orientation. (Comstock 46)

How much of this hostility can be attributed to latent homosexuality is unknown. In 1914 Sandor Ferenczi, the Hungarian psychoanalyst, hypothesized that feelings of disgust toward gay men by heterosexual men are defensive, a denial against their own unconscious attraction to other men (Goleman). Ferenczi's theory fell into disrepute in the 1970s, but it has recently received tenuous support from researchers at the University of Georgia. Adams, Wright, and Lohr recruited 64 Caucasian heterosexual male volunteers from the Psychology Department Research Subject Pool, who were then screened by the Kinsey Heterosexual-Homosexual Ratings Scale. Only those men who reported exclusive heterosexual arousal and experiences were allowed to participate. They were further divided into two groups—homophobic and non-homophobic men—using the Index of Homophobia Test, a group of 25 questions, developed by Hudson and Ricketts, which assesses how much discomfort the respondent would antic-ipate feeling interacting with homosexuals. An Aggression Questionnaire showed that the two groups did not differ from one another in terms of gen-eral aggressiveness; only hostility towards homosexuals was being appraised. A rubber circumferential strain gauge was then strapped around each subject's penis to measure swelling while three different videotapes were shown: one of nude men engaging in sex, one of lesbian women engaging in sex, and one of a heterosexual couple engaging in sex. Both groups of men—homophobic and non-homophobic alike—responded to the heterosexual and lesbian erotic scenes with erections; but only the homophobic men experienced significant swelling when shown gay male sex scenes. In the homophobic group, 20% showed no significant swelling, 26% showed moderate swelling, and 54% showed definite erections in response to the male homosexual video; in the non-homophobic group, the scores were the reverse: 66% showed no significant swelling, 10% showed moderate swelling, and only 25% showed definite erections. None of these subjects reported being *conscious* of having same-sex impulses, which may suggest either Freudian-style repression and denial or an unspoken cultural imperative.

Thus, binary thinking unites these strange bedfellows, Himmler, Robert-son, and Farrakhan, each insisting on rigidly structured social relations to control desires within individuals, each needing a perversely desiring enemy to distinguish his position in social/moral/racial structures. Even though each man is the ideological enemy of the other two, they agree on homo-sexuality as a common threat because it occupies the distaff position of binaries linked together with a hierarchy of values that structures how we understand sex, God, self, and race. But because homosexuality has tradi-tionally been defined by its presumed opposite, pro-gay rhetoric has been contaminated by binary thinking too. In the 1970s radical gays and lesbians celebrated their "deviancy," making the distaff position that the heterosex-ist binary placed them in a revolutionary virtue, as Case notes:

. . . the queer, unlike the rather polite categories of gay and lesbian, revels in the discourse of the loathsome, the outcast, the idiomatically-proscribed position of same-sex desire. Unlike petitions for civil rights, queer revels constitute a kind of activism that attacks the dominant notion of the natural. The queer is the taboo-breaker, the monstrous, the uncanny. Like the Phantom of the Opera, the queer dwells underground, below the operatic overtones of the dominant; frightening to look at, desiring, as it plays its own organ, producing its own music. (3)

When Pat Califia denigrates heterosexuals as intellectually and socially stunted because they have limited themselves to "vanilla sex" ("Identity" 98), she has written them off as the unredeemable "other," unable to engage fully in the gay rights debate because their position on the sexual binary reduces them to incompetence.

Is there any other way to theorize social relations, or do we always need a demon to define what is good? If we must have a demon, will violence always follow? And if the "other," who must be despised because binary thinking requires it, is always already inside us, who should be held responsible for the violence?

THE PRACTICE OF PERSECUTION

As overall serious crime in the United States decreased for the eighth consecutive year in 1999, hate crimes based on sexual orientation have generally risen every year since 1991 (Table 11.1). Hate crimes based on sexual orientation now rank as the third highest category after race and religion. It is widely recognized that hate crimes against LGBs are underreported, so incidence numbers are low. The private National Coalition of Anti-Violence Programs reported 1,965 incidents in 1999 in only 25 cities/jurisdictions across the country while the FBI reported only 1,317 collected from 12,122 reporting agencies ("New FBI").

Harassment based on sexual orientation ranges from name-calling and spray-painting hateful epithets on homes, slashing tires, vandalizing offices, to beatings with clubs and brass knuckles, arson and murder. A recent study of 151 anti-gay slayings revealed that 60% of the murders were marked by "extraordinary and horrific violence" of the sort "fueled by rage and hate" (Button et al. 60). Dr. Stewart Flemming, at the Ralph E. Davies Medical Center in San Francisco, reported that the attacks on gays that his Emergency Room has seen

are vicious in scope and the intent is to kill and maim. . . . Weapons include knives, guns, brass knuckles, tire irons, baseball bats, broken bottles, metal chains, and metal pipes. Injuries include severe lacerations requiring extensive plastic surgery; head injuries, at times requiring surgery; puncture wounds of the chest, requiring insertion of chest tubes; removal of the spleen for traumatic rupture; multiple

TABLE 11.1   Hate Crimes Based on Sexual Orientation, 1991–1999*

Year	1991	1992	1993	1994	1995	1996	1997	1998	1999
Incidents	—	767	860	685	1,019	1,016	1,102	1,260	1,317
All hate crimes, %	8.9	11.6	11.3	11.5	12.8	11.6	13.7	16.2	16.7

*Reported by the FBI.
Source: Human Rights Campaign

fractures of the extremities, jaws, ribs, and facial bones; severe eye injuries, in two cases resulting in permanent loss of vision; as well as severe psychological trauma the level of which would be difficult to measure. (Quoted in Comstock 46)

Groups of young men periodically cruise gay communities hunting for victims, but it can also happen without premeditation. As one teenage basher told an interviewer: "We would never make a decision to go beat up fags. But if we were walking down the street and some guy passed that look 'queer,' we'd let him have it" (Comstock 70). "Looking queer" is an unreliable method of selection, however; as a recent study shows, only 21% of young gay men are recognizably "effeminate" in their behavior, so heterosexuals are attacked as well (McCary and McCary 253).

LGBTs feel doubly harassed when light sentences are given to gay bashers. Some judges excuse victimizers as "just all-American boys." One District of Columbia judge gave only suspended sentences to queer bashers whose victim had been stalked, beaten, slashed, kicked, and urinated on, because the judge thought the assailants were "good boys at heart" since they went to a religious prep school. A murderer of Midwestern drag performer Stephen L. Jones received the lightest possible sentence under the law with eligibility for parole after one year. Dan White, a law-and-order conservative, received a seven year prison term for assassinating Harvey Milk, San Francisco's first openly gay city supervisor. A Texas judge justified leniency in sentencing the convicted murderer of two gay men on the grounds that "I put prostitutes and queers on the same level. . . . And I'd be hard put to give somebody life for killing a prostitute." In 1989 a Dallas judge reduced the sentence for an 18-year-old killer of two gay men because he had killed them in a gay cruising zone, where the victims, the judge speculated, could have been looking for children to molest (Thompson 214; Herek and Berrill 3; Mohr 5; Thomas 1483.n186). Bashing by the police themselves is also a concern for LGBTs. Surveys show that, on average, 20% of gays and lesbians have been victimized by the police for their sexual orientation (Herek and Berrill 32).

Because binary thinking is fundamental to cultural logic, children learn fairly quickly that LGBTs are inferior, even if they haven't been specifically instructed. Surveys suggest that 80% of gay and lesbian students are victims of verbal insults; 44% report being threatened by physical attack; 22% of boys and 29% of girls report being physically attacked by other students; 7% report being physically hurt by a teacher (Pilkington and D'Augelli). In 1993 the Massachusetts Governor's Commission on Gay and Lesbian Youth distributed a survey to Lincoln-Sudbury High School students and found that 97.5% had heard their classmates use anti-gay slurs. At Concord-Carlisle school, 36% of students said that verbal insults based on sexual orientation occurred at the high school on a daily basis (Blumenfeld et al). Graffiti on college campus buildings include threats like "Rape a lesbian, kill a queer," "Kill a fag before he rapes your son," and the initials K.A.G.O.S. ("Kill All Gays On Sight") (Scanzoni and Mollenkott 2). Nor does anti-gay bias diminish in college: in one survey, half of college students said they considered homosexuality more deviant than murder and drug addiction (Evans and Wall 40).

Young gays and lesbians may come to believe these stereotypes, which can lead to profound feelings of self-loathing. Unlike other minorities who may be harassed for their racial or ethnic characteristics, LGBTs often can not rely on their biological families for support because their orientation is usually not shared. Indeed, they report a higher incidence of verbal and physical abuse from parents and siblings than other youth (Tenney 1611). As Lee Fearnside, a lesbian teen, testified at the Massachusetts Governor's Commission Hearings:

I couldn't and still can't think of a single positive image of lesbians in our main-stream society. I am forced to rely on negative stereotypes for role models. How could I identify with these images and maintain a shred of self-respect? This initi-ated a downward spiral of self-hatred and anger motivated by homophobia. I hated myself for being what seemed to be everyone's worst nightmare: a Homosexual. (Blumenfeld et al.)

Suicide attempts, drug and alcohol abuse or other high-risk behaviors may be part of a vulnerable LGBT teenager's downward spiral (Human Rights Watch 74). A Minnesota survey of teenagers revealed that 28.1% of gay or bisexual boys and 20.5% of lesbian or bisexual girls reported that they had attempted suicide, as compared to 4.2% of heterosexual boys and 14.5% of heterosexual girls (Remafedi et al. 57) As Mark Ayers testified:

I began to realize I was gay at about age 12 or 13 when I became aware of my attraction to the other boys in my class. I attended parochial school and was well-versed in the "sinful" nature of homosexuality. I was so scared and confused; I tried desperately to bury my feelings. . . . The biggest cost of my denial of my sexuality was a deep entanglement with addiction. It was a journey that got progressively worse and nearly killed me. (Blumenfeld et al.)

Since 1970, a number of studies of LGB youth have reported high attempted suicide rates ranging from 7% to 30% (Cabaj and Stein 832). Why such variation? Getting a truly random sampling of all American teens is difficult (Sell and Petrulio), as is ascertaining the sexuality of the deceased, since a desire to conceal orientation may have motivated the suicide (Bull 336). Transgendered individuals are also more likely to commit suicide, be mur-dered, fired, or assaulted than heterosexuals (Nangeroni). Significantly, Hershberger and D'Augelli studied LGB youths 15 to 21 years old and found that victimization alone was not directly related to the likelihood of suicide: rather, how well the individual coped with harassment depended upon family support and self-acceptance. Although gay bashing is intended to push LGBTs back into the closet, it only intensifies their need for visibility.

Perhaps because LGBTs are commonly thought to be obsessed with sex, heterosexual students sometimes use rape to terrorize and punish other students or staff for their sexual orientation. In a review of several studies, Comstock found that 4% to 18% of lesbian students were raped, and 4% to 14% of gay male students were raped (40). When interviewed, the rapist often justified his actions as a divine act of retribution for the sin of sodomy; moreover, he did not see his active participation in anal sex as equivalent to sodomy, as an act of perversion. His actions still conformed metaphorically to his anatomy, using his penis as his gender-role deemed proper—to penetrate. It was only the victim who was dishonored (Whitam and Mathy 3–4). Thus, the gay basher sends a message to all students, straight or gay: anyone who defies the narrowly defined gender roles is a potential target. Boys who do not fit the masculine stereotype are derided first as "sissies" and then as "faggots." Girls who are too assertive risk being labeled as "bitches" or "dykes." Androgynous individuals can be bashed simply for creating confusion. Actress Winona Ryder reported to *The Tennessean* newspaper on October 15, 1996:

I was beat up pretty badly on the third day of school [when I was 12-years-old] because three guys thought I was a gay boy. I got six stitches in my head, was slammed into a locker, got a fractured rib. I insisted I was a girl. I had really short hair and stuff, and so they beat me up. (Wockner 77)

Transgendered children are easier for bashers to identify because they *do* feel like they are the opposite sex, and may act out behaviors associated with the opposite sex. One boy, John, recalled constant physical attacks by other boys:

Until the time I was nine, they would chase me, call me names like "queer," throw rocks at me, or beat me up. Once I even had a brick thrown at me. They attacked me so often that I began to feel like I had a bull's-eye painted on my back. But then I got smart and started hanging out with the largest bullies I could find. Even though I still got beaten up, at least I had protectors of sorts. It's true I was their personal punching bag, but at least I knew only they would be hitting me and no one else would. (Brown and Rounsley 45)

Gay rights advocates are convinced that gay bashing has increased because demonizing statements by religious leaders put God's seal of approval upon hating gays. Falwell has described homosexuals as "brute beasts . . . part of a vile and satanic system [that] will one day be utterly annihilated" (Niebuhr). Pat Robertson warned his television audience that homosexuals "want to destroy all Christians" (Boston, *Dangerous,* 161). Both men justify their comments as consonant with biblical teachings and rhetoric, and that they are protected as free speech. Pro-gay critics argue that if the effect of inflammatory language on viewers results in violence, it is hate speech. Gregory Herek's interviews with gay bashers, for instance, suggest that they tend to think of gays as a proxy for all that is evil in the world; hating LGBTs becomes a litmus test for being a moral person, and so even rape can be conceived as a moral act (Herek and Berrill 154). As one victim, a university employee, Kathleen Sarris, remembers:

I was leaving my office and I turned to lock the door, I felt the barrel of a gun in the back of my head. He pushed me back with his fists, his gun, and his belt. I was sexually molested and, ultimately, I was raped. Throughout the assault, he talked about how he was acting for God: that what he was doing to me was God's revenge on me because I was a "queer" and getting rid of me would save children and put an end to the [gay] movement in Indiana. (202)

A recent study has found that in 39% of the cases of verbal harassment of gay people, explicit references were made to God, religion, or the Bible (Comstock 142). During the campaign for the anti-gay Amendment Two in Colorado in 1992, the public was inundated with inflammatory and false accusations from Paul Cameron's Family Research Institute claiming that half of all child molestations were committed by gay men; after Amendment Two's successful passage, reports of gay bashing increased by 275% (Gallagher, "Colorado," 302).

But are Falwell and Robertson responsible for what others do? Anti-gay rights activists generally deny there is any connection between publically condemning LGBTs on moral grounds and the violence against them, and, indeed, most Christians deplore both name-calling and violence. Just as LGBTs feel oppressed by slurs like "faggot" or "dyke," anti-gay Christians feel unjustly disparaged by words like "bigot" and "homophobic" (Smith and Windes 116–117). But the two sides disagree sharply about how to tone down the rhetoric. Many heterosexuals feel imposed upon by "in your face" gay activists, and some even claim that violence would decline if LGBTs went back into the closet:

Homosexuals are . . . committed to destroying the traditional Christian values . . . on which this nation is founded. . . . If these deviates chose to keep their sins to themselves . . . perhaps it could be tolerated. But as it is, they are seeking rights that are reserved for normal citizens . . . such as marriage and adoption. These people are unfit to live, let alone to raise children. (Herek and Berrill 108)

Gay activists consider invisibility not only a denial of oneself as a person but a denial of one's right to participate actively in democracy. Anti-gay groups contend that visible homosexuals promote sin, crime, sickness, recruitment, and social disorder; gay groups argue that society imposes a double standard, allowing heterosexuals to exhibit their sexuality much more freely in public than homosexuals can. Campaigning against a Florida anti-discrimination ordinance, Anita Bryant reasoned:

If this ordinance is allowed to become law, you will, in fact, be infringing on my rights and discriminating against me as a citizen and a mother to teach my children and set examples and to point to others as examples of God's moral code as stated in the Holy Scriptures. (Smith and Windes 85)

A mother of a gay son expressed the pro-gay attitude:

Straight people get to run around and be visible, sexually, all over the place and if gay people are visible in that way, they're accused of flaunting. About a month after Brian came out to me, I was in this coffee house and there was this young heterosexual couple in front of me holding hands, arms around each other, heads on shoulders, nuzzling. And I was thinking, if this was my gay kid with his boyfriend, he would get harassed, stoned, maybe arrested. This is offensive to me—not what they were doing, but the double standard. It's offensive to me that some damned straight people say, "Why do those queers have to flaunt it?" (Bass and Kaufman 80)

Is visibility a privilege or a right? How much control over citizens should government exert in order to provide mothers with examples of Christian virtue for their children's instruction, or for shaping the morals of the people by repressing the "other" if that nemesis is already inside them, the thought that must be killed by killing its living embodiment? How much visibility does any group need to pursue happiness, to represent itself and its interests in the political arena? In a 1994 survey, the Human Rights Campaign found that support for equal rights for LGBTs increased from 65% to 87% when the respondent knew someone who was gay (Mills). Button et al. report that anti-discrimination laws tend to make LGBTs feel safer, especially in their jobs, more valued as members of society, and where states adopt such laws, incidents of police harassment, arrests, and violence decrease. Anti-discrimination laws also encourage LGBTs to become more politically active and less afraid to report crimes committed against them (119–124). Visibility wins political support, but for that reason both pro-gay and anti-gay groups fear the increased visibility of their opponents. Is it even possible for government to determine and protect equal access to public influence when each side finds the other side's influence threatening and unfair?

12

Pluralism versus Dogma: Public Spaces and Private Beliefs

What do religious conservatives really want? They want a place at the table in the conversation we call democracy. Their commitment to pluralism includes a place for faith among the many other competing interests in society. For too long, we have left politics to the special interests. It is time for the values of middle America to have their place at the table.
—*Ralph Reed*

In his 1994 book, *Politically Incorrect,* Ralph Reed renounced demonizing tactics and called for more civil discussions with his opponents. Reed's turnabout was unexpected because as recently as 1991 his rhetoric had been ominous:

"I want to be invisible," he bragged. "I do guerrilla warfare. I paint my face and travel at night. You don't know it's over until you're in a body bag." (Gallagher and Bull 258)

Gay activists are uncertain how to respond. Is he disarming the opposition by appearing to be more centrist, or will he act as a moderating force on more radical elements within the Christian Coalition who reject pluralism? The Interfaith Alliance issued a challenge to Reed to match his words with actions. The Reverend Dr. Albert Pennybacker, Chairman of TIA, said:

As hard as he may try, Ralph Reed can't have it both ways. If he is truly intent on turning towards tolerance and civility, we applaud him. But his first step should not be to write a book about the tactics of unnamed religious conservatives. He needs to examine his own tactics; specifically to distance himself from the well documented extreme language of his very own boss, Pat Robertson. Anything less leaves his writings suspect. ("Ralph Reed")

Reed may very well be serious about his change of heart, and, as he asserts, some conservative Christian groups are adopting a more "pragmatic politics" approach to appeal to moderate audiences (Schmidt 170–171), but he is also a casualty of the gay rights war. Years of disinformation and vilification has left LGBTs skeptical of good will in an orthodox Christian.

Pluralism itself is a tricky goal, because it is interpreted in two very different ways in the gay rights debate: some liberals, libertarians and Goldwater (secular) conservatives tend to define it as a "live and let live" tolerance, decriminalizing (but not necessarily promoting) sexual behavior between consenting adults in the privacy of the bedroom; theocratic and cultural conservatives tend to see pluralism as amorality, an abandonment of government's obligation to protect social order by encouraging virtue and discouraging vice (Ralph Smith 103; J. D. Hunter 46; Smith and Windes 31). Many evangelical and mainline Christians live according to their own dogma, but they prefer a pluralistic government that protects the conflicting beliefs of various religions, and they tend to make careful distinctions between sin and crime (homosexuality may be a "sin," but need the state make it a crime?) (Toulouse 31–32). To some orthodox Christians such neutrality is unacceptable because there can be only one Truth, as Randall Terry claims:

I want you to just let a wave of intolerance wash over you. I want you to let a wave of hatred wash over you. Yes, hate is good. . . . Our goal is a Christian nation. We have a Biblical duty, we are called by God, to conquer this country. We don't want equal time. We don't want pluralism. ("Quotes")

The Judeo-Christian God has often been an activist God, and if the practice of an orthodox faith requires active resistance against evil, then pro-gay laws are necessarily anti-religious laws.

The issue of "special rights" versus "equal rights" illustrates these conflicting views of pluralism. LGBTs frame the issue of legal protection against discrimination as seeking the security that heterosexuals already enjoy: the right to get and keep a job based on merit, to rent an apartment, stay in a hotel, be served food in a restaurant, keep their children. As Justice Kennedy noted, from a strictly secular view, these are ordinary rights, not special (O'Rourke and Dellinger 134). If Oregon's Measure 9 had passed, citizens who are gay (or even those just *perceived* to be gay—the proposition offered no rationale for how to determine a person's sexual orientation) could be fired or evicted; public libraries, television programs, and radio stations would have been required to remove books or censor programs that portrayed or mentioned homosexuality; doctors, lawyers, and other professionals could have their state licenses revoked (White 253–254). By discouraging individuals from revealing their orientation, the law would erode the general right to participate publically and politically in the life of one's community. And since invisibility is not required of other minority groups, does it not constitute an inequality for LGBTs?

The Christian Coalition defends its opposition to anti-discrimination laws by arguing that protecting LGBTs' freedom to live openly by their own beliefs infringes upon Christians from living openly by theirs. As Attorney Richard F. Duncan reasons:

When a legislature acts to protect homosexual behavior under anti-discrimination laws, it elevates homosexual practices to the status of protected activities while at the same time branding many mainstream religious institutions and individuals as outlaws engaged in antisocial and immoral behavior. ("Who" 397–398)

Reed cites an illustrative case in Massachusetts, in which state law forbade two Roman Catholic brothers who declined to rent an apartment to an unmarried couple, even though fornication was still illegal in that state (36). Ironically, what strikes Reed as unfair is that anti-discrimination laws have put Christians in the same legal contradiction that sodomy laws put LGBTs: they can escape prosecution only if they do not act on or express their private beliefs or feelings. Both closets are demoralizing, but neither side feels confident that there is enough room outside the closet for both groups. Samuel Marcosson (University of Missouri-Kansas City School of Law) responds to Duncan simply by turning the situation around:

It is ironic that Professor Duncan defends religiously-motivated discriminators on the ground that they should not be held to be "engaged in antisocial and immoral behavior," when the whole basis for their discrimination is the desire to brand *others* as being "engaged in antisocial and immoral behavior." Similarly, there is rich irony in his statement that government should not force "religiously-motivated individuals . . . merely . . . trying to live out their faith" to refrain from discriminating against gay men and lesbians because "it is illegitimate for a political majority 'to use the power of government to express its moral values by stigmatizing another group.'" (146n.23)

The rights question is framed as an either/or binary: one side *must* reap the lion's share of rights at the expense of the other. Reed objects to material loss for the sake of his own beliefs, but so do LGBTs. Anti-discrimination laws and sodomy laws both impose values. States are put in the paradoxical position of protecting each group's core beliefs while simultaneously outlawing acting on those beliefs.

To protect Christians against legal action for acting out their beliefs, the Christian Coalition backed the 1996 Religious Liberty Protection Act

(RLPA), which the House of Representatives approved by a vote of 306 to 118. RLPA would have raised the legal test for challenges to religiously-based discrimination from "rational" to "compelling," making it harder for LGBTs to win court cases. The bill was intended to counter a 1990 Supreme Court ruling that favored the government's right to deny a Native American group's right to use the otherwise illegal drug peyote in its religious rituals. The bill gained strong support from liberal, conservative, and centrist religious groups, who do not use peyote, but, as *Planet Out* reporter, Richard Kinz, observed, the bill risked unpredictable repercussions far beyond the Native Americans:

[as] various religious groups testified in committee hearings, this has left religious practice at the mercy of zoning laws, school dress codes, prison regulations against alcohol, requirements for autopsies and myriad other burdens of bureaucracy, not to mention limitations on speech and denial of accreditation to a Catholic hospital that would not teach medical students abortion procedures.

Gay rights groups also saw a sinister purpose behind it. Reports circulated that an attorney for the Pat Robertson-founded American Center for Law and Justice named Jay Sekulow

brags openly that this law would enable Christians to rid the workplace and our schools from "the gay agenda"; that "employers would not be able to violate [Christians'] firmly held religious beliefs . . . that a Christian who was offended by the presence of a GLBT or perceived GLBT co-worker would be able to have that person fired."

Protecting religion through government intervention turned out to be more complicated than legislators imagined. An earlier version of RLPA, the 1993 Religious Freedom Restoration Act, was struck down by conservative justices on the U.S. Supreme Court for exceeding Congress' authority at the expense of rights at the state and city level—a likely fate for RLPA as well (Kinz).

So which governmental role would better serve a fairer pluralism, an intrusive government that prohibits discrimination through the force of law (and entangle itself in the conflicting claims of each group), or a neutral government that provides no exempt or protected status for any group? As Steven Seidman reasons, government intervention risks a micro-management style that may be as unwieldy as it is unjust:

To the extent that discriminatory practices impede an individual from exercising his or her civil rights, the state can legitimately act to prevent such practices. However, anti-discriminatory legislation is legitimate only if it applies equally to all individuals. To enact anti-discriminatory policies that single out particular social groups for protection would be a breach in the liberal social contract. It would violate the principle of the equal moral worth and political rights of all citizens. Indeed, a state that singles out individuals for the ways they are different risks creating a nation composed of hierarchically ranked groups. (238)

But, at the same time, government neutrality may be equally difficult to achieve, as Seidman continues:

The decision to secularize the educational curriculum in the US has been justified principally on the grounds that this avoids the alignment of the state with any specific religious denomination. However, government neutrality with regard to religion can, from a different perspective, be interpreted as displacing religion from public education. In other words, the state is not neutral in educational policy because it is aligned with a culture of secularity. . . . From the standpoint of an American for whom Christianity is primary in his or her self-identity, a state-enforced secular educational curriculum would be oppressive since it devalues that person's core beliefs and excludes or marginalizes the culture that gives shape and purpose to his or her life. . . . If the impartiality of the public sphere is impossible, if, for example, decisions about what knowledges should be taught, indeed what counts as knowledge and what or whose standards should guide such decisions . . . then such decisions about the structure of public life inevitably privilege some individuals and communities and subordinate others. (243–44)

This is a classic catch-22 situation from which there is no clear escape. Libertarians and Goldwater conservatives argue that a plethora of regulations, ballot initiatives, politically expedient legislation, and court decisions eventually erode freedom. If the state got out of the business of legislating values (sodomy laws, state-sanctioned marriages, anti-discrimination statutes, secular liberal agendas, religious conservative agendas), it could avoid the "special rights" argument. LGBTs would be free to voice their views, orientations, and commitments without fear of imprisonment or prosecution (Massaro 70–72, 80), and gay marriages would be left entirely up to churches, not state agencies or popular opinion. The libertarian's answer to democracy's ills may simply be more democracy. But what makes this issue so tricky is that private discrimination can be just as effective at marginalizing a despised group as institutionalized disenfranchisement. Although Reed frames his example as merely two Roman Catholics who want to live according to their religious beliefs by refusing to service two other people with different beliefs, what would be the consequences of millions of citizens withholding public accommodation from a particular group they deem sinners? Some products, services, and accommodations are not luxury items but necessary needs: if an unmarried cohabiting couple—straight or gay—can not find housing, a restaurant, a supermarket, or a doctor to serve them, they would essentially be forced to adopt a morality alien to their beliefs. A libertarian government might simply unleash a flood of discriminatory practices, resulting in a segregation policy of "straights only." Reed argues that antidiscrimination laws force Christians to do business with sinners, effectively erasing the boundary between private belief and public acts that protects their "family values culture." Landlords, restaurateurs, employers, hotel managers, whoever provides services or products to the public, have traditionally argued that they should be able to deny any service or product to anyone for whatever reason. Such a view was articulated by Justice Harlan in the 1963 Supreme Court case, *Peterson v. Greenville:*

Freedom of the individual to choose his associates or neighbors, to use and dispose of his property as he sees fit, to be irrational, arbitrary, capricious, even unjust in his personal relations are things all entitled to a large measure of protection from governmental interference. This liberty would be overridden, in the name of equality, if the strictures of the Amendment were applied to governmental and private action without distinction. (373 U.S. 250 [1963])

Greenville, however, was not about excluding LGBTs from legal protections, but barring African American diners from a segregated restaurant. In the 1960s, civil-rights legislation to protect blacks was also denounced as granting a "special right" because it forced whites to act against their belief that integration was socially and morally harmful (Keen and Goldberg 10). Giving blacks equal access to public accommodations owned by whites endangered "white culture." But since white culture included entire states in its boundaries, blacks paid a high price to protect it from contact with non-whites, and many moved to other states to find equal access. Since anti-gay groups see gay rights as a nationwide danger to social order, where will LGBTs go to seek asylum?

The theocratic argument that civil pluralism is already invasive, a transgression by the State upon religious belief, is as thorny as it is important. Easy in the abstract, pluralism is difficult to turn into practice. The First Amendment states: "Congress shall make no law respecting an establishment of religion or prohibiting the free exercise thereof." But if the "free exercise" of Christianity is to save others and prevent sin, then pro-LGBT laws legalize sin, invalidating the separation of Church and State they are supposed to protect. Liberal constitutional lawyers argue that Thomas Jefferson established the doctrine of the separation of Church and State not only to prevent government from unfairly favoring one religion over others but also to prevent a particular religion from imposing its unquestioned beliefs on everyone else *through* their government by majority rule. But Christian conservatives interpret the First Amendment to mean that the Founding Fathers intended to forbid *only* the official establishment of a state religion, like the British Anglican Church, not to encourage the secularization of laws. For Pat Robertson, laws that depart from biblical values lack divine authority and wisdom: "Government was instituted by God to bring His laws to people and to carry out His will and purposes" (*Answers* 185). Both pro-gay and anti-gay groups represent the opposition as totalitarian, supporting the intrusion of the state into private life (Smith and Windes 122).

The Constitution does give government the right to limit social actions for the public good, at least on secular grounds—equality, justice, happiness, security, and public order, among others—but it is not clear to what extent religious belief should determine what is "good" or what constitutes "justice." American laws are based on varied amalgams of religious values and secular values derived from experience, common sense, philosophy, or practicality. But how do we judge the proportional influence that each of these values should exert on governmental policy? Walter Barnett argues that a formula for judgement lies in the First Amendment which

imposes neutrality on the state where religion is concerned, so that government may not follow a policy of preferring one religion over another or of aiding all religions at the expense of irreligion. One application of this principle is that the state may not impose a rule of conduct on its citizens for basically religious objectives. If such a law can be shown to have a religious origin, it is immediately suspect and a burden of justification rests upon the state to show that its objective is really secular. (75)

Sodomy laws, Barnett concludes, are clearly religious in origin and intent. Their history in European and American law has always been framed in theological arguments. When Pope Gregory IX created the Inquisition in 1233, heretics and homosexuals simultaneously were the target. One of these heretical groups was the Albigensians, who originated in Bulgaria under the leadership of an early 10th century priest named Bogomil. Bogomil's followers believed that life was fundamentally evil and so they condemned any sexual acts which would result in procreation. Believers were free to practice any form of sexual activity as long as conception was prevented. The English word for sodomy, "buggery," is a corruption of the word "Bulgarian." England's Buggery Act of 1533 was originally intended to prosecute religious heretics, but it gradually lost its religious aim and became solely a law against male-male sex (Greenberg 269, 323). American statutes are based on English law, describing sodomy as "the abominable and detestable crime against nature" (81). But the "moral order" of nature is a theological construct, as Barnett argues:

so much of what we once supposed to be [natural] instinct in man has turned out to be the result of cultural conditioning. Here again religion is likely to be a major causative factor: The liberal, emancipated citizen of modern India may no longer be conscious of the Hindu religion as a real influence on his life, but he may still feel an "instinctive" revulsion for eating beef. (104)

The physical revulsion some heterosexuals feel for homosexuals may or may not be shared by God, and it is certainly not shared by all heterosexuals, so can it be a legal basis for civil penalties? The fact that revulsion is experienced as an intrinsic part of being does not guarantee it is not a conditioned, cultural response. Religions and individuals are, of course, free to define what they feel are their "natures," but if LGBTs do not share the heterosexual or Christian perspective of what is in accord with or against their being, why should they be forced to act as if it is? On the other hand, how broadly can individual citizens justify their actions if only they can define their being? At what point does freedom become license?

Liberal constitutional scholars reject the argument that America is necessarily a Christian nation or that our laws are essentially Christian by pointing out that the Constitution does not mention God, Jesus Christ or Christianity. Although a divine rationale for having inalienable rights appears in the first line, the only specific reference to religion occurs in Article VI, where the founders provided that there could be no religious test for public office. But did the framers of the Constitution intend to imply that all civil rights should accord with God's will? Like Boswell, who compared ancient texts with the Bible to determine Scriptural meaning, legal historians try to reconstruct the original intentions behind the Constitution and Bill of Rights by exploring contemporaneous material. Robert Boston cites colonial documents that contain even stronger statements about the desirability of a clear separation of Church and State. In an 1802 letter to a Connecticut Baptist Association, then-President Thomas Jefferson declared that the First Amendment had erected a "wall of separation between church and state"; James Madison, considered to be the Father of the Constitution and author of the First Amendment, said in an 1819 letter, "[T]he number, the industry and the morality of the priesthood, and the devotion of the people have been manifestly increased by the total separation of the church and state"; Madison also wrote, "Strongly guarded . . . is the separation between religion and government in the Constitution of the United States." Finally, Boston argues, an early draft of the First Amendment had read in part, "The civil rights of none shall be abridged on account of religious belief, nor shall any national religion be established," but this draft was rejected as too weak ("Bad History"). Stanford University historian Jack N. Rakove's research shows that neither Jefferson nor Madison denied that the State had an interest in regulating some aspects of behavior on behalf of religiosity, but their primary concern was to prevent the kind of religious war that had devastated England during the seventeenth century:

For at the heart of their support for disestablishment and free exercise lay the radical conviction that nearly the entire sphere of religious practice could be safely deregulated, placed beyond the cognizance of the state, and thus defused as both a source of political strife and a danger to individual rights. . . . The free exercise of religion was the most "liberal" of all the rights Americans could claim, the one right that placed the greatest trust in the capacity of private choice, and the one least dependent on positive law. . . . And this meant that the problem of rights was no longer to protect the people as a collective whole *from* government but to defend minorities and individuals against popular majorities acting *through* government. (312–313)

Gay rights has become the twentieth century's religious war, pitting church against church, each inviting the state to step in to keep the peace. Is it too late to return to the deregulation the Founding Fathers preferred? Have sodomy laws, gay bashing, secularism and marketplace exclusions made it impossible for the State to be uninvolved? If incompatible conceptualizations have become immutable dogma, must state regulations multiply to keep citizens from harming each other?

Or can religious strife be creative? Is progress, in fact, being made? W. Kenneth Williams and William E. Estep argue that the Founding Fathers specifically separated Church and State because they believed that out of free dissent within religious communities would come additional revelations to enhance, correct, or replace traditional understanding of God's plan for the world. Rather than believe that God had revealed all truth at once to the ancient Hebrews and apostles, to be observed as the final authority for all generations, the framers of the Constitution hypothesized that the future might be open to further divine revelation that would reinvigorate spirituality:

This made possible a degree of humility that tempered the exclusivism that some faiths might otherwise hold as absolute over others. In their passion for freedom, and with their notion of divine revelation yet to come, the builders of the foundation of America proposed and fought for a society in which religion would stand on its own merits, free of state sponsorship or control. God's ultimate reality supersedes any earthly authority. So it is that in government's eyes, the religious convictions of the smallest sect would be on equal footing with those embraced by the greatest majority. With tolerance for all and preference for none, the religions of all people could be practiced freely. . . . In political society the corollary is freedom of conscience. To abridge the first denies the intention of God. To abridge the second is to replace liberty with tyranny. (W. Kenneth Williams)

The Constitution guarantees that each citizen is free to define his or her own understanding of the mystery and meaning of human life—whether it is called a religion or a secular philosophy (Nava and Dawidoff 10–11, 14). Indeed, David Richards argues that sexual identity should be thought of as *a religion* and given equal protection status on that basis: since the Constitution protects the individual's right "to explore, define, express, and revise the identifications central to free moral personality," Richards reasons that the state cannot impose sanctions on LGBTs' right to define themselves and the meaning of their lives even if these meanings are viewed as heretical by orthodox churches (514).

Deciding between religious views may be impossible anyway. Ralph Reed seeks a compromise position between withdrawal and warfare that recognizes the different duties of believer and citizen. But Reed underestimates just how spiritually diverse Americans are. "Religious conservatives," Reed proposes,

do not want a "Christian" nation, a "Jewish' nation, or a "Moslem" nation. They want a nation of strong families and basic goodness, that respects the rights of all individuals to express their faith and which does not prohibit faith to inform the laws that govern society. (132)

Reed mentions only three religions to denote diversity, but, in fact, there are approximately 1,200 different religious sects in the United States, including Confucianism, Judaism, Taoism, Buddhism, Hare Krishna, Shintoism, Native-American spiritualists, and the sacred teachings of mystics and preachers of hundreds of other religions or sects—Korean, Laotian, Vietnamese, Thai, African, Hawaiian, Samoan. Although surveys suggest that 93% of Americans believe in God or a universal spirit, only 34% think that the Bible is God's literal word (Herman 193). Nearly every major city in America has seen increasing numbers of non-Christian places of worship being built. There are now 300 Buddhist temples in Los Angeles alone, 70 Moslem mosques in Chicago, 62 Islamic, Buddhist, or Hindu centers in Seattle, and in Houston another 50. Six million Americans believe in Islam; there are now more Moslems in the U.S. than Episcopalians or Presbyterians, and, if the numbers continue to increase, in a few years there will be more Moslems in America than there will be Jews. America today is facing an unprecedented polyglot of belief systems each deserving to be heard.

Which gods will sit at America's dinner table to inform government policy? Doubtless, consensus between religions can be achieved on some issues through mutual respect, but the most vocal anti-gay rights leaders also tend to be the least tolerant of competing religions. In 1980 the Reverend Bailey Smith, then president of the 13-million-strong Southern Baptist Convention, claimed publicly that God responds to the prayers of Christians, but "God Almighty does not hear the prayer of a Jew, for how in the world can God hear the prayer of a man who says that Jesus Christ is not the true Messiah?" Many Christians were shocked at Smith's remarks, but 8 out of 10 Baptist ministers interviewed in Macon, Georgia, admitted that they agreed with him (Cohen 8–9). Pat Robertson has argued that the religious beliefs of the Mormons and the Jehovah's Witnesses can be ignored because they don't accord with the Bible, and claims that "demons lurk behind the Hindu and other oriental religions" (*Answers* 136–137, 141–142). On his televised show, "The 700 Club," Robertson confessed on January 14, 1991:

You say you're supposed to be nice to the Episcopalians and the Presbyterians and the Methodists and this, that, and the other thing. Nonsense! I don't have to be nice to the spirit of the Antichrist. I can love the people who hold false opinions, but I don't have to be nice to them. (Boston, *Dangerous*, 149)

Pat Robertson embraces constitutional protections but only for those whose thinking is uncorrupted by heresy:

The Constitution of the United States, for instance, is a marvelous document for self-government by Christian people. But the minute you turn the document into the hands of non-Christian and atheistic people they can use it to destroy the very foundation of our society. ("Religious Political")

There are also deep divisions within the Christian Coalition that could make a substantial governmental role unpredictably divisive. Bob Jones, a leading fundamentalist and founder of the Bob Jones University, has condemned Jerry Falwell as "the most dangerous man in America" because he tries to "rally Jews, Catholics, Protestants, and nothings" for conservative causes (Liebman and Wuthnow 42). In textbooks used at the Bob Jones University, Unitarianism is portrayed as "uniquely evil"; Mormonism is described as a "false cult"; the Quakers are "unbiblical," living in "spiritual darkness"; Anglicans and Episcopalians are repeatedly denounced as "effete, corrupt" and spiritually "dead"; Islam and Hinduism are treated with contempt; and Asian religions (Confucianism, Buddhism, Taoism, and Shintoism) are deemed "worthless." Fundamentalist textbook writers consider the Catholic Church as a "wholly corrupt institution" dedicated to the destruction of biblical Protestantism. Virtually the entire spectrum of faith is seen as an enemy, not as fellow searchers after truth or a better world but as heretics doomed to eternal punishment (Menendez). For evangelical Christian William D. Rodgers, "The law is plain: 'Thou shalt have no other gods before me' (Exodus 20:3)" (42). In a democracy, a theocratic religion has every right to hold such views. But how could these antagonistic views be written into the law of the land so that each set of religious values is protected *and* represented?

These issues of group identity and majoritarian power were put to the test in 1992 when Colorado voters approved Amendment Two. Sponsored by Colorado for Family Values, Traditional Values Coalition, Focus on the Family, and Beverly LaHaye's Concerned Women for America, Amendment Two nullified local city ordinances that banned discrimination against men and woman who were—or who were thought to be—gay, lesbian, or bisexual. The measure would also have prohibited the future passage of antidiscrimination laws and prevented government agencies from considering any claim of discrimination for all time. CFV promoted the amendment by claiming that LGBTs would otherwise enjoy "special rights" that heterosexuals would not, and that such power imperiled America:

Their inspiration, as the *Denver Post* put it, was their feeling that "America has deteriorated because it has turned away from literal interpretations of the Bible, and fundamentalist church teachings must play a bigger role in government." (Keen and Goldberg 7)

In response, groups representing minorities, such as the Colorado Hispanic League, the Anti-Defamation League of B'nai B'rith, Colorado Black Women for Political Action, and the National Organization for Women, fearful that their civil rights might be targeted next, declared their opposition to Amendment Two. It passed with 53.4% of the vote (O'Rourke and Dellinger 133–135).

Opponents appealed all the way to the U.S. Supreme Court where it was declared unconstitutional on May 20, 1996 in a 6-to-3 ruling. Known as *Romer v. Evans*, it was a stunning defeat, partly because conservative justices joined liberal, partly because of the language used:

> . . . the amendment imposes a special disability on [gay] persons alone. Homosexuals are forbidden the safeguards that others enjoy or may seek without constraint. . . . We find nothing special in the protections Amendment Two withholds. These are protections taken for granted by most people either because they already have them or do not need them; these are protections against exclusion from an almost limitless number of transactions and endeavors that constitute ordinary civil life in a free society. . . . We must conclude that Amendment 2 classifies homosexuals not to further a proper legislative end but to make them unequal to everyone else. This Colorado cannot do. A State cannot so deem a class of persons a stranger to its laws.

Justice Kennedy, who wrote the majority opinion, noted that Amendment Two raised "the inevitable inference that the disadvantage imposed is born of animosity toward the class of persons affected" (O'Rourke and Dellinger 137–138). The initiative was motivated by prejudice, not justice.

The ruling was criticized by Justice Antonin Scalia, who argued that Amendment Two did no more than enforce the "moral and social disapprobation of homosexuality" which traditionally has been a part of American legal history (O'Rourke and Dellinger 138) and which is still legal in the sodomy laws approved by *Bowers v. Hardwick* eight years before:

> If it is rational to criminalize the conduct, surely it is rational to deny special favor and protection to those with a self-avowed tendency or desire to engage in the conduct. (Fajer)

Indeed, *Evans* does not invalidate the criminal sanctions that *Bowers* allows because it does not define any fundamental right pertaining to homosexuality per se. *Evans* does not directly address the question of whether there is a fundamental right to participate in the political process: it simply rules that Amendment Two failed to provide a reasonable basis for the exclusion of gays and lesbians (Herman 157). Once again, the Supreme Court cautiously avoided the central issue of how gay rights relate to civil rights. Since only formal legal proceedings can justify denying civil freedom, perhaps the Court was thinking in terms of a fundamental right. Claude Millman has pointed out that *Evans* is in accord with *Powell v. Texas* (392 U.S. 514 [1968]), which found a distinction between a status (in this case, a man who was a chronic alcoholic) and an act (being drunk in public). Powell could not be prosecuted for his condition, it was reasoned, but he could be arrested for public drunkenness (Millman 277). This suggests that Scalia was right to point out the discrepancy between the Court's judgement and sodomy laws, but wrong to argue that the freedom to participate in the political life of the country can be denied without a trial, evidence, or arrest. But can *Evans* or *Powell* serve as a rationale for invalidating sodomy laws? Gay rights scholars are divided on the issue: some argue that the distinction between being homosexual and performing same-sex acts is "false, arbitrary, and theoretically untenable" because it desexualizes sexual diversity. Others argue that arrest should be viewed as a form of political exclusion (Herman 160).

In spite of granting LGBTs a "status," *Romer v. Evans* does not define LGBTs as a "suspect class," as racial or ethnic groups are, which would have been necessary if the Court intended to overturn *Bowers v. Hardwick*. State laws can be declared unconstitutional if they fulfill two criteria: they target members of a traditionally recognized suspect class, or they infringe on a fundamental constitutional right enjoyed by everyone. *Bowers v. Hardwick* has already ruled that homosexual behavior itself is not a constitutional right, and federal circuit courts have consistently decided that homosexuals do not constitute a suspect or protected class under the Equal Protection Clause. As Paul J. Weithman, Assistant Professor of Philosophy at Notre Dame, reports, for a group of citizens to be considered a suspect class, it must resemble race to some (as yet unspecified) degree: it must exhibit a trait that is immutable and visible which invites discrimination; it must have suffered under a history of pervasive discrimination on the basis of stereotyped characteristics not truly indicative of the abilities of its members; it must suffer such political powerlessness that it requires judicial protection from a persecuting majority ("A Propos" 98–100). Although LGBTs have historically been discriminated against and suffered from unjust stereotypes, it is not clear if sexual orientation is an immutable trait, nor is it a visible trait, like gender or the color of skin. Amendment Two fell, not because of a new understanding of the nature of homosexuality but because it denied the fundamental right to participate fully in the political system—a right any citizen possesses (Duncan and Young 107). In this way the Supreme Court avoided most of the central issues in the gay rights debate. What does it *mean* to be gay? What value does it have for the individual or society? Equal protection was tended solely on the basis of citizenship, not on a new judicial understanding of sexual orientation.

That work is still left to be done, and it will involve much more than discovering a "gay" gene. Attorney Nan D. Hunter maintains that even if homosexuality is proven to be immutable, biological and innate, states could still argue that regulating their sexual lives served the public interest (552). Toni M. Massaro, Professor of Law at the University of Arizona, believes this argument can be countered by forcing states to explain exactly why sodomy laws are required:

The lesson of *Evans* is that, when advancing arguments for gay rights, advocates should avoid thick doctrinal arguments that alter existing legal categories, extend the upper echelon tiers of review, or construct gay rights as such. Rather, they should emphasize thin doctrinal statements that merely say that homosexuality cannot and should not be a basis for official discrimination. Such a nondiscrimination policy involves only minimal modification of existing legal doctrine. Specifically, litigants should focus attention on the ways in which such discrimination violates minimal—"thin"—principles of neutrality, conventionally understood, and avoid arguments that require the courts to define, or appear to endorse, homosexual or bisexual identities. In short, litigants should address the following question: "What is wrong with homosexuality?", not "What is homosexuality?" (47)

As I hope this book has demonstrated, both questions are extremely complex and presently unanswerable, at least in scientific or evidentiary terms. A great deal of controversy surrounds even the definitions used in the debate—what do the words "gay," "lesbian," "bisexual," "sexual orientation," "sexual identity," "transgenderism," or "gender" mean when theology, science, and politics are constantly redrawing the center and the boundaries of these terms? Laws must have reasons behind them, must be able to pass a "rationality review," but the rational parameters of the LGBT question are continuously evolving and expanding. Attorneys Lisa Keen and Suzanne B. Goldberg ask a difficult question: "how can a civil rights law related to sexual orientation be administered fairly" if both science and the gay community disagree about what it means to be gay or lesbian or straight (144)? Stanford University Law School Professor Janet Halley is more optimistic when she argues that

until recently, gay rights advocates have fairly consistently argued that homosexual orientation is so unitary, fundamental, irresistible, and inalterable that homosexuals meet a supposed requirement of suspect classifications, that of immutability. [But] after *Hardwick,* the argument for heightened scrutiny under the equal protection clause is now undermined, not bolstered, by claims that homosexuality is a fixed and immutable attribute of a rigidly demarcated class. . . . Both sides are empirically right: homosexuality is sometimes mutable and sometimes not. . . . Clearly, it is time for gay advocates to rethink that argument—but even if it were not, the sheer facts demand that the argument be abandoned. . . . The patterns that emerge from recent empirical and theoretical work on the subject compel the conclusion that homosexual identity . . . is constituted in precisely the political process which, under the equal protection clause, the courts are pledged to protect. Far from closing constitutional debate on this issue, *Hardwick* opened it. ("Politics" 920–922)

Halley insists that proving the immutability of sexual orientation as an innate, unchangeable characteristic is not required by equal protection precedents: "a proper reading of these precedents demonstrates that the equal protection clause vigilantly protects not monolithic groups but rather the dialogue that generates group identity" (923). A homosexual identity can be non-biologically based, culturally constructed, a personal decision, a provisional state, a political act, and still be protected because the first amendment guarantees free speech and unfettered participation in public life. As the product of the individual's participation in social discourse, the "gay self," unique to modern culture, accrues the rights of participation (968).

The Constitution gives no specific formula for recognizing group identities or for reconciling manifestly diverging beliefs (Barnett 95). The Founding Fathers provided protections against the evils they knew and left adjustments to future generations. The Ninth Amendment alluded to this when it asserted: "The enumeration in this Constitution of certain rights shall not be construed to deny or disparage others retained by the people," which, Jack N. Rakove argues, "suggests that fundamental rights not mentioned in the Constitution can secure [eventually] constitutional recognition" (289). During ratification of the Bill of Rights, the delegates were deeply concerned that future jurists might mistakenly assume that the only legitimate rights Americans could claim were the ones listed. As Benjamin Rush told the convention: "Our rights are not yet all known."

Whether you are liberal or conservative, heterosexual or gay, lesbian, bisexual or transgendered/transsexual, the gay-rights debate asks you to think about the very nature of democracy. If God is the source of our inalienable rights, how should these rights be understood and circumscribed by divergent religious beliefs, and can we do so without discriminating against those who do not believe? Can science provide compelling evidence for discussions of religious and social values? Should government legislate these values? All these questions dovetail: the debate about gay rights is part of a much larger debate about how we understand the world and ourselves. St. Paul warns Orthodox Christians against straying from the path of One Truth: "Be not carried about with divers and strange doctrines" (KJV Hebrews 13:9). Chaos is scary, but so is a repressive order. A certain amount of order is the precondition of freedom, but freedom is the goal of a responsible order. There is no easy answer to this paradox. As James Davison Hunter concludes in his survey of the contemporary American culture wars:

Pluralism is not the bland arithmetic mean of what everyone in a society believes, nor tolerance the obligation to make one's deepest beliefs tolerable to others. We are dealing with the sacred after all. By its very nature, the principles that derive from it are non-negotiable. A principled pluralism and a principled toleration is what common life in contemporary America should all be about. But this is only possible if all contenders, however much they disagree with each other on principle, do not kill each other over these differences, do not desecrate what the other holds sublime, and do not eschew principled discourse with the other. (325)

Hunter's phrasing reveals just how difficult it will be to forge a consensus. To become "principled" one must first understand. But the gay rights debate has not yet provided common intellectual ground, a conceptual framework that allows each side to understand how the other side translates "the sacred" into their conflicting perspectives. Until we can understand how "difference" (in religious perspectives, in gender, in sexuality) is produced and what it means, the debate will continue to labor in legal skirmishes, cascading ideological schisms, and mutual suspicion.

Works Cited

Adam, Barry D. "Age, Structure, and Sexuality: Reflections on the Anthropological Evidence on Homosexual Relations." *Anthropology and Homosexual Behavior.* Edited by Evelyn Blackwood. New York: Haworth, 1986. 19–33.

Adams, Henry E., Lester W. Wright, Jr., and Bethany A. Lohr. "Is Homophobia Associated with Homosexual Arousal?" *Journal of Abnormal Psychology* 105.3 (1996): 440–445.

Adams, William E., Jr. "Can We Relax Now? An Essay About Ballot Measures and Lesbian, Gay and Bisexual Rights after *Romer v. Evans.*" *The National Journal of Sexual Orientation Law* 2.2 (1996): n.p. Online posting. The National Journal of Sexual Orientation Law. http://www.ibiblio.org/gaylaw/issue4/adams2.html. 17 January 2002.

Allen, Garland E. "The Double-Edged Sword of Genetic Determinism: Social and Political Agendas in Genetic Studies of Homosexuality, 1940–1994." *Science and Homosexualities.* Edited by Vernon A. Rosario. New York: Routledge, 1997. 242–270.

Alpert, Rebecca T. "In God's Image." *Twice Blessed: On Being Lesbian, Gay, and Jewish.* Edited by Christine Balka and Andy Rose. Boston: Beacon, 1989. 61–70.

American Civil Liberties Union. " 'Abominable and detestable crimes against nature': An ACLU Lesbian and Gay Rights Project Update on the Status of Sodomy Laws." July 2001. Online posting. ACLU. http://www.aclu.org/issues/gay/sodomy_update.html. 17 January 2002.

———. " 'Crime' and Punishment in America: State-by-State Breakdown of Sodomy Laws." July 2001. Online posting. American Civil Liberties Union. http://www.aclu.org/issues/gay/sodomy.html. 17 January 2002.

American Psychological Association. "Answers to Your Questions About Sexual Orientation and Homosexuality." July 1998. Online posting. APA Public Information Home Page. http://www.apa.org/pubinfo/answers.html. 17 January 2002.

Ammerman, Nancy T. "North American Protestant Fundamentalism." *Fundamentalisms Observed*. Edited by Martin E. Marty and R. Scott Appleby. Chicago: University of Chicago Press, 1991. 1–65.

Angier, Natalie. "Report Suggests Homosexuality is Linked to Genes." *New York Times* (16 July 1993): A1, D21.

———. "Study Links Brain to Transsexuality." *New York Times* (2 November 1995): National section, n.p.

Aquinas, Thomas. *Summa Theologiae*. New York: McGraw-Hill, Eyre and Spottiswoode, 1968.

Bagemihl, Bruce. *Biological Exuberance, Animal Homosexuality and Natural Diversity*. New York: St. Martin's, 1999.

Bailey, J. Michael, David Bobrow, Marilyn Wolfe and Sarah Mikach. "Sexual Orientation of Adult Sons of Gay Fathers." *Developmental Psychology* 31.1 (1995): 124–129.

Baird, Robert M., and M. Katherine Baird, eds. *Homosexuality: Debating the Issues*. Amherst, NY: Prometheus, 1995.

Balch, David L., ed. *Homosexuality, Science, and the "Plain Sense" of Scripture*. Grand Rapids, MI: Eerdmans, 2000.

Barnett, Walter. *Sexual Freedom and The Constitution: An Inquiry into the Constitutionality of Repressive Sex Laws*. Albuquerque, NM: University of New Mexico Press, 1973.

Barret, Robert L., and Bryan E. Robinson. *Gay Fathers: Encouraging the Hearts of Gay Dads and their Families*. San Francisco, CA: Jossey-Bass, 2000.

Barthel, Manfred. *What the Bible Really Says*. Translated by Mark Howson. 1980; rev. ed. New York: Wings, 1998.

Bass, Ellen, and Kate Kaufman. *Free Your Mind: The Book for Gay, Lesbian and Bisexual Youth—and Their Allies*. New York: Harper Perennial, 1996.

Batey, Richard A. *New Testament Nuptial Imagery*. Leiden: Brill, 1971.

Bawer, Bruce. *A Place at the Table: The Gay Individual in American Society*. New York: Poseidon, 1993.

Bell, A. P., and M. S. Weinberg. *Homosexualities: A Study of Human Diversity Among Men and Women*. New York: Simon and Shuster, 1978.

Bell, Shannon. "Kate Bornstein: A Transgender Transsexual Postmodern Tiresias: An Interview with Kate Bornstein." *The Last Sex: Feminism and Outlaw Bodies*. Edited by Arthur and Marilouise Kroker. New York: St. Martin's, 1993. 104–120.

Berenbaum, Sheri A., and Elizabeth Snyder. "Early Hormonal Influences on Childhood Sex-Typed Activity and Playmate Preferences: Implications for the Development of Sexual Orientation." *Developmental Psychology* 31.1 (1995): 31–42.

Bergler, Edmund. *Homosexuality: Disease or Way of Life?* New York: Hill and Wang, 1956.

Bieber, Irving, et al. *Homosexuality: A Psychoanalytic Study*. New York: Basic, 1962.

Blair, Ralph. *Ex-gay*. New York: Homosexual Community Counseling Center, 1982.

Blasius, Mark, and Shane Phelan. *We Are Everywhere: A Historical Sourcebook of Gay and Lesbian Politics*. New York: Routledge, 1997.

Bleys, Rudi C. *The Geography of Perversion: Male-to-Male Sexual Behaviour Outside the West and the Ethnographic Imagination: 1750–1918*. Washington Square, NY: New York University Press, 1995.

Blumenfeld, Warren J., Laurie Lindop, and Anne Greenbaum. "Violence Prevention." 1996. Online posting. Queer Resources Directory. http://www.qrd.org/www/orgs/glstn/violence.prevention. 17 January 2002.

Bornstein, Kate. *Gender Outlaw: On Men, Women and the Rest of Us*. New York: Routledge, 1994.

Boston, Robert. "Bad History: What the Right Says About the Constitution: Facts to Help You Set the Record Straight." *Church and State* 45.3 (March 1992): n.p. Online posting. Ashlynn's Grove Pagan Information Resource. http://www.paganism.com/ag/articles/rightsfaq.html. 17 January 2002.

———. *The Most Dangerous Man in America? Pat Robertson and the Rise of the Christian Coalition*. Amherst, NY: Prometheus, 1996.

Boswell, John. *Christianity, Social Tolerance, and Homosexuality: Gay People in Western Europe from the Beginning of the Christian Era to the Fourteenth Century*. Chicago: University of Chicago Press, 1980.

Boughton, Lynne C. "Biblical Texts and Homosexuality: A Response to John Boswell." *Irish Theological Quarterly* 58 (1992): 141–153.

Bradshaw, David. "A Reply to Corvino." *Same Sex: Debating the Ethics, Science, and Culture of Homosexuality*. Edited by John Corvino. New York: Rowman & Littlefield, 1997: 17–30.

Brennan, Shannon. "Falwell, White Open Dialogue on Acceptance." 24 October 1999. Online posting. *Lynchburg News & Advance*. http://www.newsadvance.com. 29 December 1999.

Brooten, Bernadette J. *Love Between Women: Early Christian Responses to Female Homoeroticism*. Chicago: University of Chicago Press, 1997.

———. "Paul's Views on the Nature of Women and Female Homoeroticism." *Immaculate and Powerful: The Female in Sacred Image and Social Reality*. Edited by Clarissa W. Atkinson, Constance H. Buchanan, and Margaret R. Miles. Boston: Beacon, 1985. 61–87.

Brow, Reverend Robert. "A Biblical Response to Latimer Comment Number 45." Online posting. 18 August 1996. Gay Christian Channel. http://www.bway.net/~halsall/lgbh/lgbh-brow-resplat.txt. 13 February 2002.

Brown, Mildred L., and Chloe Ann Rounsley. *True Selves: Understanding Transsexualism—For Families, Friends, Coworkers, and Helping Professionals*. San Francisco, CA: Jossey-Bass, 1996.

Brown, Raymond E. "The Contribution of Historical Biblical Criticism to Ecumenical Church Discussion." *Biblical Interpretation in Crisis: The Ratzinger Conference on Bible and Church*. Edited by Richard John Neuhaus. Grand Rapids, MI: William B. Eerdmans, 1989. 24–49.

Brown, Robert D., and James K. Cole. "Letter to the Editor." *Nebraska Medical Journal* 70 (November 1985): 410–414.

Brownmiller, Susan. *Against Our Will: Men, Women, and Rape*. New York: Simon and Schuster, 1975.

Bruce, F. F. *The English Bible: A History of Translations*. London: Lutterworth, 1961.

Bryant, Steve, and Demian. "Partners National Survey of Lesbian & Gay Couples." 1995. Online posting. Partners Task Force for Gay & Lesbian Couples. http://www.eskimo.com/~demian/survey.html. 17 January 2001.

Bryant, Wayne M. *Bisexual Characters in Film, from Anais to Zee*. New York: Haworth, 1996.

Bull, Chris, ed. *Witness to Revolution: "The Advocate" Reports on Gay and Lesbian Politics, 1967–1999*. New York: Alyson, 1999.

Bullough, Vern. L., Bonnie Bullough and James Elins, eds. *Gender Blending*. Amherst, NY: Prometheus, 1997.

Burr, Chandler. *A Separate Creation: The Search for the Biological Origins of Sexual Orientations*. New York: Hyperion, 1996.

Butler, Judith. *Gender Trouble: Feminism and the Subversion of Identity*. New York: Routledge, 1990.

———. "Imitation and Gender Insubordination." *The Lesbian and Gay Studies Reader*. Edited by Henry Abelove, Michele Aina Barale, and David M. Halperin. New York: Routledge, 1993. 307–320.

Button, James W., Barbara A. Rienzo, and Kenneth D. Wald. *Private Lives, Public Conflicts: Battles over Gay Rights in American Communities*. Washington, DC: Congressional Quarterly, 1997.

Byne, William, and Bruce Parsons. "Biology and Human Sexual Orientation." *Harvard Mental Health Letter* 10.8 (February 1994): 5–7.

Byne, William, and Mitchell Lasco. "The Origins of Sexual Orientation: Possible Biological Contributions." *Same Sex: Debating the Ethics, Science, and Culture of Homosexuality*. Edited by John Corvino. New York: Rowman & Littlefield, 1997. 107–120.

Cabaj, Robert P., and Terry S. Stein. *Textbook of Homosexuality and Mental Health*. Washington, DC: American Psychiatrist, 1996.

Cahill, Paul Thomas. "An Investigation into the Bible and Homosexuality: *Malakoi* and *Arsenokoitai*." N.D. Online posting. Gay Christian Home Page. http://www.yougogirl.com/gaychristians/cahill6.html. 17 January 2002.

Califia, Pat. "Gay Men, Lesbians, and Sex: Doing It Together." *Advocate* (7 July 1983): 24–27.

———. "Identity Sedition and Pornography." *PoMoSexuals: Challenging Assumptions about Gender and Sexuality*. Edited by Carol Queen and Lawrence Schimel. San Francisco, CA: Cleis, 1997. 87–106.

Cameron, Paul, et al. "Child Molestation and Homosexuality." *Psychological Reports* 58 (1986): 327–337.

———. et al. "Sexual Orientation and Sexually Transmitted Diseases." *Nebraska Medical Journal* 70 (1985): 292–299.

———, et al. *The Homosexual Lifespan*. Washington, DC: Family Research Institute, 1992.

Carlston, Erin G. " 'A Finer Differentiation': Female Homosexuality and the American Medical Community, 1926–1940." *Science and Homosexualities*. Edited by Vernon A. Rosario. New York: Routledge, 1997. 177–196.

Carrier, Joseph M. "Cultural Factors Affecting Urban Mexican Male Homosexual Behavior." *Homosexuality in the Ancient World*. Edited by Wayne R. Dynes and Stephen Donaldson. New York: Garland, 1992. 89–110.

"Catholic Clergy join the Interfaith Alliance in warning to America's Catholics." 3 July 2001. Online posting. Interfaith Alliance. http://www.interfaithalliance. org/Newsroom/Narchive/cathol.htm. 17 January 2002.

Chambers, Barbara L. "Transsexuals in the Work Place—A Guide for Employers." 1990. Online posting. Renaissance Transgender Association. http://www.ren. org/tgwork.html. 17 January 2002.

Christensen, Cornelia V. *Kinsey: A Biography*. Bloomington: Indiana University Press, 1971.

Churchill, Wainwright. *Homosexual Behavior Among Males: A Cross-Cultural and Cross-Species Investigation*. New York: Hawthorn Books, 1967.

Clowes, Brian. "The Pro-Life Activist's Encyclopedia." N.D. Online posting. The American Life League. http://www.rlbm.tripod.com/allcontents.html. 17 January 2002. Parenthetical number refers to chapter number.

Cohen, Naomi. *Natural Adversaries or Possible Allies? American Jews and the New Christian Right*. New York: American Jewish Committee, 1993.

Coleman, Eli, Walter O. Bockting, and Louis Gooren. "Homosexual and Bisexual Identity in Sex-Reassigned Female-to-Male Transsexuals." *Archives of Sexual Behavior* 22 (1993): 37–50

Comstock, Gary David. *Violence Against Lesbians and Gay Men*. New York: Columbia University Press, 1991.

Congregation for the Doctrine of the Faith. *Persona humana: Declaration on Certain Questions Pertaining to Sexual Ethics. Acta Apostolicae Sedis* 68 (1976): 77–96.

Corvino, John, ed. *Same Sex: Debating the Ethics, Science, and Culture of Homosexuality*. New York: Rowman & Littlefield, 1997.

Countryman, L. William. *Biblical Authority or Biblical Tyranny? Scripture and the Christian Pilgrimage*. Valley Forge, PA: Trinity, 1994.

Crew, Louie. "The Situation in the Episcopal Church." 1994. Online posting. Lesbian, Gay, and Bisexual Catholic Handbook. http://www.bway.net/~halsall/ lgbh/lgbh-episc.txt. 17 January 2002.

Dallas, Joe. *A Strong Delusion: Confronting the "Gay Christian" Movement*. Eugene, OR: Harvest House, 1996.

D'Augelli, Anthony R., and Scott L. Hershberger. "Lesbian, Gay, and Bisexual Youth in Community Settings: Personal Challenges and Mental Health Problems." *American Journal of Community Psychology* 21.4 (1993): 321–348.

Davies, Bob. "About Exodus: Policy on Homosexuality." N.D. Exodus International. http://www.exodusnorthamerica.org/aboutus/aboutdocs/ a0000048.html. 17 January 2002.

———, and Lori Rentzel. "Roots of Homosexuality." 27 December 1995. Online posting. Messiah College Home Page. http://www.messiah.edu/hpages/facstaff/ chase/h/articles/index.htm. 17 January 2002.

Davis, Natalie. "The Other Side of the Rainbow: Behind the Curtain of Ex-Gay Ministries." 10 March 1999. Online posting. Free Speech TV. http://www. freespeech.org/nd/exgay.html. 12 March 1999.

Dawn, Marva J. "Are Christianity and Homosexuality Incompatible?" *Caught in the Crossfire: Helping Christians Debate Homosexuality.* Edited by Sally B. Geis and Donald E. Messer. Nashville, TN: Abingdon, 1994. 89–98.

D'Emilio, John. "Cycles of Change, Questions of Strategy: The Gay and Lesbian Movement after Fifty Years." *The Politics of Gay Rights.* Edited by Craig A. Rimmerman, Kenneth D. Wald, and Clyde Wilcox. University of Chicago Press, 2000. 31–53.

Denny, Dallas. "Transgender: Some Historical, Cross-Cultural, and Contemporary Models and Methods of Coping and Treatment." *Gender Blending.* Edited by Vern L. Bullough, Bonnie Bullough, and James Elias. Amherst, NY: Prometheus, 1997. 33–47.

———, and Jamison Green. "Gender Identity and Bisexuality." *Bisexuality: The Psychology and Politics of an Invisible Minority.* Edited by Beth A. Firestein. Thousand Oaks, CA: Sage, 1996. 84–102.

D'Entremont, James. "Purification Equals Silence: Censorship of Queer Expression by the Theocratic Right." *Journal of Gay, Lesbian and Bisexual Identity* 1.3 (1996): 213–234.

De Young, James B. *Homosexuality: Contemporary Claims Examined in Light of the Bible and other Ancient Literature and Law.* Grand Rapids, MI: Kregel, 2000.

Diamond, Milton. "Homosexuality and Bisexuality in Different Populations." *Archives of Sexual Behavior* 22.4 (1993): 291–310.

———. "Self-Testing: A Check on Sexual Identity and Other Levels of Sexuality." *Gender Blending.* Edited by Vern L. Bullough, Bonnie Bullough, and James Elias. Amherst, NY: Prometheus, 1997. 103–125.

Diamond, Sara. *Spiritual Warfare: The Politics of the Christian Right.* Boston: South End, 1989.

Dignity/USA. "Statement of Position & Purpose." N.D. Online posting. Dignity/USA. http://www.dignityusa.org/purpose.html. 18 January 2002.

Doan, Laura, ed. *The Lesbian Postmodern.* New York: Columbia University Press, 1994.

Dobson, James. "Why I Use 'Fighting Words.'" *Christianity Today* (19 June 1995): 27–30.

Dollimore, Jonathan. *Sexual Dissidence: Augustine to Wilde, Freud to Foucault.* Oxford: Clarendon, 1992.

Dolphin, Lambert. "Jesus and the Homosexual." 10 August 2001. Online posting. Lambert Dolphin Library. http://www.ldolphin.org/Homo.shtml. 17 January 2002.

Duncan, Richard F. "Who Wants to Stop the Church?" *Notre Dame Law Review* 69.3 (January 1994): 393–445.

———, and Gary L. Young. "Homosexual Rights and Citizens Initiatives: Is Constitutionalism Unconstitutional?" *Notre Dame Journal of Law, Ethics and Public Policy* 9.1 (1995): 95–135.

Dworkin, Andrea. *Intercourse.* New York: Free, 1987.

Dynes, Wayne R., and Stephen Donaldson, eds. *Homosexuality in the Ancient World.* New York: Garland, 1992.

Edwards, Mickey. "Conservatives Betrayed on the Right." *The Boston Herald* (13 February 1996): 21.

Eliason, Michele J., and Kris S. Morgan. "Lesbians Define Themselves: Diversity in Lesbian Identification." *Journal of Gay, Lesbian, and Bisexual Identity* 3.1 (1998): 47–63.

Eron, Rabbi Lewis John. "Early Jewish and Christian Attitudes toward Male Homosexuality as Expressed in the Testament of Naphtali." *Homophobia and the Judaeo-Christian Tradition*. Edited by Michael L. Stemmeler and J. Michael Clark. Dallas: Monument, 1990. 25–50.

Estep, William E. *Revolution Within the Revolution: The First Amendment in Historical Context 1612–1789*. Grand Rapids, MI: Eerdman's, 1990.

Estlund, David M., and Martha C. Nussbaum, eds. *Sex, Preference, and Family: Essays on Law and Nature*. New York: Oxford University Press, 1997.

Evans, Nancy J., and Vernon A. Wall, eds. *Beyond Tolerance: Gays, Lesbians and Bisexuals on Campus*. Alexandria, VA: American College Personnel Association, 1991.

Fajer, Marc A. "*Bowers v. Hardwick, Romer v. Evans,* and the Meaning of Anti-Discrimination Legislation." *The National Journal of Sexual Orientation Law* 2.2 (1996). Online posting. The National Journal of Sexual Orientation Law. http://www.ibiblio.org/gaylaw/issue4/fajer.html. 17 January 2002.

Falk, Patricia J. "Lesbian Mothers: Psychosocial Assumptions in Family Law." *American Psychologist* 44.6 (June 1989): 941–947.

Fausto-Sterling, Anne. "The Five Sexes: Why Male and Female are Not Enough." *The Sciences* (March/April 1993): 20–24.

———. "How to Build a Man." *Science and Homosexualities*. Edited by Vernon A. Rosario. New York: Routledge, 1997. 219–224.

Finnis, John M. "Law, Morality, and 'Sexual Orientation.'" *Notre Dame Journal of Law, Ethics and Public Policy* 9.1 (1995): 11–39.

Firestein, Beth A. *Bisexuality: The Psychology and Politics of an Invisible Minority*. Thousand Oaks, CA: Sage, 1996.

Fisher, Seymour, and Roger P. Greenberg. *The Scientific Credibility of Freud's Theory and Therapy*. New York: Columbia University Press, 1985.

Ford, Clellan S., and Frank A. Beach. *Patterns of Sexual Behavior*. New York: Harper and Row, 1951.

Foucault, Michel. *The History of Sexuality: Volume 1: An Introduction*. Translated by Robert Hurley. New York: Random House, 1978.

Fox, Ronald C. "Bisexuality in Perspective: A Review of Theory and Research." *Bisexuality: The Psychology and Politics of an Invisible Minority*. Edited by Beth A. Firestein. Thousand Oaks, CA: Sage, 1996. 3–52.

Freud, Sigmund. *The Standard Edition of the Complete Psychological Works of Sigmund Freud*. 24 vols. Translated and Edited by James Strachey. London: Hogarth, 1953–74.

Gagnon, Robert A. J. *The Bible and Homosexual Practice: Texts and Hermeneutics*. Nashville, TN: Abington, 2001.

Galatowitsch, Paul. "N.T." 4 August 1998. Online posting. Gay/Lesbian/Queer Social Sciences List. GLQSOC-L%BINGVMB.BITNET@crcvms.unl.edu. 5 August 1998.

Gallagher, John. "Blacks and Gays: The Unexpected Divide." *Witness to Revolution: "The Advocate" Reports on Gay and Lesbian Politics, 1967–1999*. Edited by Chris Bull. New York: Alyson, 1999. 398–401.

———. "Colorado Goes Straight to Hell." *Witness to Revolution: "The Advocate" Reports on Gay and Lesbian Politics, 1967–1999*. Edited by Chris Bull. New York: Alyson, 1999. 294–305.

———, and Chris Bull. *Perfect Enemies: The Religious Right, The Gay Movement, and the Politics of the 1990's*. New York: Crown, 1996.

van Gelder, Lindsy. "The 'Born That Way' Trap." *Homosexuality: Debating the Issues*. Edited by Robert M. Baird and M. Katherine Baird. Amherst, NY: Prometheus, 1995. 80–82.

VanGemeren, Willem A., ed. *New International Dictionary of Old Testament Theology and Exegesis*. Grand Rapids, MI: Zondervan House, 1997.

George, Robert P., and Gerard V. Bradley. "Marriage and the Liberal Imagination." *Georgetown Law Journal* 84.1 (1995): 301–320.

Geslin, Reverend Dan. "How can Someone be both Christian and Homosexual?" Online posting. 19 March 1996. Carlton University. http://www.ncf.carleton.ca/ip/sigs/life/gay/religion/bible. 17 January 2002.

Gibbs, Elizabeth D. "Psychosocial Development of Children Raised by Lesbian Mothers: A Review of Research." *Women and Therapy* 8.1–2 (1988): 65–75.

Gilder, George F. *Sexual Suicide*. New York: Quadrangle, 1973.

Gilson, Etienne. *Moral Values and the Moral Life: The Ethical Theory of St. Thomas Aquinas*. Translated by Leo Richard Ward, C.S.C. N.P.: Shoe String, 1961.

GLAAD. "Special: Tell Dr. Laura The Truth." Online posting. 3 August 1999. Gay and Lesbian Alliance Against Defamation. http://www.glaad.org. 18 August 1999.

Goetze, Rob. "Homosexuality and the Possibility of Change: An Ongoing Research Project." 2001. New Direction for Life Ministries for Canada. http://www.newdirection.ca/research/index.html. 17 January 2002.

Golden, Carla. "Diversity and Variability in Women's Sexual Identities." *Lesbian Psychologies: Explorations and Challenges*. Edited by Boston Lesbian Psychologies Collective. Chicago: University of Illinois Press, 1987. 18–34.

Goldstein, Anne B. "Reasoning about Homosexuality: A Commentary on Janet Halley's 'Reasoning about Sodomy': Act and Identity in and after *Bowers v. Hardwick.*'" *Virginia Law Review* 79.7 (1993): 1781–1832.

Goleman, Daniel. "Studies Discover Clues to the Roots of Homophobia." *New York Times*. 10 July 1990. Online posting. 22 January 1996. Person Project. http://www.youth.org/loco/PERSONProject/Resources/ResearchStudies/homophobia.html. 17 January 2002.

Good News Bible: Catholic Study Edition. Imprimatur by Archbishop John Whealon. New York: Thomas Nelson, 1976.

Gooren, L. "Biomedical Theories of Sexual Orientation: A Critical Examination." *Homosexuality/Heterosexuality: Concepts of Sexual Orientation*. Edited by D. P. McWhirter, A. S. Sanders, and J. M. Reinisch. New York: Oxford University Press, 1990.

Goss, Robert. *Jesus Acted Up: A Gay and Lesbian Manifesto*. San Francisco: Harper, 1993.

Gotestam, K. O., T. J. Coates, and M. Ekstrand. "Handedness, Dyslexia and Twinning in Homosexual Men." *International Journal of Neuroscience* 63 (1992): 179–186.

Green, Richard, Jane Barclay Mandel, Mary E. Hotvedt, James Gray, and Laurel Smith. "Lesbian Mothers and Their Children: A Comparison with Solo Parent Heterosexual Mothers and Their Children." *Archives of Sexual Behavior* 15.2 (1986): 167–184.

Greenberg, David F. *The Construction of Homosexuality*. Chicago: University of Chicago Press, 1988.

Groth, A. Nicholas, and H. Jean Birnbaum. "Adult Sexual Orientation and Attraction to Underage Persons." *Archives of Sexual Behavior* 7:3 (1978): 175–181.

Grunbaum, Adolf. *The Foundations of Psychoanalysis: A Philosophical Critique*. Berkeley: University of California Press, 1984.

Gudorf, Christine E. "The Bible and Science on Sexuality." *Homosexuality, Science, and the "Plain Sense" of Scripture*. Edited by David L. Balch. Grand Rapids, MI: Eerdmans, 2000. 121–141.

Haeberle, Steven H. "Gay and Lesbian Rights: Emerging Trends in Public Opinion and Voting Behavior," *Gays and Lesbians in the Democratic Process: Policy, Public Opinion, and Public Representation*. Edited by Ellen D. B. Riggle and Barry Tadlock. New York: Columbia University Press, 1999. 146–169.

Haider-Markel, Donald P. "Creating Change—Holding the Line: Agenda Setting on Lesbian and Gay Issues at the National Level." *Gays and Lesbians in the Democratic Process: Policy, Public Opinion, and Public Representation*. Edited by Ellen D. B. Riggle and Barry Tadlock. New York: Columbia University Press, 1999. 242–268.

———. "Lesbian and Gay Politics in the States: Interest Groups, Electoral Politics, and Policy." *The Politics of Gay Rights*. Edited by Craig A. Rimmerman, Kenneth D. Wald, and Clyde Wilcox. University of Chicago Press, 2000. 290–346.

Halberstam, Judith. "F2M: The Making of Female Masculinity." *The Lesbian Postmodern*. Edited by Laura Doan. New York: Columbia University Press, 1994. 210–228.

———. *Female Masculinity*. Durham: Duke University Press, 1998.

Haldeman, D. C. "Sexual Orientation Conversion Therapy for Gay Men and Lesbians: A Scientific Examination." *Homosexuality: Implications for Public Policy*. Edited by J. C. Gonsiorek and J. D. Weinrich. Newbury Park, CA: Sage, 1991.

Hall, James Alan. "Sodom." N.D. Online posting. Lesbian, Gay, and Bisexual Catholic Handbook. http://www.bway.net/~halsall/lgbh/lgbh-gen19.html. 17 January 2002.

Haller, Tobias S. "An Abominable Article." N.D. Online posting. Lesbian, Gay, and Bisexual Catholic Handbook. http://www.bway.net/~halsall/lgbh/lgbh-lev18.html. 17 January 2002.

Halley, Janet E. "The Politics of the Closet: Towards Equal Protection for Gay, Lesbian, and Bisexual Identity." *UCLA Law Review* 36.5 (1989): 915–976.

———. "Reasoning about Sodomy: Act and Identity in and after *Bowers v. Hardwick*." *Virginia Law Review* 79.7 (1993): 1721–1780.

———. "Sexual Orientation and the Politics of Biology: A Critique of the Argument from Immutability." *Stanford Law Review* 46 (1994): 503–568.

Halperin, David. "Is There a History of Sexuality?" *The Lesbian and Gay Studies Reader.* Edited by Henry Abelove, Michele Aina Barale, and David M. Halperin. New York: Routledge, 1993. 416–431.

——. "Sex Before Sexuality: Pederasty, Politics, and Power in Classical Athens." *Same Sex: Debating the Ethics, Science, and Culture of Homosexuality.* Edited by John Corvino. New York: Rowman & Littlefield, 1997. 203–219.

Halsall, Paul. "The Background to Leviticus." N.D. Online posting. Lesbian, Gay, and Bisexual Catholic Handbook. http://www.bway.net/~halsall/lgbh/lgbh-lev18.html. 17 January 2002.

——. "John Boswell on Romans I—The Criticism of Richard Hays." 23 September 1993. Online posting. Lesbian, Gay, and Bisexual Catholic Handbook. http://www.bway.net/~halsall/lgbh/lgbh-rom1–boswell.txt. 17 January 2002.

——. "Moral Law and Ritual Law in the Old and New Testaments." 19 July 1993. Online posting. Lesbian, Gay, and Bisexual Catholic Handbook. http://www.bway.net/~halsall/lgbh/lgbh-moralritual.txt. 17 January 2002.

——. "Syllabus of Papal and Magisterial Errors." 18 December 1995. Online posting. Lesbian, Gay, and Bisexual Catholic Handbook. http://www.bway.net/~halsall/radcath/syl.txt. 17 January 2002.

Hamer, Dean, Stella Hu, Victoria Magnuson, Nan Hu, and Angela Pattatucci. "A Linkage Between DNA Markers on the X Chromosome and Male Sexual Orientation." *Science* 261 (July 1995): 321–327.

Harvey, John F. "Homosexuality." *New Catholic Encyclopedia: Volume 7.* New York: McGraw Hill, 1967. 116–119.

Haste, Helen. *The Sexual Metaphor.* Cambridge, MA: Harvard University Press, 1994.

Hays, Richard B. "Relations Natural and Unnatural: A Response to John Boswell's Exegesis of Romans I." *Journal of Religious Ethics* 14 (1986): 184–215.

Helminiak, Daniel. "The Jewish Testament Text on Homosexuality." N.D. Lesbian, Gay, and Bisexual Catholic Handbook. http://www.bway.net/~halsall/lgbh/lgbh-lev18.html. 17 January 2002.

——. *What the Bible Really Says about Homosexuality.* San Francisco: Alamo Square, 1994.

Helms, Kathryn J. "Religion and Cross-Gender Behavior: Wellspring of Hope or Swamp of Despair?" *Gender Blending.* Edited by Vern L. Bullough, Bonnie Bullough, and James Elias. Amherst, NY: Prometheus, 1997. 398–404.

Henry, William A., III. "Born Gay?" *Time* (26 July 1993): 36–39.

Herdt, Gilbert. "Fetish and Fantasy in Sambia Initiation." *Rituals of Manhood: Male Initiation in Papua New Guinea.* Edited by Gilbert H. Herdt and Roger M. Kessing. Berkeley: University of California Press, 1982.

——, ed. *Ritualized Homosexuality in Melanesia.* Berkeley: University of California Press, 1984.

——. *Same Sex, Different Cultures: Exploring Gay and Lesbian Lives.* Boulder, CO: Westview, 1997.

Herek, Gregory, and Kevin T. Berrill. *Hate Crimes: Confronting Violence Against Lesbians and Gay Men.* Newbury Park, CA: Sage, 1992.

Herman, Didi. *The Antigay Agenda: Orthodox Vision and the Christian Right.* Chicago: University of Chicago Press, 1997.

Hershberger, Scott L., and Anthony R. D'Augelli. "The Impact of Victimization on the Mental Health and Suicidality of Lesbian, Gay Male and Bisexual Youths." *Developmental Psychology* 31.1 (1995): 65–74.

Hooker, Evelyn. "The Adjustment of the Male Overt Homosexual." *Journal of Projective Techniques* 21 (1957): 18–31.

———. "Male Homosexuality in the Rorschach." *Journal of Projective Techniques* 22 (1958): 33–54.

"Hostile Climate: Antigay Politics and the Religious Right." 1998. Online posting. People for the American Way. http://www.pfaw.org/issues/right/rtvw.antigay.shtml. 17 January 2002.

Hu, Stella, A. M. L. Pattatucci, C. Patterson, L. Li, D. W. Fulker, S. S. Cherny, L. Kruglyak, and D. H. Hamer. "Linkage Between Sexual Orientation and Chromosome Xq28 in Males but not in Females." *Nature Genetics* 11 (1995): 248–256.

Hudson, W. W., and W. A. Ricketts. "A Strategy for Measurement of Homophobia." *Journal of Homosexuality* 5 (1980): 356–371.

Human Rights Campaign. "Gays, Lesbians and Bisexuals Rank Third in Reported Hate Crimes—1999." 22 October 2001. Online posting. Human Rights Campaign. http://www.hrc.org/issues/hate_crimes/background/stats/stats1999.asp. 17 January 2002.

Human Rights Watch. *Hatred in the Hallways: Violence and Discrimination Against Lesbian, Gay, Bisexual, and Transgender Students in U.S. Schools.* New York: HRC, 2001.

Hume, Basil. "Note on Church Teaching Concerning Homosexual People." *Origins* 24.45 (27 April 1995): 765–769.

Hunter, James Davison. *Culture Wars: The Struggle to Define America.* New York: Basic, 1991.

Hunter, Nan D. "Life After *Hardwick.*" *Harvard Civil Rights and Civil Liberties Law Review* 27.2 (1992): 531–554.

Hutchins, Loraine. "Bisexually: Politics and Community." *Bisexuality: The Psychology and Politics of an Invisible Minority.* Edited by Beth A. Firestein. Thousand Oaks, CA: Sage, 1996. 240–262.

Inness, Sherrie A., and Michele E. Lloyd. "G.I. Joes in Barbie Land: Recontextualizing Butch in Twentieth-Century Lesbian Culture." *Queer Studies: A Lesbian, Gay, Bisexual and Transgender Anthology.* Edited by Brett Beemyn and Mickey Eliason. New York: New York University Press, 1996. 9–34.

Jagose, Annamarie. *Queer Theory: An Introduction.* Washington Square, NY: New York University Press, 1996.

Jenny, C., T. A. Roesler, and K. L. Poyer. "Are Children at Risk for Sexual Abuse by Homosexuals?" *Pediatrics* 94.1 (July 1994): 41–44.

Johnstone, William. "Biblical Study and Linguistics." *The Cambridge Companion to Biblical Interpretation.* Edited by John Barton. New York: Cambridge University Press, 1998. 129–142.

Jones, Alexander. *The Jerusalem Bible.* Garden City, NY: Doubleday, 1966.

Jones, Stanton L., and Mark A. Yarhouse. "The Use, Misuse, and Abuse of Science in the Ecclesiastical Homosexuality Debates." *Homosexuality, Science, and the "Plain Sense" of Scripture.* Edited by David L. Balch. Grand Rapids, MI: Eerdmans, 2000. 73–120.

Jordan, Mark D. *The Invention of Sodomy in Christian Theology.* Chicago: University of Chicago Press, 1997.

———. *The Silence of Sodom: Homosexuality in Modern Catholicism.* Chicago: University of Chicago Press, 2000.

Kader, Reverend Samuel. *Openly Gay, Openly Christian: How the Bible Really Is Gay Friendly.* San Francisco, CA: Leyland, 1999.

Kandel, E. R., and R. D. Hawkins. "The Biological Basis of Learning and Individuality." *Scientific American* 267 (1992): 53–60.

Kaplan, Morris B. "Constructing Lesbian and Gay Rights and Liberation." *Virginia Law Review* 79.7 (1993): 1877–1902.

Keen, Lisa, and Suzanne B. Goldberg. *Strangers to the Law: Gay People on Trial.* Ann Arbor: University of Michigan Press, 1998.

Kehoe, Monika. *Lesbians Over 60 Speak for Themselves.* New York: Haworth, 1989.

Kenen, Stephaine H. "Who Counts When You're Counting Homosexuals? Hormones and Homosexuality in Mid-Twentieth-Century America." *Science and Homosexualities.* Edited by Vernon A. Rosario. New York: Routledge, 1997. 197–218.

Kinsey, Alfred. *Sexual Behavior in the Human Female.* Philadelphia: W. B. Saunders, 1953.

———. *Sexual Behavior in the Human Male.* Philadelphia: W. B. Saunders, 1948.

Kinz, Richard. "Religion Protected, Not Rights (Be afraid!!)." 16 July 1999. *Planet Out News.* Online posting. http://www.planetout.com/pno/news/. 19 July 1999.

Kitzinger, Celia, and Sue Wilkinson. "Transitions from Heterosexuality to Lesbianism: The Discursive Production of Lesbian Identities." *Developmental Psychology* 31.1 (1995): 95–104.

(KJV) *The Holy Bible: The Authorized or King James Version of 1611 now reprinted with the Apocrypha.* 3 vols. London: Nonesuch Press, 1963.

Klein, Marty. "The Sex Lies of the Religious Right: How Conservatives Distort the Facts of Life." *Playboy Forum* (January 1996): n.p. 22 April 1996. Online posting. Charles Haynes's Radical Sex Page. http://www.radical-sex.com/marty.html. 17 January 2002.

Koppelman, Andrew. "Homosexual Conduct: A Reply to the New Natural Lawyers." *Same Sex: Debating the Ethics, Science, and Culture of Homosexuality.* Edited by John Corvino. New York: Rowman & Littlefield, 1997. 44–57.

LaHaye, Tim. *The Unhappy Gays.* Wheaton, IL: Tyndale, 1978.

Lamos, Colleen. "The Postmodern Lesbian Position: *On Our Backs.*" *The Lesbian Postmodern.* Edited by Laura Doan. New York: Columbia University Press, 1994. 85–103.

Laumann, Edward O., John H. Gagnon, Robert T. Michael, and Stuart Michaels. *The Social Organization of Sexuality: Sexual Practices in the United States.* Chicago: University of Chicago Press, 1994.

Law, Sylvia A. "Homosexuality and the Social Meaning of Gender." *Wisconsin Law Review* 1988.2 (1988): 187–235.

Lawrence, Jill. "Political Attacks on Gays Heat Up." *USA Today,* 17 July 1998: 5A.

Leland, John, et al. "Bisexuality Emerges as a New Sexual Identity." *Newsweek* (17 July 1995): 44–50.

"Lesbian Appeals Child's Custody to Convicted Murderer." *The Orlando Sentinel* (1 February 1996): n.p.

LeVay, Simon. "A Difference in Hypothalamic Structure Between Heterosexual and Homosexual Men." *Science* 253 (1991): 1034–1037.

———. "Sexual Orientation and Its Development." *Homosexuality: Debating the Issues.* Edited by Robert M. Baird and M. Katherine Baird. Amherst, NY: Prometheus, 1995. 62–70.

Lewes, Kenneth. *The Psychoanalytic Theory of Male Homosexuality.* New York: Meridian, 1988.

Lewis, Gregory B., and Marc A. Rogers. "Does Public Support Equal Employment Rights for Gays and Lesbians?" *Gays and Lesbians in the Democratic Process: Public Policy, Public Opinion, and Political Representation.* Edited by Ellen D. B. Riggle and Barry L. Tadlock. New York: Columbia University Press, 1999. 118–145.

Lewis, Jack P. *The English Bible from KJV to NIV: A History and Evaluation.* 2nd ed. Grand Rapids, MI: Baker, 1991.

"Lez Opinions on Bi's—It's Political." 8 September 1995. Online posting. newsgroup.soc.women.lesbian-and-bi. 16 September 1995.

Lidz, Theodore. "Reply to 'A Genetic Study of Male Sexual Orientation.'" *Archives of General Psychiatry* 240 (1993): 240.

Liebman, Robert C., and Robert Wuthnow, eds. *The New Christian Right.* New York: Aldine, 1983.

Lockard, Denyse. "The Lesbian Community: An Anthropological Approach." *Anthropology and Homosexual Behavior.* Edited by Evelyn Blackwood. New York: Haworth, 1986. 83–96.

Logan, Colleen R. "Homophobia? No, Homoprejudice." *Journal of Homosexuality* 31.3 (1996): 31–53.

Loulan, JoAnn. *The Lesbian Erotic Dance: Butch, Femme, Androgyny, and Other.* San Francisco, CA: Spinsters, 1990.

MacDonald, A. P. "A Little Bit of Lavender Goes a Long Way: A Critique of Research on Sexual Orientation." *Journal of Sex Research* 9.1 (February 1983): 94–100.

Macedo, Stephen. "Homosexuality and the Conservative Mind." *The Georgetown Law Journal* 84.1 (1995): 261–300.

———. "Sexuality and Liberty: Making Room for Nature and Tradition?" *Sex, Preference, and Family: Essays on Law and Nature.* Edited by David M. Estlund and Martha C. Nussbaum. New York: Oxford University Press, 1997. 86–101.

Mallon, Gerald P. "Counseling Strategies with Gay and Lesbian Youth." *Helping Gay and Lesbian Youth: New Policies, New Program, New Practice.* Edited by Teresa DeCrescenzo. New York: Haworth, 1994. 75–91.

Malloy, Edward A. *Homosexuality and the Christian Way of Life.* Washington, DC: University Press of America, 1981.

Marcosson, Samuel A. "The 'Special Rights' Canard in the Debate Over Lesbian and Gay Civil Rights." *Notre Dame Journal of Law, Ethics and Public Policy* 9.1 (1995): 137–183.

Marcus, Eric. *Is It a Choice? Answers to 300 of the Most Frequently Asked Questions about Gays and Lesbians.* San Francisco, CA: Harper, 1993.

Martin, Dale B. "*Arsenokoites* and *Malakos:* Meanings and Consequences." *Biblical Ethics and Homosexuality: Listening to Scripture.* Edited by Robert L. Brawley. Westminster: John Knox, 1996. 117–136.

Mason-Schrock, Douglas. "Transsexuals' Narrative Construction of the 'True Self.'" *Social Psychology Quarterly* 59.3 (1996): 176–192.

Massaro, Toni M. "Gay Rights, Thick and Thin." *Stanford Law Review* 49 (1996): 45–110.

May, Herbert Gordon. *Our English Bible in the Making: The Word of Life in Living Language.* Rev. ed. Philadelphia, PA: Westminster, 1965.

McCaffrey, Phillip. *Freud and Dora: The Artful Dream.* New Brunswick, NJ: Rutgers University Press, 1984.

McCary, S. P., and J. L. McCary. *Human Sexuality.* Belmont, CA: Wadsworth, 1984.

McNeill, John J., S.J. *The Church and the Homosexual.* Kansas City, KS: Sheed Andrews and McMeel, 1976.

Menendez, Albert J. *Visions of Reality: What Fundamentalist Schools Teach.* Buffalo, NY: Prometheus Books, 1993.

Meyer-Bahlburg, Heino F. L., Anke A. Ehrhardt, Laura R. Rosen, and Rhoda S. Gruen. "Prenatal Estrogens and the Development of Homosexual Orientation." *Developmental Psychology* 31.1 (1995): 12–21.

Milgrom, Rabbi Jacob. "Does the Bible Prohibit Homosexuality?" *Bible Review* 9.6 (December 1993): 11.

Millman, Claude. "Sodomy Statues and the Eighth Amendment." *Columbia Journal of Law and Social Problems* 21.3 (1988): 267–307.

Mills, Kim I. "Mission Impossible: Why Reparative Therapy and 'Ex-Gay' Ministries Fail." February 1999. Online posting. Human Rights Campaign. http://www.hrc.org/pubs/change.html. 10 September 2000.

Mohr, Richard D. *A More Perfect Union: Why Straight America Must Stand up for Gay Rights.* Boston: Beacon, 1994.

Monette, Paul. "My Priests." *Last Watch of the Night: Essays too Personal and Otherwise.* New York: Harcourt Brace, 1994. 54–88.

Morantz, Regina Markell. "The Scientist as Sex Crusader: Alfred C. Kinsey and American Culture." *American Quarterly* 29 (1977): 563–589.

Murphy, Caryle. "Falwell and Gays Meet but Don't Eat." *Washington Post* (30 October 1999): B09.

Nakamura, Karen. "Narrating Ourselves: Duped or Duplicitous?" *Gender Blending.* Edited by Vern L. Bullough, Bonnie Bullough, and James Elias. Amherst, NY: Prometheus, 1997. 74–86.

Nancy. *Homosexual Struggle.* Downers Grove, IL: Inter-Varsity Christian Fellowship, 1980.

Nangeroni, Nancy R. "Transgenderism." 1996. Online posting. International Foundation for Gender Education. http://www.altsex.org/transgender/Nangeroni.html. 18 November 2001.

Nava, Michael, and Robert Dawidoff. *Created Equal: Why Gay Rights Matter to America.* New York: St. Martin's, 1994.

Neuhaus, Richard John. "In the Case of John Boswell." *First Things* 41 (November 1994): 56–59.

"New FBI Data Show Anti-gay Hate Crimes are on Rise." 16 October 2001. Human Rights Campaign. Online posting. Human Rights Campaign. http://www.hrc.org/newsreleases/2000/001016HC.asp. 17 January 2002.

Nichols, Margaret. "Lesbian Sexuality: Issues and Developing Theory." *Lesbian Psychologies: Explorations and Challenges*. Edited by The Boston Lesbian Psychologies Collective. Chicago: University of Illinois Press, 1987.

Niebuhr, Gustav. "Falwell Finds Accord With a Gay Rights Advocate." *The New York Times* (23 October 1999): National Desk.

Norman, Stuart. "How to Fight the Right Wing." 1995. Online posting. Queer Resources Directory. http://www.qrd.org/religion/anti/how.to.fight.the.right.txt. 17 January 2002.

Ochshorn, Judith. *The Female Experience and the Nature of the Divine*. Bloomington, IN: Indiana University Press, 1981.

O'Hanlan, Kate. "Lesbian Health and Homophobia: Perspectives for the treating Obstetrician/Gynecologist." *Current Problems in Obstetrics and Gynecology* 18.4 (July/August 1995): 96. N.D. Online posting. Kate O'Hanlan Home Page. http://www.ohanlan.com/lhr.htm. 17 January 2002.

O'Rourke, Sean Patrick, and Laura K. Lee Dellinger. "*Romer v. Evans*: The Centerpiece of the American Gay-Rights Debate." *Anti-Gay Rights: Assessing Voter Initiatives*. Edited by Stephanie L. Witt and Suzanne McCorkle. Westport, CT: Praeger, 1977. 133–139.

Orth, Kathryn. "A bridge to tolerance: Falwell, gay activist exchange apologies, vow to oppose hatred." *Richmond Times-Dispatch* (24 October 1999): A1.

Patrick, Lord Bishop Simon et al. *A Critical Commentary and Paraphrase on the Old and New Testament and the Apocrypha*. 4 vols. Philadelphia, PA: Carey and Hart, 1844.

Pattatucci, A. M., C. Patterson, L. Li, D. W. Fulker, S. S. Cherny, L. Kruglyak, and D. H. Hamer. "Linkage between Sexual Orientation and Chromosome Xq28 in Males but not in Females." *Nature Genetics* 11.3 (November 1995): 248–256.

Patterson, Charlotte J. "Children of Lesbian and Gay Parents." *Annual Progress in Child Psychiatry and Child Development* 63.5 (1993): 33–62.

Perry, Michael J. "The Morality of Homosexual Conduct: A Response to John Finnis." *Notre Dame Journal of Law, Ethics and Public Policy* 9.1 (1995): 41–74.

Peters, Julie. "Transgender Diversity." 1995. Online posting. Julie Elizabeth Peters Home Page. http://home.mira.net/~janie/essays/tgdiversity.html. 17 January 2002.

Peters, Peter J. "The BIBLE: Handbook for Survivalists, Racists, Tax Protesters, Militants, and Right-Wing Extremists." 9 February 1997. Online posting. http://www.logoplex.com/resources/sfa/files/handbook.html. 21 September 1998.

Petersen, William L. "Can *ARSENOKOITAI* be Translated by 'Homosexuals'? (I Cor. 6:9, I Tim 1:10)." *Vigiliae Christianae* 40 (1986): 187–191.

PFLAG. "Is Homosexuality a Sin?" N.D. Online posting. Queer Resources Directory. http://www.qrd.org/religion/judeochristian/is.homosexuality.a.sin. 17 January 2002.

Phelps, Reverend Fred. "More Bible Commentary on Current Events." 12 June 1996. Online posting. Fred Phelps Home Page. http://godhatesfags.com/judge_06-12-96.gif. 22 June 1998.

———. "Week 181 of the Great Gage Park Decency Drive." Online posting. 2 December 1994. Fred Phelps Home Page. http://godhatesfags.com/week181_12-02-94.gif. 22 June 1998.

Pilant, Craig Wesley. "The Evolution of Pastoral Thought Concerning Homosexuality in Selected Vatican & American Documents from 1975–1986." *Homophobia and the Judaeo-Christian Tradition.* Edited by Michael L. Stemmeler and J. Michael Clark. Dallas: Monument, 1990. 117–146.

Pilkington, Neil. W., and Anthony D'Augelli. "Victimization of Lesbian, Gay, and Bisexual Youth in Community Settings." *Journal of Community Psychology* 23 (January 1995): 34–56.

Pillard, Richard C. "The Search for a Genetic Influence on Sexual Orientation." *Science and Homosexualities.* Edited by Vernon A. Rosario. New York: Routledge, 1997. 226–241.

———, and J. Michael Bailey. "A Genetic Study of Male Sexual Orientation." *Archives of General Psychiatry* 48 (December 1991): 1089–1096.

———. "The Innateness of Sexual Orientation." *Harvard Mental Health Letter* 10.7 (January 1994): 4–6.

Porteous, Skipp. *Jesus Doesn't Live Here Anymore.* Buffalo, NY: Prometheus, 1991.

———. "Inside Glen Eyrie Castle: The Organized Assault on Gay Rights." August 1994. Online Posting. Institute for First Amendment Studies. http://www.ifas. org/fw/9408/gleneyrie.html. 17 January 2002.

Porter, Jack Nusan. *Sexual Politics in the Third Reich: The Persecution of the Homosexuals during the Holocaust.* Newton, MA: Spencer, 1994.

Price, Ira Maurice. *The Ancestry of Our English Bible: An Account of Manuscripts, Texts, and Versions of the Bible.* 3rd rev. ed. Edited by William A. Irwin and Allen P. Wikgren. New York: Harper & Brothers, 1956.

Queen, Carol, and Lawrence Schimel, eds. *PoMoSexuals: Challenging Assumptions about Gender and Sexuality.* San Francisco, CA: Cleis, 1997.

"Quotes From the Religious Right." 8 March 1999. Online posting. The Anti-Pat Robertson/Christian Coalition Site. http://www.geocities.com/CapitolHill/ 7027/quotes.html. 17 January 2002.

Rakove, Jack N. *Original Meanings: Politics and Ideas in the Making of the Constitution.* New York: Knopf, 1996.

"Ralph Reed's Change of Heart Challenged by TIA." 7 May 1996. Online posting. The Interfaith Alliance. http://www.interfaithalliance.org/Newsroom/ press/050796.html. 17 January 2002.

Ray, Colonel Ronald D. *Gays: In or Out? The U.S. Military and Homosexuals— A Sourcebook.* New York: Brassey's (U.S.), 1993.

Raymond, Katherine. "Confessions of a Second-Generation . . . Dyke? Reflections on Sexual Non-Identity." *PoMoSexuals: Challenging Assumptions about Gender and Sexuality.* Edited by Carol Queen and Lawrence Schimel. San Francisco, CA: Cleis, 1997. 53–61.

Reed, Ralph. *Politically Incorrect: The Emerging Faith Factor in American Politics.* Dallas: Word, 1994.

Reinisch, June, Ruth Beasley, and Debra Kent. *The Kinsey Institute New Report on Sex: What You Must Know to be Sexually Literate.* New York: St. Martin's, 1990.

Reisman, Judith A. and Edward W. Eichel. *Kinsey, Sex, and Freud: The Indoctrination of a People.* Edited by J. Gordon Muir and John H. Court. Lafayette, LA: Lochinvar-Huntington, 1990.

"Religious Political Extremist Monitor: Quotes on Separation of Church and State." N.D. Online posting. Interfaith Alliance. http://www.interfaithalliance. org/Rr/separation.html. 17 January 2002.

Remafedi, Gary, S. French, M. Story, M.D. Resnick, R. Blum. "The Relationship Between Suicide Risk and Sexual Orientation: Results of a Population-Based Study." *American Journal of Public Health* 88 (1998): 57–60.

Richards, David A. J. "Sexual Preference as a Suspect (Religious) Classification: An Alternative Perspective on the Unconstitutionality of Anti-Lesbian/Gay Initiatives." *Ohio State Law Journal* 55 (1994): 491–514.

Riggle, Ellen D. B., and Barry L. Tadlock, eds. *Gays and Lesbians in the Democratic Process: Public Policy, Public Opinion, and Political Representation.* New York: Columbia University Press, 1999.

Rist, Darrell Yates. "Are Homosexuals Born That Way?" *Homosexuality: Debating the Issues.* Edited by Robert M. Baird and M. Katherine Baird. Amherst, NY: Prometheus 1995. 71–79.

Roberts, B. C. " 'The Many Faces of Bisexuality': The 4th International Bisexual Symposium." *Journal of Gay, Lesbian, and Bisexual Identity* 2.1 (1997): 65–76.

Robertson, Pat. *Answers to 200 of Life's Most Probing Questions.* Nashville, TN: Thomas Nelson, 1984.

Robinson, Bruce A. "Christian Reconstructionism, Dominion Theology, and Theonomy." 19 October 2001. Ontario Consultants on Religious Tolerance. http://www.religioustolerance.org/reconstr.htm. 17 January 2002.

———. "Homosexuality and Bisexuality." 17 January 2002. Ontario Consultants on Religious Tolerance. http://www.religioustolerance.org/homosexu.htm. 17 January 2002.

Roche, Pat, compiler. "Highlights of Dignity/USA's History, 1990–present." N.D. Dignity/ USA. http://www.dignityusa.org/archives/1990s.html. 17 January 2002.

Rodgers, William D. *The Gay Invasion: A Christian Look at the Spreading Homosexual Myth.* Denver: Accent Books, 1977.

Rofes, Eric E. "Innocence, Perversion, and Heather's Two Mommies." *Journal of Gay, Lesbian, and Bisexual Identity* 3.1 (1998): 3–26.

Rogers, Susan M., and Charles R. Turner. "Male-Male Sexual Contact in the U.S.: Findings from Five Sample Surveys, 1970–1990." *Journal of Sex Research* 28.4: (1991) 491–519.

Rosario, Vernon A., ed. *Science and Homosexualities.* New York: Routledge, 1997.

Roscoe, Will. *Living the Spirit: A Gay American Indian Anthology.* New York: St. Martin's, 1988.

Rubin, Gayle. "Thinking Sex: Notes for a Radical Theory of the Politics of Sexuality." *Pleasure and Danger: Exploring Female Sexuality.* Edited by Carole S. Vance. Boston: Routledge and Kegan Paul, 1984. 267–319

Rudy, Kathy. *Sex and the Church: Gender, Homosexuality, and the Transformation of Christian Ethics.* Boston: Beacon, 1997.

Rueda, Enrique T., and Michael Schwartz. *Gays, AIDS, and You.* Old Greenwich, CT: Devin Adair, 1987.

Ruether, Rosemary Radford. *Sexism and God-Talk: Toward a Feminist Theology.* Boston: Beacon, 1983.

Rust, Paula C. *Bisexuality and the Challenge to Lesbian Politics: Sex, Loyalty, and Revolution.* New York: New York University Press, 1995.

———. "Monogamy and Polyamory: Relationship Issues for Bisexuals." *Bisexuality: The Psychology and Politics of an Invisible Minority.* Edited by Beth A. Firestein. Thousand Oaks, CA: Sage, 1996. 127–148.

"Safeguarding Religious Liberty." 20 June 1998. Online posting. Interfaith Alliance. http://www.interfaithalliance.org/AboutUs/issues.html. 17 January 2002.

Saghir, Marcel T., and Eli Robins. *Male and Female Homosexuality: A Comprehensive Investigation*. Baltimore: Williams & Wilkins, 1973.

Sample, Tex S. "Should Gays and Lesbians Be Ordained?" *Caught in the Crossfire: Helping Christians Debate Homosexuality*. Edited by Sally B. Geis and Donald E. Messer. Nashville, TN: Abingdon, 1994. 121–131.

Satinover, Jeffrey. *Homosexuality and the Politics of Truth*. Grand Rapids, MI: Baker, 1996.

Savin-Williams, Ritch C. "An Exploratory Study of Pubertal Maturation Timing and Self-Esteem Among Gay and Bisexual Male Youths." *Developmental Psychology* 31.1 (1995): 56–64.

Scanzoni, Letha Dawson, and Virginia Ramey Mollenkott. *Is the Homosexual My Neighbor? A Positive Christian Response*. Rev. ed. San Francisco: Harper, 1994.

Schapiro, Mark. "Who's Behind The Culture War: Contemporary Assaults on the Freedom of Expression." 1994. The Public Eye: Website of Political Research Associates. http://www.publiceye.org/theocrat/Schapiro.html. 17 January 2002.

Schmidt, Thomas E. *Straight and Narrow? Compassion and Clarity in the Homosexuality Debate*. Downers Grove, IL: Inter-Varsity, 1995.

Schoedel, William R. "Same-Sex Eros: Paul and the Greco-Roman Tradition." *Homosexuality, Science, and the "Plain Sense" of Scripture*. Edited by David L. Balch. Grand Rapids, MI: Eerdmans, 2000. 43–72.

Schor, Naomi, and Elizabeth Weed, eds. *Feminism Meets Queer Theory*. Bloomington: Indiana University Press, 1997.

Schroedel, Jean Reith. "Elite Attitudes Toward Homosexuals." *Gays and Lesbians in the Democratic Process: Public Policy, Public Opinion, and Political Representation*. Edited by Ellen D. B. Riggle and Barry L. Tadlock. New York: Columbia University Press, 1999. 89–117.

Schuklenk, Udo, and Michael Ristow. "The Ethics of Research into the Cause(s) of Homosexuality." *Journal of Homosexuality* 31.3 (1996): 5–30.

Schuster, Rebecca. "Sexuality as a Continuum: The Bisexual Identity." *Lesbian Psychologies: Explorations and Challenges*. Edited by Boston Lesbian Psychologies Collective. Chicago: University of Illinois Press, 1987. 56–71.

Schwanberg, Sandra L. "Health Care Professionals' Attitudes Toward Lesbian Women and Gay Men." *Journal of Homosexuality* 31.3 (1996): 71–83.

Scott, D. Travers. "Le Freak, C'est Chic! Le Fag, Quelle Drag!" *PoMoSexuals: Challenging Assumptions about Gender and Sexuality*. Edited by Carol Queen and Lawrence Schimel. San Francisco, CA: Cleis, 1997. 62–69.

Scruton, Roger. *Sexual Desire: A Moral Philosophy of the Erotic*. New York: Free, 1986.

Seidman, Steven. *Difference Troubles: Queering Social Theory and Sexual Politics*. New York: Cambridge University Press, 1997.

Sell, Randall, and Christian Petrulio. "Sampling Homosexuals, Bisexuals, Gays, and Lesbians for Public Health Research: A Review of the Literature from 1990 to 1992." *Journal of Homosexuality* 30.4 (1996): 31–47.

Sell, Randall, James A. Wells, and David Wypij. "The Prevalence of Homosexual Behavior and Attraction in the United States, the United Kingdom and France:

Results of National Population-Based Samples." *Archives of Sexual Behavior* 24.3 (1995): 235–248.

Sherrill, Kenneth. "The Youth of the Movement: Gay Activists in 1972–1973." *Gays and Lesbians in the Democratic Process: Public Policy, Public Opinion, and Political Representation*. Edited by Ellen D. B. Riggle and Barry L. Tadlock. New York: Columbia University Press, 1999. 269–296.

Silva, Moises. *Biblical Words and Their Meaning: An Introduction to Lexical Semantics*. 1983; rev. ed. Grand Rapids, MI: Zondervan, 1994.

Simmel, Georg. "The Relative and the Absolute in the Problem of the Sexes." *Georg Simmel*. Translated by Guy Oakes. New Haven: Yale University Press, 1984. 102–132.

Simmons, Ron. "Some Thoughts on the Challenges facing Black Gay Intellectuals." *Brother to Brother: New Writings by Black Gay Men*. Edited by Essex Hemphill. Boston: Alyson, 1991. 211–228.

Simon, William. *Postmodern Sexualities*. New York: Routledge, 1996.

Smith, David M. "HRC Polls America." *Human Rights Campaign Quarterly* (Winter 1997): 8–9.

Smith, Ralph R. "Secular Anti-Gay Advocacy in the Springfield, Missouri, Bias Crime Ordinance Debate." *Anti-Gay Rights: Assessing Voter Initiatives*. Edited by Stephanie L. Witt and Suzanne McCorkle. Westport, CT: Praeger, 1977. 95–106.

———, and Russel R. Windes. *Progay/Antigay: The Rhetorical War Over Sexuality*. Thousand Oaks, CA: Sage, 2000.

Smith, Robin. *Living in Covenant with God and One Another*. Geneva: World Council of Churches, 1990.

Socarides, Charles W. "The Erosion of Heterosexuality: Psychiatry falters, America sleeps." 8 September 1995. Online posting. Messiah College Home Page. http://www.messiah.edu/hpages/facstaff/chase/h/articles/art6.htm. 17 January 2002.

Sorenson, Arthur P. "Linguistic Exogamy and Personal Choice in the Northwest Amazon." *Illinois Studies in Anthropology* 14 (1984): 180–193.

Steakley, James D. "*Per scientiam ad justitiam*: Magnus Hirschfeld and the Sexual Politics of Innate Homosexuality." *Science and Homosexualities*. Edited by Vernon A. Rosario. New York: Routledge, 1997. 133–154.

Stein, Edward. *The Mismeasure of Desire: The Science, Theory, and Ethics of Sexual Orientation*. New York: Oxford University Press, 1999.

Stemmeler, Michael L., and J. Michael Clark, eds. *Homophobia and the Judaeo-Christian Tradition*. Dallas: Monument, 1990.

Stoller, Robert J. *Presentations of Gender*. New Haven: Yale University Press, 1985.

Stone, Sandy. "The 'Empire' Strikes Back: A Posttranssexual Manifesto." *BodyGuards: The Cultural Politics of Gender Ambiguity*. Edited by Kristina Straub and Julia Epstein. New York: Routledge 1991. 280–304.

Stuart, Bill. "faq2TS FAQ." N.D. 24 January 2001. Online posting. Transgendered Ireland. http://indigo.ie/~transgen/faq2.htm. 17 January 2002.

———. "Transvestites." N.D. Online posting. Transgendered Ireland. http://indigo.ie/~transgen/tv.htm. 17 January 2002.

Stuart, Elizabeth. *Just Good Friends: Towards a Lesbian and Gay Theology of Relationships*. London: Mowbray, 1995.

Stuart, Sharon, and Tom Heitz. "About Our Transgendered Children and Their Families." N.D. TGS-PFLAG. http://tensegrity.critpath.org/pflag-talk/tgKIDfaq.html. 17 January 2002.

"Stupid Things Christians Say." N.D. Online posting. Planet Newark. http://www.angelfire.com/de/planetnewark/christianquotes.html. 17 January 2002

Sullivan, Andrew. *Virtually Normal: An Argument About Homosexuality.* New York: Knopf, 1995.

Sunstein, Cass R. "Homosexuality and the Constitution." *Sex, Preference, and Family: Essays on Law and Nature.* Edited by David M. Estlund and Martha C. Nussbaum. New York: Oxford University Press, 1997. 208–226.

Tafoya, T., and R. Rowell. "Counseling Gay and Lesbian Native Americans." *The Sourcebook on Lesbian/Gay Health Care.* Edited by M. S. and W. A. Scott. Washington, DC: National Lesbian/Gay Health Foundation, 1988.

Tasker, Fiona, and Susan Golombok. "Adults Raised as Children in Lesbian Families." *American Journal of Orthopsychiatry* 65.2 (April 1995): 203–215.

Tate, W. Randolph. *Biblical Interpretation: An Integrated Approach.* Peabody, MA: Hendrickson, 1991.

Tenney, Nancy. "The Constitutional Imperative of Reality in Public School Curricula: Untruths about Homosexuality as a Violation of the First Amendment." *Brooklyn Law Review* 60.3 (1994): 1599–1651.

Terry, Jennifer. "The Seductive Power of Science in the Making of Deviant Subjectivity." *Science and Homosexualities.* Edited by Vernon A. Rosario. New York: Routledge, 1997. 271–295.

Thomas, Kendall. "Beyond the Privacy Principle." *Columbia Law Review* 92.6 (1992): 1431–1516.

Thompson, Mark, ed. *Long Road to Freedom: The Advocate History of the Gay and Lesbian Movement.* New York: St. Martin's, 1994.

Thurston, Thomas M. "Leviticus 18:22 & the Prohibition of Homosexual Acts." *Homophobia and the Judaeo-Christian Tradition.* Edited by Michael L. Stemmeler and J. Michael Clark. Dallas: Monument, 1990. 7–24.

"TIAF Issues a report on Pat Robertson's Radical Agenda." N.D. Online posting. Interfaith Alliance. http://www.interfaithalliance.org/Newsroom/Narchive/report.htm. 17 January 2002.

Toulouse, Mark G. "Muddling Through: The Church and Sexuality/Homosexuality." *Homosexuality, Science, and the "Plain Sense" of Scripture.* Edited by David L. Balch. Grand Rapids, MI: Eerdmans, 2000. 6–42.

Tremblay, Pierre J. "The Homosexuality Factor in the Youth Suicide Problem." 19 January 1996. Online posting: Queer Resources Directory. http://www.qrd.org/qrd/www/youth/tremblay/. 17 January 2002.

Turner, William J. "Homosexuality, Type 1: An Xq28 Phenomenon." *Archives of Sexual Behavior* 24.2 (1995): 109–134.

Two Spirit Laughing. "Fartwell's ambush of no real consequence." 30 October 1999. Internet posting. FIGHT. http://members.home.net/trubble. 17 January 2002

Udis-Kessler, Amanda. "Challenging the Stereotypes." *Bisexual Horizons: Politics, Histories, Lives.* Edited by Sharon Rose, Cris Stevens, et al. London: Lawrence & Wishart, 1996. 45–57.

Voeller, Bruce. "AIDS and Heterosexual Anal Intercourse." *Archives of Sexual Behavior* 20.3 (1991): 233–276.

Weeks, Jeffrey. *Sexuality and its Discontents: Meanings, Myths and Modern Sexualities.* London: Routledge & Kegan Paul, 1986.

Weinberg, Martin S., Colin J. Williams, and Douglas W. Pryor. *Dual Attraction: Understanding Bisexuality.* New York: Oxford University Press, 1994.

Weithman, Paul J. "A Propos of Professor Perry: A Plea for Philosophy in Sexual Ethics." *Notre Dame Journal of Law, Ethics and Public Policy* 9.1 (1995): 75–94.

———. "Natural Law, Morality, and Sexual Complementarity." *Sex, Preference, and Family: Essays on Law and Nature.* Edited by David M. Estlund and Martha C. Nussbaum. New York: Oxford University Press, 1997. 227–249.

Whitam, Frederick L., and Robin M. Mathy. *Male Homosexuality in Four Societies: Brazil, Guatemala, the Philippines, and the United States.* New York: Praeger, 1986.

White, Mel. *Stranger at the Gate: To Be Gay and Christian in America.* New York: Simon and Schuster, 1994.

Williams, David. *A Study of Two Tabloids Disseminated by Freedom's Heritage Forum During the 1993 Primary and General Election Campaigns in Louisville, Kentucky.* Louisville, KY: Kentucky Gay and Lesbian Education Center, 1994.

Williams, W. Kenneth. "Theological Arguments Against Intolerance." 1994. Online posting. Radical Right Task Force. http://thewatch.paganteahouse.com/guide/d/guided03.html. 17 January 2002.

Williams, Walter L. *The Spirit and the Flesh: Sexual Diversity in American Indian Culture.* Boston: Beacon, 1992.

Wockner, Rex. "Quote Unquote #75." 1 October 1996. Online posting. Owner-glb-news@LISTSERV.AOL.COM. 28 October 1996.

———. "Quote Unquote #77." 29 October 1996. Online posting. Owner-glb-news@LISTSERV.AOL.COM. 11 November 1996.

———. "Quote Unquote #80." 10 December 1996. Online posting. Owner-glb-news@LISTSERV.AOL.COM. 5 August 1998.

Woodbridge, John D. "Culture War Casualties." *Christianity Today* (6 March 1995): 20–33.

Wright, David. F. "Homosexuality: The Relevance of the Bible." *Evangelical Quarterly* 61.4 (1989): 291–300.

Wright, J. Robert. "Boswell on Homosexuality: A Case Undemonstrated." *Anglican Theological Review* 66 (1984): 79–94.

Index

African Americans, 9, 105, 112, 200; attitudes towards LGBTs, 31, 182; and gay culture, 111, 183; and racism, 179, 181, 196; and segregation laws, 196

AIDS: and brain studies, 106; and "dirtiness" of sex, 89; and gay liberation, 17; in radical left rhetoric, 2, 176; in radical right rhetoric, 165, 181; and sex surveys, 119–120, 155–156

American Psychiatric Association, 151

American Psychological Association, 95, 151, 170

anal sex: and AIDS, 120; among animals, 98; biblical story of Sodom, 57, 59–62, 70, 115; cultural attitudes toward, 92, 112–117; in definition of sodomy, 3–4, 23, 42, 54, 59–60, 65–67; and gays, 5, 120; among heterosexuals, 5, 81, 188; and same-sex rape, 188

animals: and Jewish Law, 51–53, 56–57; sexual diversity in, 76, 98–99;

anti-Christian rhetoric, 2, 166; from Martin Dubermann, 2; as homophobes, 16, 45, 47, 58, 166, 168, 189; Paul Monette, 2; as pathological, 6–7; portraying CR as fascistic, 2, 8, 87–88, 166, 168; Michael Swift, 166; as theocratic, 2, 12, 14, 168; Two-Spirit Laughing, 176; use of hyperbole in, 1, 166–167

anti-discrimination laws, 192–198, 201–205; anti-gay views of, 9, 14, 15, 30, 116, 190, 193–196; "Don't Ask, Don't Tell" military policy, 7; pro-gay views of, 9, 14, 16, 93, 116, 153, 190, 192, 194–106; *Romer v. Evans,* 201–203

anti-gay arguments: biblical basis of (*see also* Bible), 33–34; in Christian theology, 27–30;

disapproval in world cultures, 23–27, 92–93, 117, 180, 197; gays as anti-family, 56, 66, 86–88, 89, 92, 154, 166, 180, 182, 196; as anti-religious, 2, 13, 32–33, 56, 87, 167–168, 189; as anti-social, 5–6, 57, 59, 86–87, 167, 173, 193; as biological mistakes, 169; as dangerous to children, 7, 9, 92, 117, 145, 152, 171–172, 176–177, 186, 189–190; as fascistic, 166–167, 181; as gender dysphoric, 85, 89, 106, 148–149; as narcissistic, 83, 126, 147–149; as pathological or depraved; 17, 77–84, 126, 137, 139, 141, 145–147, 154, 165, 170, 172–173, 182; as radically liberal, 13–14; as satanic, 2, 13, 23, 59, 167, 174, 181, 188; as sexually addicted, 126, 154; as violent, 165, 173; in natural law, 3, 24, 27, 29–30, 57, 63–66, 71, 75–82, 91, 93–94

anti-gay rhetoric: from ex-gay ministries, 157; from Paul Cameron, 169–172, 175, 189, Brian Clowes, 32, 121, 152, 154, 167, 172–173, William Dannemeyer, 2, Jerry Falwell, 2, 165, 175–176, 188–189, Tim LaHaye, 167, *The Lambda Report,* 167, Steve Largent, 21, Trent Lott, 1, 95, Fred Phelps, 6, 165, Pat Robertson, 59, 92, 167–168, 175, 181, 188–189, 192, William Rodgers, 143, 154, R. S. Rushdoony, 58–59, Laura Schlessinger, 169; use of apocalyptic or hyperbolic imagery, 2, 167; use in Nazi propaganda, 180–181

anti-gay rights initiatives: from 1974–1997, 8–9, 176; Colorado's Amendment Two, 9, 189, 201–203; in Idaho, 171; Oregon's Measure Nine, 2, 9, 166, 172, 192

Aquinas, Thomas, 6, 63, 76, 91–94, 157

Bible: King James Version, 35, 41–45; contested translations in, "abomination," 23, 48, 50–51, 53–55, 60, 66; *anomia,* 52, 56, *arsenokoitai,* 66–69, *asebes,* 62, *bdelygma,* 52, 56, 62, *chamakoites,* 68, *doulokoites,* 68–69, "impurity," 38, 51–53, 56, 58, 77, *ishshah,* 53, *kata physin,* 64–66, koite, 68–69, *malakoi,* 66–67, *malthakos,* 67, *pais,* 70, *para physiken (physin),* 63–65, *pornos,* 68, *porneiai,* 69–70, *qadheshim (kadeshim),* 48–50, *raca,* 44–45, *shakab,* 61, *sheqets,* 57, *toevah,* 50–53, 56–58, 69, *yada (yadha),* 61, *zakar,* 53, *zimah,* 51, 57

Bible: original manuscripts, 35–41; Massoretes revisions, 36

Bible passages (in **bold**): **Acts 15:1–29,** 57; **Colossians 2:21,** 38, **3:22–4:1,** 55; **I Corinthians 5:11,** 176, **6:9–10,** 63, 66, 7, 77, **6:15–16,** 68, **11:14,** 56, 64, 65, **11:8,** 91, **12:4–5,** 40, **15:43,** 64; **II Corinthians 2:17,** 41, **7:10,** 40, **8:1,** 41, **11:4,** 40; **Daniel 11:37,** 167; **Deuteronomy 14:3,** 57, **22:5,** 55, **23:1–2,** 55, **23:10,** 51, **23:17–18,** 48–50, **31:1,** 36, **32:17,** 62; **Ecclesiastes 2:25,** 41; **Ephesians,** 8, **6:5–9,** 55; **Exodus 20:3,** 201, **22:25,** 55; **Ezekiel,** 56, **16:48–50,** 60, **18:13,** 55, **18: 52,** 65–67, 56; **Galatians 1:6,** 40–41, **3:4,** 43; **Genesis 9:6,** 57, **12:19,**

41, **19:1–11**, 60–63, **47:16**, 36, **50:20**, 40; **Hebrews 13:4**, 68, 69, **13:9**, 205; **Hosea 4:14**, 50, **2:19–20**, 50; **Isaiah 1:10**, 60, **3:9**, 60, **31:1**, 41, **57:3–13**, 53; **Jeremiah 16:18**, 56, **17:9**, 143, **23:14**, 60; **Job 26:5** 41, **32:6**, 45, **36:2**, 45, **36:33**, 41; **John 1:1–4**, 37, **8:44**, 165, **16:12–13**, 33; **I Kings 12:18**, 36, **14:24**, 48, 51, **22:46**, 48; **II Kings 23:7**, 48; **Leviticus 1:3**, 53, **3:1**, 53, **18:3**, 49, **18:6**, 49, **18:19**, 30, **18:20**, 57, **18:22**, 50, 52, 53, 56, 62, **18:23**, 53, **18:26–30**, 56, **19:27**, 56, **20:9**, 55, **20:10**, 55, **20:13**, 50, **20:18**, 30, 62, **20:26**, 54–55, **21:9**, 55, **23:3**, 54, **23:30**, 55, **24:16**, 55, **25:44–46**, 55; **Luke 2:22–24**, 31, **7:25**, 67; **Mark 6:20**, 41, **7:21–23**, 69, **10:17**, 40; **Matthew 5:22**, 44, **5:17–18**, 69, **5:27–28**, 71, **5:31–32**, 71, **8:4**, 57, **8:5–13**, 70, **11:8**, 67, **10:5–15**, 60, **15:2**, 57, **15:10–15**, 52, 81, **15:14**, 59, **18:33**, 40, **19:16**, 40, **21:23**, 40, **25:46**, 40, **28:18**, 40; **Numbers 4:15**, 72, **30:2–8**, 91; **1 Peter 2:18**, 55; **2 Peter 2:6**, 62, **2:7, 8, 12**, 165; **Philemon 2:6,7**, 41, 55; **Proverbs 6:12–14**, 43; **Psalm 15**, 55; **Revelations 12:9**, 174, **21**, 13; **Romans 1:26–27**, 63, 66, **1:28**, 6, **5:2, 3, 11**, 40, **11:21, 24**, 65; **Ruth**, 54; **1 Samuel 6:1–8**, 72, **15**, 55; **2 Samuel 6:7**, 72; **1 Timothy 1:10**, 63, **2:11–15**, 92; **2 Timothy 3:16**, 46; **Titus 1:14–15**, 52

Bible: *Septuagint* version, 36, 39, 52, 56, 61

biological origins of homosexuality: animal studies, 76, 98–99, 103, 106; brain structure, 101–106; determinism, 25, 106–110; endocrinology, 102–103; genes, 97–105, 110, 112; LGBT attitudes toward, 17, 106–107, 109–110; and left–handedness, 27; objections to biological approach, 103–110; as a trait, compared to alcoholism, 1, 95, 107, 203

bisexuality, 125–131: in animals, 98; category issues, 122, 125–131; and choice, 107, 116–117, 204–205; discrimination against by heterosexuals, 7, 126; discrimination against by homosexuals, 121, 125–131; and gender, 26; and heterosexuality, 124, 147, 150; incidence of, 120, 124; innateness of, 16, 26, 147, 150; misrepresented in scientific studies, 101, 103, 107, 123, 125; pomosexuality, 135–136; and reparative therapy, 158–159; and sexual activity, 87, 125–126; stereotypes about, 125–126, 152; a "Sexually Incorrect Lesbian," 128; in transsexuals, 19

celibacy, as perversion, 78, 94

censorship, of homosexuality and Christianity in schools, 7–10, 166, 172, 192

children: in the Bible, 55, 61; child custody issues, 120, 177, 192; in definition of *sodomia*, 42; as restraint on/redemption of sexual desire, 6, 76, 78–79, 86–88, 94, 159; vulnerability of, 7, 9, 25, 100, 114, 117, 132, 145–148, 150, 152, 158, 171–172, 176–177, 182, 186, 189–190

Christ, Jesus: as anti-gay, 57, 69–71, 157, 167; as pro-gay, 28, 52–53, 60, 69–70

Christians, centrist, 12, 14, 82, 84, 107–108, 194

Christians, liberal, 12, 14, 28, 31–32, 46, 54, 56, 59, 70–73, 107–108, 182, 194; on gay rights, 28, 58, 70–71, 199; Interfaith Alliance, 32, 191; on revelation, 33, 46, 54, 56, 58, 70–73; on science, 29, 31, 58, 107–108

Christians, orthodox, 2, 11–14, 27, 32, 45–46, 54, 56, 58–59, 61, 66–67, 69, 71–72, 75, 78, 80, 160–161, 165–166, 174, 179–181, 192, 199, 205; and the Anti-Christ (Satan), 2, 13, 59, 167–168, 174, 201; Christian Coalition and allied groups, 7, 11–12, 32, 157, 166–167, 172, 191, 193, 201; Christian Reconstructionism, 12, 181; on contraception, 3; *detente* with, 175–176, 200–201; and evangelical traditions, 11–12, 14, 28, 31–32, 72, 91, 174–176, 192, 201; on evil, 27, 71, 80, 173, 176, 181; on gay rights, 14, 32, 160–161, 167, 172, 193–194; and hate speech/crimes, 1, 166, 173–175, 179, 183–190, 192; and homophobia, 16, 45, 58, 174, 189; on pluralism, 32, 192–196, 205; premillenialists and postmillenialists, 12–13; relations with other religions, 201; on revelation, 12, 30, 33, 39, 46, 58, 71–73, 94, 200–201; on separation of church and state, 196–197; on science, 29–31, 80, 107–109, 173; social/political influence of, 11,

32; Theocratic Right, 12, 14, 16, 192, 196, 201; on women and gender roles, 12, 55, 71, 76–78, 86–89, 91–92, 129, 133–134, 151–152

constitutional issues: and Amendment Two, 9, 201–203; multiculturalism, 13, 181, 200–201; protections offered, 4, 5, 93, 205; religious basis of sodomy laws, 197; separation of church and state, 196–198; tyranny of majority, 15, 193, 198–199

cross-dressing. *See* transvestism

culture wars, 2–3, 6, 12, 16, 17, 87–88, 174, 192, 196, 205–206

discrimination: anti-discrimination laws, 1, 14–15, 190, 193–196, 201, 203–204; against Christians, 7–8, 168, 190, 193–196; against LGBTs, 1, 5, 7–9, 30, 93, 116–117, 153, 168–169, 175, 190, 192, 195; "Don't Ask, Don't Tell" policy, 7

effeminacy, 19, 26, 33, 44, 66–67, 89, 100, 112, 115, 132, 147, 159, 180, 182, 186

Equal Protection Clause of the Fourteenth Amendment, 203

"Ex-Gay" movement. *See* reparative therapy

family: as exclusive ideal, 56, 66, 79, 86–87, 92, 112, 180, 182, 196; as practical restraint on desire, 86–89, 166; and sexual diversity, 112–115, 122

fellatio: among animals, 98; among heterosexuals, 5, 81; among homosexuals, 42, 92, 120; legal

status of, 3–4, 42; ritualized,
113, 117; as "sodomy," 3, 42
feminism: and butches, 139;
denigration of women, 89–92;
and gay liberation, 16–17, 32,
86, 92, 116, 123, 128
Finnis, John, 79–82, 86, 89, 90
Freud, Sigmund, 83, 97, 131,
133–134, 144–150, 157, 184

gay activists: 2, 4, 104, 119, 130,
152, 166, 189, 191; politics/
organizations, 2, 13–17
"Gay Agenda": anti-gay version
of, 2, 12–13, 27–28, 32–33,
71, 81–84, 87, 92, 108–109,
122, 143, 152, 154, 161,
165–168, 172–174, 189–194;
pro-gay version of, 2, 16–17,
28, 70–71, 81–82, 87–88,
151, 154, 161, 169, 190,
192, 204
"gay brain," 101–103,
105–106, 172
"gay gene," 99–101, 103–105,
109–110, 112
gay identity: as essential,
immutable, or unified, 29, 89,
107, 109–113, 116–117, 127,
135, 138, 141–143; legal
implications of, 2, 4, 106–107,
110, 112, 113, 116–117, 179,
203–205; as multiple, mutable,
or socially constructed, 17, 42,
89, 97, 99, 111–118, 122–125,
127–131, 135–139
gay males, 18; and biological
etiology, 97, 99, 100, 116; and
drag queens, 19; and effeminacy,
19, 44, 66–68, 89, 92, 100, 115,
147–148, 159, 186, 188;
ideological tensions between gay
men and lesbians, 17; and
masculinity/male desire unleashed

in, 86–89, 92, 114–115, 149,
171; and promiscuity, 15, 82, 87,
126, 155–156; and racism, 17, 88,
182; in relationships, 83–84, 87,
89, 155–156; sexual practices of,
5, 120, 124, 137, 155; and
transexuality, 136–137; in world
cultures, 23–26, 91, 112–117, 197
gay politics: assimilationists, 2,
16–17, 19, 88–89, 116; Gay Pride,
8, 16, 162, 167; separatists,
16–17, 87–89, 128
gender: anatomy and gender roles,
16–19, 24, 42, 57–58, 80–81,
84, 90–93, 101–102, 114, 132,
135–139, 147, 188; and desire,
17–18, 26, 86–89, 92, 128–129,
132–135, 139, 147–149,
151–152; gender identity as
fixed, 71, 82–85, 87–89, 93,
116–117, 148, 157, 158; gender
identity as fluid, 114, 131–139,
204; genital romance of
heterosexuality ("one flesh"),
76–88, 85, 90, 92–93, 129, 133,
136, 174; Greek myth of origin
of, 78; as related to a structured
universe, 28, 76–78, 88,
180–181, 184; reversals of,
114–116, 135–137; spiritual
symbolism of conception, 29, 66,
79–83, 89–90, 197; subversion of
in butch/femme role playing, 85,
89, 111, 128–129, 133–139
Greek attitudes towards same-sex
love, 23–25, 42, 78, 111–113,
116, 146

hate crimes: bashing, 179, 185;
effect on self-esteem and suicide,
187–188; harassment in schools,
186; laws, 1; statistics, 185;
theory of, 180–185; use of rape,
188–189

heterosexuality: denaturalization of
by psychoanalysis, 149; by
cultural studies, 111, 115–116
homophile movement, 16, 110
homophobia: and Christianity, 29,
66; versus homoprejudice, 16,
58, 146; as latent homosexuality,
183–184; or displaced unease
about sex, 90; and opposition to
gay rights, 16, 45, 58, 66, 166;
psychological effects of, 153,
175, 187; and violence, 179,
185–190
homosexuality: in ancient times,
23–25, 42, 70, 111–112; cross-
cultural considerations of, 23–27,
110–118; de/criminalization of,
3–5, 117, 179–181, 190, 193,
197, 202–204; and education,
7–10; genetic studies of, 99–110;
hate crime laws protecting, 1, 9,
93, 190; as an inadequate label,
17, 42, 111, 113–116, 119, 120,
122–125, 135–139; among
Native-Americans, 25–27;
neuroanatomical studies of,
101–103, 105–107; and
pedophilia, 171, 176–177;
and physical traits, 103;
psychoanalytic studies of,
145–150; psychological studies
of, 150–152; public opinion polls
concerning, 1, 3, 14, 187;
ritualized kinship forms of, 25,
112–116; sexual practices as
definitive of orientation, 5, as not
definitive, 120; statistical
frequency of, 119–125; theories
of causality, biological
predisposition, 25, 97–110,
astrological, 24, psychogenic, 83,
141, 143, 146–150, 153–154,
sociogenic, 110–118,
theological, 26, 27, 157–162;

and transgenderism, 18–19,
131–132
homosexuals: and alcohol, 153,
187; childhoods of, 141–143,
152–153, 175, 177, 187; and
gender issues, 16–18, 42, 83–89,
106, 114–116, 126, 129–131,
133–137, 147–148, 177, 183,
188; in the military, 6–7, 14–15,
23, 88, 93, 117, 171; in
relationships, 15, 82–84, 87–88,
154–156; in religious
organizations, 2, 13; political
beliefs of, 14–16, 87–88,
127–129; as parents, 120, 177

identity: in animals, 99; and
essentialism, 109–110; gender,
16–19, 102, 132; mutable/
immutable, 42, 86–87, 107, 110,
116–117, 127–128, 134–138,
141–143, 203–204; political, 15;
sexual, 16–17, 29, 89, 115–131;
and social constructionism,
111–112, 116
interpretive communities, 39,
143–146;

Jews: ancient texts of, 35–37, 39;
attitudes toward animal sacrifices,
53; gender display, 55–56;
homosexuality, 24, 27, 49–50,
54, 56–57, 62; involuntary
ejaculation, 51; lesbians, 13, 48,
54; menstruation, 30–31, 53;
mixing different substances,
53–54; non-procreative sex, 56,
77–78; pagans, 49–51, 53–54;
slavery, 55; as a "chosen" people,
54–55; interpretation of story of
Sodom and Gomorrah, 59–62;
Jewish LGBTs, 13; Orthodox
sects, 12, 24, 77, 78; Progressive
sects, 27, 54; Purity Laws of, 38,

51–58; use of figurative, euphemistic, or untranslatable language in OT, 37, 41, 43–45, 49–50, 61–62; as victims of prejudice, 180

Kinsey, Alfred: research, 75, 119–123, 125, 159, 171–172, 183; criticisms of, 121–122

lesbians: attitudes towards butch/femme role playing, 85, 87, 89, 111, 128, 133–134, 136–139; in Bible, 48, 54; and biological studies, 97, 99–101, 105, 109; "elective" vs. "born," 17, 97, 99–100, 107, 110, 122–123, 143, 204–205; and feminism, 17, 92, 116, 123, 128, 139; gender issues, 87–89, 91–92, 148; motherhood, 88, 176–177; policing of group boundaries, 126–131; politics of, 13–14, 16–17, 184; quality of medical treatment for, 120–121; relationships, 91, 156; religious affiliation of, 13–14, 28; sexual activity of, 120, 123, 126, 155; sexual identity issues, 5, 81–82, 111, 121–137, 142, 154; surveys of, 120–124; and violence, 170, 186–188; in world cultures, 25–26, 42, 48, 54, 91, 115

marriage: between heterosexuals, 1, 3, 5, 27, 29, 69, 77, 86, 91, 112, 118, 156; between homosexuals, 1, 5, 15, 24, 26, 28, 31, 154, 156, 195; compatible with same-sex relations, 112–115; as exclusive, ideal relationship, 6, 27, 29, 77–81, 87, 92, 182; as practical restraint on sexual desires, 6, 76, 78, 83, 86–88,

155–156; rejection of, by lesbians and gay men, 87–89, 91–92; and transsexuals, 19, 133–135
masculinity: and gender nonconformity, 133–139, 149–150; in traditional bipolar gender roles, 16–17, 71, 84–85, 88, 117, 133, 147, 150, 180–182, 188; not a factor in pedophilia, 171; in transgendered persons, 18, 136–137; in women, 85, 89, 102–103; in world cultures, 67, 112–115
masturbation, 42, 67, 78, 98, 136
menstruation, 30–31, 42, 53, 58, 64, 114

natural law: in ancient times, 56–58, 63–64, 66, 76, 91; and contraception, 3; in Middle Ages, 75–76, 82–83, 94; in modern times, 29–30, 58, 71, 79–81, 88, 93, 108, 114–115, 157, 180, 197

oral sex, included in definition of sodomy, 3, 42, 65; prevalence among heterosexuals, 5, 81, 113; prevalence among homosexuals, 92, 120, 136; in *Bowers v. Hardwick*, 4–5, 42
orientation vs. desire, fantasy, identity, 99, 103–104, 112, 114, 116–119, 122–125, 127, 131, 136–137, 154, 158–159, 188, 204–205

parents, of homosexuals, 17, 100, 147–150, 152, 158; homosexuals as parents, 120, 176–177
pedophilia, 3, 9, 71, 116, 167, 171–172, 177
police harassment, 16, 17, 186, 190

politics: centrist, 2, 7, 16, 17, 54,
    82, 84, 107, 168–169, 194;
    conservative, 4, 7, 12–17, 32,
    122, 171, 191–192, 194–196,
    200–202; disaggregation of
    major political parties, 15;
    differences within anti-gay rights
    movement, 1, 12, 14; differences
    within gay rights movement, 2, 8,
    13–17, 88, 117, 127–128, 131;
    liberal, 7, 8, 12–14, 16–17, 32,
    54, 166–168, 173, 182, 192,
    194, 195, 196, 198, 202;
    libertarian, 14, 15, 192, 195; and
    pluralism, 87, 191–196,
    205–206; and religion, 12–14,
    166, 176, 190–195, 204; and
    science, 104–110, 121, 122, 152,
    161, 169, 172–173, 204
privacy issue in constitutional law,
    3, 4, 179, 181, 192
pro-gay arguments, 2; approval in
    world cultures, 23–27; biblical
    basis of (see Bible); homosexuality
    as not intrinsically anti-family,
    88, 112–115; congruent with
    principles of freedom, 14–15,
    191–206; noncriminal, 3–5; not
    dangerous to children; 171–172,
    176, personally fulfilling, 5,
    153–154; psychologically healthy,
    150–156; religious and moral,
    13, 27–28, 31–32; socially
    beneficial, 15, 23, 94; and
    violence, 175, 179, 181, 183,
    185–190

race, and homosexuality, 7, 15, 17,
    83, 87–88, 111, 116, 180–182,
    185, 203; Rev. Louis Farrakhan,
    182–184
reparative therapy, 143, 148, 154,
    157–162; confusion of religious
    values and psychotherapeutic
principles, 157, 160–162; ex-gay
    ministries, 157–160; focus on
    denial, 57, 71, 72, 126, 143,
    145, 148, 154, 157, 159, 162;
    success rates for, 158–160, use of
    abstinence in, 160; theories of
    homosexuality, 146–150,
    157–158, use of aversion
    techniques, 25, 150; use of
    psychoanalysis, its limitations,
    143–146
Roman Catholicism: anti-gay
    Catholics, 2, 12, 14, 25, 28–29,
    32, 59–60, 76, 83–84, 121, 154,
    167, 172–173; interpretive
    policies regarding Scripture,
    30–31, 38, 108; attitude toward
    menstruation, 30–31; Cardinal
    Basil Hume, 29; Cardinal Joseph
    Ratzinger, 2, 33, 59, 76; Pope
    Gregory IX, 197; Pope John Paul
    II, 2; Pope Paul XI, 28; Pope Pius
    XII, 31; pro-gay Catholics,
    28–32, 50, 108; St. Thomas
    Aquinas, 6, 63, 76, 91–94, 157

science: as anti-Christian, 108, 109,
    173; as anti-gay, 109–110, 119,
    169–172, 204; in discussions of
    moral values, 2, 29–31, 58,
    80–81, 106–109, 161–162; as
    politically contaminated, 97,
    108–109, 112, 121–122, 152,
    162, 172–173; as pro-gay, 58,
    107–109, 135, 151, 177
sexism, 7, 17, 88, 91
sodomy: American sodomy laws, 3,
    93, 181, 193, 202–204;
    definition of, 3–5, 42, 60; history
    of sodomy laws, 4, 25, 66, 75,
    92–93, 197–199; and violence,
    179, 188
"special rights," 192–193,
    195–196, 201–202

suicide, 170, 182, 187–188
Supreme Court, United States,
  cases: Religious Freedom
  Restoration Act, 194; *Bowers v.
  Hardwick*, 3–5, 23, 42, 93, 179,
  202–204; *Dahl v. Secretary of the
  United States Navy*, 117;
  Eisenstadt v. Baird, 3; *Griswold v.
  Connecticut*, 3; *Keyishian v.
  Board of Regents*, 9; *Olmstead v.
  United States*, 3–4; *Peterson v.
  Greenville*, 196; *Powell v. Texas*,
  203; *Romer v. Evans*, 202–203;
  Steffan v. Aspin, 107
surveys: 1, 5, 12–14, 19, 23,
  31–32, 119–125, 130, 131, 138,
  142, 152–156, 158, 169–170,
  172, 185–188

transgenderism/transsexuality:
  category dissidents
  (transgenderists, gender benders),
  111, 133–137; childhood
  experiences, 132, 142, 188;
  definition of, 18–19, 131–132,
  204; distinguished from
  homosexuality, 131–132, 150;
  favorable attitudes towards,
  24–26, 28; intersexed individuals,
  18; hate crime laws protecting, 1;
  neuroanatomical and
  neuroendocrinological studies of,
  101–102, 107; psychological
  studies of, 151–152;
  requirements for sexual
  reassignment surgery 132–133;
  subcategories of, FTM, 18–19,
  131, 136–138, MTF, 18–19,
  101–102, 131–132, 135, 142,
  MTLF and FTGM, 137; the
  "true self," 132–133, 142–143;
  unfavorable attitudes towards,
  55–56, 66, 113; in world
  cultures, 24, 26, 113; violence
  against, 1, 186–187
transvestism (cross-dressing), 19,
  55, 111, 113, 131, 134–136,
  138, 150

About the Author

THOMAS C. CARAMAGNO is Associate Professor of English at the University of Nebraska–Lincoln. He is the author of *The Flight of the Mind: Virginia Woolf's Art and Manic-Depressive Illness*.